LISTENING TO MUSIC
Creatively

EDWIN J. STRINGHAM

Professor of Music
Queens College of the City of New York

New York   PRENTICE-HALL, INC.   *1946*

MT
6
.S815

Printed in the United States of America

To

DR. PAUL KLAPPER

PRESIDENT OF QUEENS COLLEGE
OF THE CITY OF NEW YORK

WHOSE VISION, LEADERSHIP, AND LOVE FOR THE
ART OF MUSIC MADE POSSIBLE THE EXPERIMENTS
OUT OF WHICH THIS BOOK DEVELOPED.

ACKNOWLEDGMENTS

IT IS not possible here to mention the names of all, or even many, of the persons who have contributed to the text in its many stages of development; but we would be ungrateful indeed if we failed to acknowledge our gratitude to President Paul Klapper of Queens College, to whom this book is dedicated, for his sympathetic interest and support; and above all others, to my wife, Alta Morrill Stringham, for her tireless and active aid and unceasing encouragement, without which this book could never have been realized. To the many unnamed others who have contributed directly or indirectly, including the students in my classes during the past score or more years, we offer our sincere thanks and appreciation.

E. J. S.

TABLE OF CONTENTS

CHAPTER   PAGE

ACKNOWLEDGMENTS vii

I. MUSIC AND THE DANCE 1

Discussion of the place dance music has in our living and a study of the basic characteristics of this type of music.

Essential Listening: A popular dance record, Turkey in the Straw (Guion), Beautiful Blue Danube (Johann Strauss), Slavonic Dance No. 1 (Dvořák), Amaryllis (Ghys), Suite No. 2 in B minor (Bach).

Additional Suggestions for Listening: Waltz in C-Sharp Minor (Chopin), Golliwog's Cakewalk (Debussy), "Rhumba" movement from Harl McDonald's Symphony No. 2.

RHYTHM: THE HEARTBEAT OF MUSIC. Discussion of rhythm and integration with painting and poetry.

II. MUSIC AND CEREMONY 10

How music serves in various formal ceremonies of life.

Essential Listening: Marche Militaire (Schubert), Pomp and Circumstance (Elgar), Stars and Stripes Forever (Sousa), Polonaise Militaire (Chopin), Triumphal March from "Aïda" (Verdi), Wedding March from "Midsummer Night's Dream" (Mendelssohn), Wedding March from "Lohengrin" (Wagner), and Funeral March (Chopin).

Additional Suggestions for Listening: Slow movement from the "Eroica" (No. 3) Symphony (Beethoven), and the third movement from Tchaikovsky's "Pathetique" (Sixth) Symphony.

MELODY AND HARMONY. Discussion of those two elements in music.

III. MUSIC AND RELIGION 17

Place and function of music in our religious worship. Brief résumé of the subject in Protestant, Catholic and Jewish faiths, with typical examples from each.

Essential Listening: "A Mighty Fortress is Our God"; selected Jewish Kaddish Chants; Gregorian (Catholic) Chants: "Kyrie," "Gloria," or "Tenebrae factae sunt"; "Sanctus" and "Gloria" from the Pope Marcellus Mass (Palestrina); Lutheran Chorales, "Jesu Joy of Man's Desiring" (Bach), "Credo," "Crucifixus," "Et Resurrexit," and "Sanctus" from The B-minor Mass (Bach).

Additional Suggestions for Listening: Excerpts from "Parsifal" (Wagner), Finale from the "Reformation" Symphony (Mendelssohn), and Finale from the Ninth Symphony (Beethoven).

VOLUME AND SPEED AS ELEMENTS IN EMOTIONAL EXPRESSION: Brief discussion of the part dynamics, accent, and tempo play in music.

IV. MUSIC, WORK AND PLAY: THE TRADITIONAL
FOLK SONG 28

Discussion of traditional folk songs from many nations. Elementary
phrase structures. Basic elements of the Ternary (three-part), A-B-A,
form. The Strophic form. Some scales.

Essential Listening: Barbara Allen, Marlborough, Home on the Range,
John Henry, Drink to Me Only, and Comin' Through the Rye.

Additional Suggestions for Listening: Selected folk songs from Germany, France, Italy, Spain, and Russia.

V. THE COMPOSED FOLK SONG: THE ARCHITEC-
TURE OF MUSIC 39

Differentiation between the "traditional" and the "composed" folk
songs. Period and Binary structures and forms.

Essential Listening: Lullaby (Brahms). The Birch Tree (Russian folk
song), and the Finale from Tchaikovsky's Fourth Symphony.

THE ARCHITECTURE OF MUSIC: FORM AND STRUCTURE. Discussion of a few
basic concepts of the function of form and structure in the allied fine
arts. Integration with poetry and painting. The Rondo form in music
and poetry.

Essential Listening: Rondino (Beethoven-Kreisler).

VI. MUSIC AS PERSONAL EXPRESSION: THE ART
SONG (LIED) 51

Historical sketch of the rise of the Art Song. The Strophic versus the
Thorough-composed song. Important function of the poem.

Essential Listening: Study of the following art songs with their Eng-
lish translations of the foreign words: Serenade (Schubert), Der Erl
König (Schubert), Ich Grolle Nicht (Schumann), Minnelied (Brahms),
Ich Liebe Dich (Grieg), The Flea (Moussorgsky), and The Sea (Mac-
Dowell).

Additional Suggestions for Listening: Selected songs by Wolf, Franz,
Richard Strauss, César Franck, Gabriel Fauré, Duparc, Debussy, Bond,
Cadman, Carpenter, and others.

SENTENCE STRUCTURE IN MUSIC: THE PHRASE, PERIOD AND CADENCE. Further
study of these aspects as they are found in simple songs.

Essential Listening: London Bridge Is Falling Down, the Farmer in
the Dell, and Swanee River.

VII. THE OPERA 70

PART ONE: OPERETTA AND LIGHT OPERA. History of Opera.
Description of different types. Typical examples of arias.

Suggestions for Listening: Selections from various popular works in
this form, including Show Boat (Kern), Rose Marie (Friml), Mlle.
Modiste (Herbert), Porgy and Bess (Gershwin), The Mikado (Sullivan), and others.

THE OPERA BUFFA:

Suggestions for Listening: Excerpts from the Marriage of Figaro
(Mozart), and The Barber of Seville (Rossini).

PART TWO: GRAND OPERA. History and description of various types of Grand Opera. Outstanding composers and their principal works in this form. Discussion of French, Italian and Wagnerian types, with pertinent suggestions for optional listening.

Essential Listening: The opera Carmen by Georges Bizet; its story and dramatic action, act by act, and descriptive study of the principal arias, ensembles, and instrumental numbers as they appear in each act.

Additional Suggestions for Listening: Selections from various Wagnerian operatic works. Selections from Aïda (Verdi), La Bohème (Puccini), Pagliacci (Leoncavallo), Cavalleria Rusticana (Mascagni), Boris Godunoff (Moussorgsky), and reference to other works by Verdi, Richard Strauss, Massenet, Charpentier, Gruenberg, Hanson, Taylor, Hageman, Herbert, Menotti, and Giannini.

VIII. THE ORATORIO 97

Survey of the backgrounds of this form. Biographical sketch of George Frideric Handel. Outline of "The Messiah," with a complete list of numbers in this work.

Essential Listening: Indicated selections from "The Messiah," either complete, or with two alternate reduction plans to meet time allowance.

Additional Suggestions for Listening: Works by Bach, Haydn, Beethoven, Mendelssohn, Liszt, Berlioz, Franck, Parry, Stanford, Stainer, Elgar, Walton, Delius, Holst, Paine, Parker, Stillman-Kelley, Loeffler, Shelley, Smith, d'Indy, Wolf-Ferrari, Pierné, and Honegger.

IX. MUSIC IN THE THEATRE; INCIDENTAL MUSIC: THE SUITE 106

Brief outline of the history pertinent to the subject.

Essential Listening: Valse Triste (Sibelius), Peer Gynt Suite No. 1 (Grieg), Midsummer Night's Dream Suite (Mendelssohn), the "Indian" Suite (MacDowell).

Additional Suggestions for Listening: "Through the Looking Glass" Suite (Taylor) with words of Lewis Carroll pertinent to each movement of the Suite. Music for the Cinema, with a few typical examples cited.

X. MUSIC AND THE BALLET 119

Brief résumé of the history of this form.

Essential Listening: Description and analysis of Ritual Fire Dance from "El Amor Brujo" (Falla), Petrouchka (Stravinsky), Skyscrapers (Carpenter), "Mother Goose" Suite (Ravel).

Additional Suggestions for Listening: Selected and appropriate works by Tchaikovsky, Delibes, Offenbach, Glazounov, Milhaud, Ravel, Glière, Stravinsky, Shostakovitch, and Aaron Copland.

XI. TONE COLOR IN MUSIC 131

PART ONE: THE INSTRUMENTS OF THE ORCHESTRA

A study of the history, description, range, transposition, and tonal characteristics of the many instruments comprising the modern sym-

CHAPTER   PAGE

phony orchestra; musical illustrations; orchestra seating plans; the Art of Orchestration; the complete orchestra score.

Essential Listening: Peter and the Wolf (Prokofieff); "Instruments of the Symphony Orchestra" from available commercial recordings of string, woodwind, brass and percussion instruments; Introduction and Allegro for Strings (Elgar).

PART TWO: THE ORCHESTRA IN ACTION 150

Essential Listening: The "Nutcracker Suite" (Tchaikovsky).

Additional Suggestions for Listening: Carnival of the Animals (Saint-Saëns).

XII. CLASSIC AND ROMANTIC ELEMENTS IN ART ... 158

Analysis and discussion of these two typical categories, or tempers, and comparisons with similar tempers in painting, poetry, and architecture. General historical implications.

THE ROMANTIC MOVEMENT IN MUSIC and its historical backgrounds; Program music. Biographical sketch of Tchaikovsky.

Essential Listening: Minuet from the Symphony in E-flat (Mozart), the Liebestod music from "Tristan and Isolde" (Wagner), and the Overture-Fantasy, Romeo and Juliet (Tchaikovsky).

XIII. THE SYMPHONIC POEM: TONE PAINTING 181

Narrative and mood depiction through musical means. Definitions of terms involved. Romanticism and the injection of the literary element into musical forms.

Essential Listening: Detailed analysis of Danse Macabre (Saint-Saëns), Night on Bald Mountain (Moussorgsky), and The Sorcerer's Apprentice (Dukas).

Additional Suggestions for Listening: the tone-poem, The Isle of the Dead (Rachmaninoff).

XIV. NATIONALISM IN MUSIC 197

Nationalism as an expression of Romanticism; biographical sketches of Smetana and Sibelius.

Essential Listening: Minute study of The Moldau (Smetana), the Overture Solennelle 1812 (Tchaikovsky), and Finlandia (Sibelius).

Additional Suggestions for Listening: Works by Sibelius, Albeniz, Grieg, Smetana, Kodály, Rimsky-Korsakoff, Liadov, German, Grofé, Enesco, and McDonald.

XV. EXOTICISM IN MUSIC: RIMSKY-KORSAKOFF 211

Romanticism and exoticism in poetry, painting, and music. Biographical sketch of Nicholas Rimsky-Korsakoff.

Essential Listening: The "Scheherezade" Symphonic Suite (Rimsky-Korsakoff); analysis of narrative and music.

Additional Suggestions for Listening: Other works by Tchaikovsky, Saint-Saëns, David, Massenet, Verdi, Puccini, Cui, Borodin, Rimsky-Korsakoff. The Caucasian Sketches (Ippolitov-Ivanov).

XVI. THE SYMPHONIC POEM: FRANZ LISZT 225

The Romantic spirit and the composer Liszt; biography of the composer and a list of his works in the symphonic poem form; his use of

CHAPTER PAGE

the "germinal motif" and thematic metamorphosis as a means of musical narrative.

Essential Listening: Les Préludes, described and analyzed in detail.

Additional Suggestions for Listening: Other works by Liszt to be chosen from the number of symphonic poems mentioned in the early paragraphs of this chapter.

XVII. **RICHARD WAGNER AND THE LEIT MOTIF TECHNIQUE** 234

Biography of Wagner and his general historical background. Enumeration of his works and statement of his ideals. The *leit motif* technique as developed by Wagner; as a means of musical narrative.

Essential Listening: The Overture to "Tannhäuser" described and analyzed from a literary as well as musical standpoint.

Additional Suggestions for Listening: Other appropriate works by Wagner to be selected from: the Prelude to "Die Meistersinger," Prelude and Entrance of the Gods into Valhalla from "Das Rhinegold," Magic Fire Scene and Ride of the Valkyries from "Die Walküre," Forest Murmurs from "Siegfried," the Rhine Journey from "Götterdämmerung," the Good-Friday Spell from "Parsifal," Siegfried's Funeral March, and the Siegfried Idyl.

XVIII. **RICHARD STRAUSS AND REALISM IN MUSIC** .. 245

Biographical sketch of the composer. The "Expressionist" composers and their ideas concerning program and descriptive music.

Essential Listening: the Symphonic Poem, the Merry Pranks of Till Eulenspiegel, with detailed analysis showing how Strauss uses the "descriptive" themes and transforms them in musical development.

Additional Suggestions for Listening: Selections to be made from other works by Strauss, including Don Juan, Don Quixote, Death and Transfiguration, Heldenleben, and Thus Spake Zarathustra.

XIX. **THE SONATA AND THE SYMPHONY** 257

A ROMANTIC SYMPHONIST: ANTONIN DVOŘÁK.

Comparisons between so-called "absolute" and "program" music. History and application of the sonata form to the symphony. Each movement of a typical work outlined and explained. The symphony as a realization of combined forms. Antonin Dvořák: his biography and his ideals.

Essential Listening: Symphony in E Minor, "From the New World" (Dvořák), with musical and formal analysis.

SCHEMATIC OUTLINE OF A SYMPHONY AS A WHOLE: The internal characteristics of each of the usual four movements of a "composite" or conventional type of symphony, with special emphasis upon the sonata-allegro form and its application. A skeletal diagram of general style and design of each movement.

XX. **BEETHOVEN: CLASSICISM AND ROMANTICISM IN IDEAL BALANCE** 281

An early Romantic symphony (the Symphony No. 5 in C Minor). Biography and general historical background of the composer and

CHAPTER   PAGE

his time; his achievements and general characteristics of Beethoven's style.

Essential Listening: Symphony No. 5 in C Minor, with musical and formal analysis.

Additional Suggestions for Listening: Beethoven's Third, Sixth, Seventh, and Ninth Symphonies.

XXI. BRAHMS: THE CLASSICAL ROMANTICIST 296

Biography and general historical background of the composer.

Essential Listening: Symphony No. 2 in D Major, with musical and formal analysis.

Additional Suggestions for Listening: In addition to the remainder of Brahms' four symphonies, selections may be made from: the "Unfinished" Symphony (Schubert), as well as his C-Major Symphony; Tchaikovsky's Fifth and Sixth Symphonies; Symphony in D Minor (Franck); the "Italian" and the "Scotch" Symphonies of Mendelssohn; the "Spring" and "Rhenish" Symphonies of Schumann; the Second Symphony in E Minor, Op. 27, by Rachmaninoff; the First, Second, Fourth, or Fifth Symphonies of Sibelius; the "Symphony Fantastique" by Berlioz; and the "London" Symphony by Vaughn-Williams.

XXII. THE CLASSICAL SYMPHONY: TWO VIENNESE MASTERS—MOZART AND HAYDN 307

Discussion of the salient characteristics of the Classical temper in painting, poetry, sculpture, and music. The Rococo versus the Classical styles. Biography and general historical backgrounds of Mozart.

Essential Listening: Symphony in G Minor, No. 40 (Mozart), with musical and structural exposition of each movement. Biography of Haydn; his style and general historical background.

Essential Listening: Symphony No. 6, in G Major, the "Surprise" (Haydn), with musical and structural analysis.

Additional Suggestions for Listening: the "Jupiter" and E-Flat Major Symphonies by Mozart; and the "Oxford," "Paris," "Clock," and "Drum-Roll" Symphonies by Haydn.

REVIEW OF SALIENT CHARACTERISTICS OF THE CLASSICAL TEMPER as they may be discovered in all the fine arts, with special emphasis upon those characteristics and traits in music.

XXIII. CLASSICAL FORM AND ROMANTIC CONTENT IN THE OVERTURE 332

The historical background of the overture; Gluck and the Classical overture; the so-called "Italian" and "French" forms of the overture; "absolute" versus "programmatic" content in the overture; the Romantic overture; the potpourri type.

Essential Listening: Overture to the opera "Der Freischütz" by Weber and the Overture "Leonora" No. 3 by Beethoven; detailed musical and formal analysis of both works.

Additional Suggestions for Listening: Overture to The Marriage of Figaro, The Magic Flute, and Don Giovanni by Mozart; the Egmont and Coriolanus Overtures by Beethoven; the Oberon and Euryanthe Overtures by Weber; and the Hebrides and Fingal's Cave Overtures by Mendelssohn.

CHAPTER   PAGE

XXIV. THE CONCERTO FOR SOLO INSTRUMENT AND ORCHESTRA 344

Musical and historical backgrounds of the Solo Concerto. Biography of Robert Schumann.

Essential Listening: Concerto for Piano and Orchestra in A Minor, Op. 54, by Robert Schumann, with historical sketch and analysis of the concerto.
Biographical review of Felix Mendelssohn.

Essential Listening: Concerto in E Minor, Op. 64, for Violin and Orchestra, by Felix Mendelssohn, with analysis of the concerto.

XXV. CHAMBER MUSIC: THE STRING QUARTET 358

History and discussion of chamber music, especially that for the string quartet. Comparisons between the orchestra and the string quartet as performing and compositional media, and their peculiar demands upon the listener. Some parallels between this type of music and the arts of drawing, painting, and sculpture.

Essential Listening: "Ein kleine Nachtmusik" by Mozart; the "Andante Cantabile" movement from String Quartet Op. 11 by Tchaikovsky; the complete String Quartet in F Major, Op. 96 (the "American"), by Antonin Dvořák. Detailed analysis of all three works.

Additional Suggestions for Listening: Selected string quartets by Haydn, Mozart, Beethoven (with representations from each of his "three periods"), Brahms, Schubert, Debussy, and Ravel, and the quintets of Schumann, Brahms, Franck, and Ernest Bloch.

XXVI. THE PIANO SOLO AND THE VIOLIN AND PIANO SONATA 371

The emergence of the solo performer and the complex relationship between the composer, performer, listener, and instrument maker.

THE PIANO: Its history and musical characteristics. Biography of Frederic Chopin; discussion of his compositional style and output.

Essential Listening: Ballade No. 3, in A-Flat Major, Op. 47, by Chopin, with detailed analysis of its contents and form.

Additional Suggestions for Listening: To be chosen from a large number of additional works of Chopin as listed in the text, together with piano compositions by Schumann, Mendelssohn, Schubert, Beethoven, Mozart, Rachmaninoff, MacDowell, Grieg, Debussy, Ravel, Franck, Scriabin, Schönberg, and others.

THE VIOLIN: THE VIOLIN AND PIANO SONATA: THE TRIO: Historical sketch of the violin; essential characteristics of the instrument and its tone. Biography of César Franck, with a discussion of his style and compositional idioms. The nature of the "idée-fixe".

Essential Listening: Sonata in A Major for Violin and Piano (Franck), with minute analysis and explanation. The three "germinal motives" underlying the entire sonata.

Additional Suggestions for Listening: A rather large list of violin and piano sonatas by Bach, Beethoven, Brahms, Corelli, Dvořák, Grieg, Handel, Mozart, Schubert, and others. Also a list of TRIOS FOR PIANO AND STRINGS by Mendelssohn, Mozart, Beethoven, Schubert, Tchaikovsky, Dvořák, and Brahms.

CHAPTER   PAGE

XXVII. BACH AND THE POLYPHONIC STYLE: THE REF-
ORMATION AND THE BAROQUE 394

Survey of the history of the contrapuntal style of music. Comparisons between homophonic and polyphonic styles. Instrumental versus
vocal means of musical expression. Bach and the Reformation.
Bach and the Baroque, with extended integration and explanation of
Baroque characteristics in painting, sculpture, architecture, and literature, and parallels with music. Descriptive analysis of the chorale,
the chorale prelude, the fugue, the Well-Tempered Clavichord, the
passacaglia, the chaconne, and the concerto grosso.

Essential Listening: Chorale preludes: "Christ Lay in the Bonds of
Death" and "Come Sweet Death"; the so-called "Little" Fugue in G
Minor, with a general explanation of the fugue form and a specific
application to this particular work; the Passacaglia in C Minor, with
explanation of its derivation and general, as well as specific, characteristics and form; the Chaconne in D Minor in its original and
orchestral versions; transcriptions of Bach's organ works.

Additional Suggestions for Listening: Rather extended list of Bach's
works to choose from in the forms of the Invention and the Prelude
and Fugue. The "Kunst der Fuge," the CONCERTO GROSSO, with brief
descriptions of the six "Brandenburg Concerti" by Bach. Additional
works by Corelli, Locatelli, Vivaldi, and Bloch, and six Concerti Grossi
by Handel.

XXVIII. IMPRESSIONISM 422

Derivation of the term and relationship to Realism, Symbolism,
Classicism, and Romanticism. Impressionism in painting, literature,
and music. Impressionism in France, England, Italy, and America.
Synthesis of the arts. Biography of Claude Debussy.

Essential Listening: Prelude to "The Afternoon of a Faun" by Debussy;
analysis from literary and musical standpoints. Brief sketch of Maurice Ravel.

Essential Listening: Daphnis and Chloé, Suite No. 2, for orchestra,
by Maurice Ravel. Program for choreography as a ballet. Ottorino
Respighi and Impressionism in Italy.

Essential Listening: "The Fountains of Rome," a symphonic poem, by
Ottorino Respighi, with literary program and musical analysis.

Additional Suggestions for Listening: In addition to other compositions
by Debussy, Ravel, and Respighi, the suggested listening includes
works by Manuel de Falla, Delius, Loeffler, Griffes, and Carpenter.

XXIX. EXPRESSIONISM AND OTHER MODERN TRENDS 440

Native and contemporary composers have been discussed throughout
previous chapters without discrimination. The present is a part of
the past as well as of the future. It is difficult to appraise contemporary works, either pro or con. Classicism, Romanticism, Realism
and symbolism co-exist now as in the past; but the manner and
means of expressing them may be different. The manner of using
techniques of music is as important as the musical idioms themselves—often more so. Neo-classicism, neo-romanticism, realism, and
primitivism. Expressionism: integration with painting. Study of pictures by Vytlacil, Picasso, and Gris. "Abstract" and non-representa-
tional art. Surrealism; Cubism. Integration of Expressionism with

literature: "Ulysses" by James Joyce, "The Hairy Ape" by Eugene O'Neill, and "Rhapsody on a Windy Night" by T. S. Eliot. Some modern techniques in music: Atonality, the twelve-tone system, the "Schönbergian Row," polytonality, poly-rhythms, modern contrapuntal techniques such as the canon, the fugue and the Canon Cancrizans. Contributors to renewed and sustaining life of art. Responsibilities of listeners; personal choices and biases inevitable and necessary.

Essential Listening: Ballet-suite, "Sacre du Printemps", by Igor Stravinsky; "Pierrot Lunaire" by Arnold Schönberg; "Mathis der Maler Suite" by Paul Hindemith; and Symphony No. 4 in A Minor, Op. 63, by Jean Sibelius.

Additional Suggestions for Listening: An extended list of works by native and foreign composers to select from as a beginning and a foundation for building the listener's own personal list of recordings; and a list of works to be heard in the concert room, as well as by radio.

POSTSCRIPT TO THE LISTENER 457

PICTORIAL ILLUSTRATIONS

SINGING BOYS FROM CHOIR GALLERY (*Della Robbia*) ...... *Frontispiece*

DANCING PEASANTS (*Brueghel*) 3

PRIMAVERA (*Botticelli*) 8

CORONATION OF NAPOLEON AND JOSEPHINE (*David*) 11

MEDIEVAL MUSIC MANUSCRIPT (*photograph*) 20

MADONNA DELLA SEDIA (*Raphael*) 23

THE FORGE (*Goya*) 31

TOMB OF GIULIANO DE' MEDICI (*Michelangelo*) 35

THE VISITATION WITH TWO SAINTS (*Piero di Cosimo*) 42

SCHOOL OF ATHENS (*Raphael*) 47

THE CAPITOL BUILDING IN WASHINGTON 48

MANUSCRIPT OF SCHUBERT'S SONG "HEIDENRÖSLEIN" (*photograph*) 57

SCENE FROM THE OPERA "AÏDA" (*Verdi*) 79

SCENE FROM THE OPERA "CARMEN" (*Bizet*) 86

MILAN CATHEDRAL (*from a photograph*) 98

PORTRAIT OF GEORGE FRIDERIC HANDEL (*from an old print*) 101

PORTRAIT OF EDWARD MACDOWELL 111

BALLET REHEARSAL ON STAGE (*Degas*) 120

A SCENE FROM THE BALLET "PETROUCHKA" BY STRAVINSKY 124

THE DOODLE-SACK PLAYER (*Dürer*) 138

A NOVEL SEATING PLAN FOR THE SYMPHONY ORCHESTRA 149

A CONVENTIONAL SEATING PLAN FOR THE SYMPHONY ORCHESTRA ... 149

FIRST PAGE OF THE FULL ORCHESTRAL SCORE OF WEBER'S OVERTURE TO
"DER FREISCHÜTZ" 151

THE PARTHENON, VIEWED FROM THE NORTHWEST (*photograph*) 159

ORPHEUS AND EURYDICE (*Poussin*) 161

ABDUCTION OF REBECCA (*Delacroix*) 163

ISLE OF THE DEAD (*Böcklin*) 183

MICKEY MOUSE AS THE SORCERER'S APPRENTICE (FROM "FANTASIA")
(*Disney*) 194

MIDNIGHT RIDE OF PAUL REVERE (*Grant Wood*) 198

THE GIRL IN THE PURPLE ROBE (*Matisse*) 212

PORTRAIT OF GEORG GISZE (*Holbein*) 246

THE BOSTON SYMPHONY ORCHESTRA (*photograph*) 260

BIRTHPLACE OF BEETHOVEN AT BONN 283

PORTRAIT OF JOHANNES BRAHMS 297

THE PURSUIT (*Fragonard*) 309

PIETÀ (*Michelangelo*) 311

A DOUBLE VIRGINAL (*old Flemish instrument*) 346

GIRL IN FEATHERED HAT (*Matisse*) 360

STRING QUARTET (*Levine*) 365

ECSTASY OF ST. THERESA (*Bernini*) 401

TOLEDO (*El Greco*) 403

ORIGINAL MANUSCRIPT OF A BACH "ORGAN PRELUDE" 407

ROUEN CATHEDRAL (*photograph*) 425

A PAINTING OF ROUEN CATHEDRAL (*Monet*) 426

NOCTURNE: A CANAL IN HOLLAND (*Whistler*) 431

STILL LIFE WITH FRUIT (*Vytlacil*) 449

THE THREE MUSICIANS (*Picasso*) 450

STILL LIFE (*Gris*) 454

Chapter I

MUSIC AND THE DANCE

SINCE music does not attempt to reproduce the exact shapes and images of the real world in the tangible way that literature and painting do, many persons have come to think of the art of sound as being remote and divorced from life. As a matter of fact, from its very beginnings in savage and primitive society, music has been an integral part of the daily life of the individual and the group. Whether to express triumph over the enemy or thanksgiving for the harvest, the praise of heroes or the pleasures of the hunt, religious feelings, incantation against evil spirits, tenderness for the beloved or lament for the dead, music is called upon to convey and at the same time to heighten the emotional side of man's experiences. Let us, by way of introduction, examine some of these uses of music, and by so doing perceive more clearly the relation of the art of music to our daily lives and its place in society as a whole.

In all times and places music has been a necessary part of the dance. On the one hand, it serves the immediate purpose of keeping the dancers in step. More important psychologically, it helps to create and sustain that mood of joy and physical well-being that finds its natural expression in rhythmic bodily movement. Wherever people come together for social purposes they require music to create the proper festive atmosphere. Naturally, the music differs with each country and century, reflecting the tastes and needs of the particular social environment. But the basic emotional responses are more or less the same everywhere.

We may begin our study and our first listening by playing a *popular dance record*, any one of the current hits. How eloquently the abrupt rhythms, the spicy harmonies and instrumental effects express the feverish tempo of modern life! This is the music of a sophisticated urban culture, breathing an air of restless gaiety and movement, awakening in the listener an almost irresistible physical response. One is immediately struck by the fact that in this modern equivalent of folk-dance music, rhythm is immeasurably more important than melody. From the first pulsation of the drums and double basses, we are in a world of ecstatic rhythm. Clarinet, saxophone, and trumpet alternate and unite in dazzling improvisations that completely wipe out the original tune. Only the harmonies and rhythm remain to make the blood run faster and the muscles flex more vigorously.

The traditional folk dance makes its appeal in somewhat simpler fashion. Try listening, as our second essential study, to our own *Turkey in the Straw*, as arranged by David Guion. The melodies go along merrily, with clusters of rapid notes and clearly marked accents, in a manner dear to generations of village fiddlers. This music, too, conjures up a definite way of life: the boisterous jollity of hard-working agricultural folk, the barn dance on Saturday night, with much clapping of hands and stamping of feet. Before long you will find yourself beating time, with a "down-up" of the hand or foot, in what is the simplest of rhythmic patterns: ONE-two, ONE-two—an accented or strong beat alternating with an unaccented or weak beat (the musical equivalent of the pattern we get when we stand marking time with LEFT-right, LEFT-right). This rhythmic grouping is known as two beats in a measure, or duple meter.

The lilting waltzes of Johann Strauss (1825-1899) sing of still another milieu, of a nineteenth-century dream city that has become the symbol of an era. Listen to his *Beautiful Blue Danube*. How well these flowing melodies combine urbanity and tenderness, gaiety and longing, the spirit of the dance with the nostalgic! Again you will find yourself beating time with the music. But the rhythmic movement is broader here, more flowing. This is waltz time, to which we can count ONE-two-three, ONE-two-three: a pattern consisting of an accented beat followed by two unaccented beats, giving us three beats in a measure, or triple meter. (This is our third essential listening project.)

Since dancing and singing are such deep-rooted human impulses and are among all people so close to the life of the folk, it was natural that each nation should develop its own musical idiom, as characteristic as its spoken language. The great composers found inspiration in the rich literature of native folk song and attempted in their art to capture and express the spirit of their homelands. The national dances that they wrote vary in mood from gentle melancholy to joyous abandon, but all breathe the spirit of the folk, the vigorous peasant rhythms, the melodic richness and pungent flavor of the countryside.

And all speak the simple language of the heart, which knows no barriers of nation, race, or time.

Fine examples of this folk-dance genre within the literature of "composed art music," to distinguish it from the traditional type, are the SLAVONIC DANCES of Anton Dvořák, of which we should now

COURTESY OF THE UNIVERSITY PRINTS, NEWTON, MASS.

DANCING PEASANTS   *Brueghel*

hear the first, that in E minor. Dvořák (1841-1904), himself of peasant stock, was an ardent nationalist and stands in European music, together with his compatriot and guide, Bedrich Smetana (1824-1884), as the voice of the Czech nation—musically speaking. (This is to be used as the fourth essential listening project of the chapter.)

The *Slavonic Dance No. 1*, originally written for piano duet, has become very popular in the orchestral version as well as in Fritz Kreisler's arrangement for violin solo. The opening section brings us a poignant melody in triple meter, with that undercurrent of melancholy so often found in the folk music of Central and Southeastern Europe, and with a strong Gypsy coloring. (As in Hungary and Rumania, the Gypsies left their imprint on the musical idiom of Bohemia.)

In the middle section the mood brightens; the pace becomes animated. A playful theme appears, followed by a broad lyrical melody, serene and folklike in character. Then we return to the somber mood of the opening theme. This music has warmth and forthrightness and is rooted—as its composer wished it to be—in the soil of his native land.

Notice how clear-cut is the contrast in mood between the opening section and the two themes in the middle part. Having achieved a pleasant diversity of effect, the composer returns to his original melody, which balances and unifies the structural scheme of the composition.

A popular dance form of the eighteenth-century composers was the *Rondo,* based upon the old French round dance (much like our ring-around-the-rosy type of dance), in which the leader's tune alternates with that sung by the dancing ring. This form might be basically described as A^1-B-A^2-C-A^3, and so on, although many variants are possible. The distinguishing feature is the recurrence throughout of the main, or first, theme, separated by episodes, or contrasting material. An excellent variant of this type is the old French rondo, *Amaryllis* (Ghys). Haydn, Mozart, Beethoven, and countless other composers have used this type of dance form in their symphonies, chamber music, and other works. Listen to *Amaryllis* and try to recognize the principal theme when it recurs.[1] (See also Chapter V, page 49.) (This is the fifth essential listening project of the chapter.)

What Mozart and Haydn did for the dance of the Classical Period, the great Johann Sebastian Bach (1685-1750) did in the early part of the eighteenth century. In his DANCE SUITES, as in those of his contemporaries, we find characteristic dance rhythms of the various na-

---

[1] Mozart and Haydn are generally referred to as the two outstanding masters of the "Classical Period." In this connection it might not be amiss to clear up some misconceptions surrounding the use of the word *classical.* In colloquial speech, the term is generally used to denote art music as opposed to popular music, or "jazz." For the musician, *classical* refers to an art style distinguished from *romantic,* the classical spirit seeking to recapture the qualities of serenity, universality, restraint, and perfection of form associated with the art of Greece in classical antiquity. The historian often applies the term "Classical Period" to the second half of the eighteenth century when the spirit of classicism was very much to the fore in European art, as distinct from the "Romantic Period," which is generally considered to have begun after the French Revolution and to have lasted for the greater part of the nineteenth century. (For a detailed discussion of the two styles and the two periods, see Chapter XII.) The schematic phrase design of *Amaryllis* is A-A-B-A-A-C-C-B-C-A-A.

tions of Europe brought together. There is the *Allemande*, or German dance, a moderately slow movement in quadruple meter; the French *Courante*, which as its name implies contains running passages and simple rhythms; the stately *Sarabande*, of Spanish or Moorish ancestry, in slow triple meter; the *Bourrée* and *Branle*, rollicking French peasant dances in vigorous duple meter; the *Polonaise*, a martial Polish dance, almost like a march, in a broad, strongly accented triple meter; the dignified but vivacious *Gavotte*, a French court dance with four beats to a measure; and the lively Italian *Giga* (*Gigue*), allied to the English *Jig*, with three or six rapidly paced beats to a measure. Let us listen to Bach's *Suite No. 2 in B minor*, for flute and strings, which contains a rondo, sarabande, bourrée, polonaise, and minuet. The suite opens with an overture, and ends with a section called *Badinerie*, which, as the title implies, is full of playfulness and mischief. Here is merry, heart-warming music, rich with the spirit of the dance. If time does not permit the playing of all the records of this suite, select accordingly. (This is the sixth, and last, listening suggestion for this chapter.)

ADDITIONAL SUGGESTIONS FOR LISTENING

The "masters" often wrote in idealized dance forms—that is, they sought to capture the spirit of the dance in art music rather than to create music for actual dancing. Thus, Frederic Chopin (1810-1849), one of the most distinctive of the Romanticists, transformed the rhythms of the waltz into something altogether personal and subtle, what the critic, James Huneker, called "a dance of the spirit rather than of the body." Listen to his *Waltz in C-Sharp Minor*, a poetic idealization of this dance form, tinged with gentle sadness. Notice the clearly defined sectional construction, similar to that found in the *Slavonic Dance*, each section introducing a melody and mood of its own. The hauntingly lovely opening theme is followed by a caressing melody in running notes. Then comes a broad, flowing theme of quiet lyricism and serenity. By introducing new melodic material, Chopin sustains our interest and achieves a pleasantly varied effect. By repeating the old, at judicious intervals, he gives coherence and unity to his structural scheme, a sense of orderly and symmetrical arrangement.

In *Golliwog's Cakewalk*, Claude Debussy (1862-1918) makes delightful use of the rollicking American dance rhythm that was popular at the turn of the century. The piece was written for piano, one of a set of five known as THE CHILDREN'S CORNER. Golliwog is an imaginary figure who, in the middle of the dance, becomes romantic, at which point the composer introduces with sly satire the opening notes of the love theme from Wagner's TRISTAN AND ISOLDE. Save for this brief interlude, the music struts and bounces along with gusto—and cleverness.

Also listen to the "Rhumba" movement from Harl McDonald's *Symphony No. 2*.

Rhythm: The Heartbeat of Music

The compositions we have just heard differ in style and content, but they all share certain basic elements. There is the melody, or tune, which caught and held our attention, and the harmony, the chords that accompany and support the melody. There is the steady pulse of the rhythm (to which some of the listeners may have responded by beating time quite unconsciously with the music). Each performing instrument has a distinctive tone color, which either blends with that of the other instruments sounding simultaneously or stands out by itself. The various themes alternate, as we saw, in accordance with a definite structural pattern. In addition, the music grows softer or louder at various times, and travels at a faster or slower pace. Let us begin with the element that plays so decisive a part in all dance music—the rhythm.

"In the beginning was rhythm," Johannes Brahms is reported to have said. Unquestionably, rhythm is one of the basic elements in music, and one with universal appeal. One has only to watch people fall into step or nod their heads as the band plays to realize how irresistible is its power. In primitive society, the rhythmic beating of the drums takes on a ritualistic or magical potency. Some writers on music go so far as to ascribe the origin of the art to the stamping, clapping, and beating that accompanied the work and play activities, the harvesting, threshing, ceremonial dances, and sacrificial rites of the primitive tribes. In any case, when we hear a haphazard succession of sounds coming at irregular intervals, we remain more or less indifferent. But as soon as these sounds are arranged in a regular sequence of accented and unaccented beats, repeated over and over, we become aware of a rhythmic pattern and respond accordingly. We begin to expect the accent in a definite place, and receive a pleasant sense of security from having our expectation fulfilled. Rhythm is the heartbeat, the pulse, of the music. The word in Greek means "flow" or "flowing." Rhythm may be defined as the element of music that regulates its forward movement through the regular recurrence of accented and unaccented beats in a pattern.

Actually, rhythm is not restricted to music. It enters into painting and all the arts of design, where the subtle repetition of a decorative pattern reinforces the relationship of the parts to the whole, balancing and unifying the composition. The great painters were masters of spatial rhythm. See (on page 8) in the "Primavera" of Sandro Botticelli (1447-1510), how subtle are the internal rhythms uniting the individual figures and the groups to the total design. Within the rectangular framework, the movement is carried in a vast oval from the figure of the wind on the right, along the curve of the trees, to the cherub on top and down again along the raised arm of the figure on the left. Within this oval are three smaller ones taking in the two groups of figures arranged symmetrically on either side, and the central figure of Spring, framed so dramatically by the arching trees and the cherub overhead. Notice how rhythmically the movement flows from one end of the canvas to the other, from the male figure on the left, along the billowing draperies and raised arms

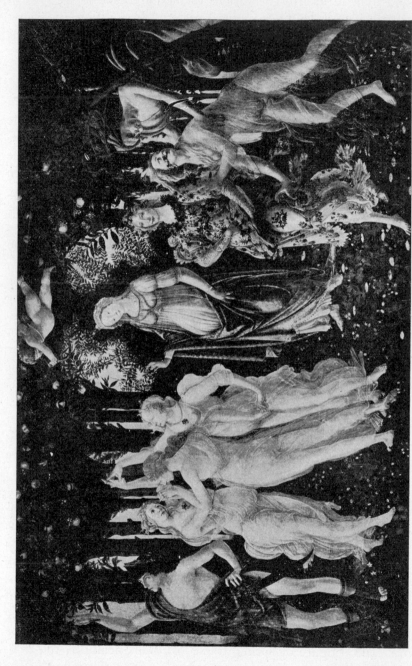

PRIMAVERA

COURTESY OF THE UNIVERSITY PRINTS, NEWTON, MASS.

Botticelli

of the nymphs, curving gently over the central figure, and sweeping on to the group at the right. Synchronized with this movement is the vertical rhythm of the trees in the background and the positions of the individual figures, the whole melting in a harmonious interplay of rhythmic design.

Rhythm figures no less prominently in the art of poetry, where the arrangement of the lines in metrical patterns adds a strange power to the music of the words. Through these patterns poets have achieved a marvelous diversity of effect and have mastered the most subtle musical cadences of which language is capable. The simpler metrical combinations are familiar to all. The sonnets of Shakespeare are superb examples of the *iambic pentameter*, two beats to a measure, accent on the second, five measures (or feet, as we call them in scanning poetry) in each line:

> Shall *I* com*pare* thee *to* a *sum*mer's *day?*
> Thou *art* more *love*ly *and* more *tem*per*ate.*

Robert Browning in his "Song" used two beats to a measure, accent on the first, four measures to a line (*trochee*):

> *Nay* but *you,* who *do* not *love* her,
> *Is* she *not* pure *gold,* my *mis*tress?

Three beats to a measure, accent on the first, three measures to a line, characterize Longfellow's "Evangeline" (*dactyl*):

> *This* is the *for*est pri*me*val,
> The *mur*muring *pines* and the *hem*locks.

Three beats to a measure, accent on the third, mark Byron's "Sennacharib" (*anapest*):

> The As*syr*ian came *down* like a *wolf* on the *fold;*
> And his *co*horts were *gleam*ing in *pur*ple and *gold.*

We see, then, that in all ages, no matter in what medium he works, man derives untold pleasure and satisfaction from the simple, orderly arrangement of the accented and unaccented pulsations upon which rhythm depends. In the ideal world that he has created for himself through art, these pulsations assume the importance of a vital force, a dynamic principle. They constitute the very heartbeat of the art of music.

Chapter II

MUSIC AND CEREMONY

MUSIC plays its part not only in moments of festivity and recreation, but also at occasions when a more lofty mood, whether of triumph, exaltation, or grief, is appropriate. From earliest times men have relied on music to heighten the impressiveness of ceremonies marking the important events of their existence as individuals and as members of the social group.

The military march, with its stirring trumpet and drum passages, its simple melodies and steady beat, has always served to arouse a festive and martial mood. An example of what this type of music can become in the hands of a great artist is the *Marche Militaire* by Franz Schubert (1797-1828). The spirited opening theme, in strongly accented duple meter, is vibrant with energy and movement.

Notice the contrast with the quieter middle section, where the music takes on grace and lightness, after which it returns (in simple, symmetrical, A-B-A formation) to the opening theme.[1] Notice, too, that the music seems to be laid out in simple symmetrical sections, a type of architecture highly appropriate to "outdoor" music.

The ceremonial march often creates an effect of great dignity, pomp, and patriotic fervor. For an example of this type, play Edward Elgar's *Pomp and Circumstance*, which has become almost a national march for Britain. Marches of this kind are most often in a rather slowly paced four-four time, which imparts a broad span to the meas-

---

[1] This A-B-A basic formation may be taken to mean, for the moment, first a statement of the principal theme, then an appearance of a contrasting section, and finally the restatement of the main theme after the contrast. Mutations and adaptations of this form will be noted in subsequent pages.

ure. For a good example of the more rapid (quick-step) type of march, listen to *Stars and Stripes Forever*, by our own "March King," John Philip Sousa. Such marches are likely to be in a fast two-four or six-eight time, with the last mentioned given only two beats to a measure.

The march, like the dance, depends upon rhythmic bodily movement, upon music with a strong pulse and with catchy melodies that are easy to whistle and hum. March and dance come together in the broad triple meter of the *Polonaise*, the stately processional dance in

COURTESY OF THE UNIVERSITY PRINTS, NEWTON, MASS.

CORONATION OF NAPOLEON AND JOSEPHINE   *David*

which the Polish nobles filed past the throne of their kings. Chopin's *Polonaise Militaire* brings us this march dance in its proudest and most military mood. Notice here, too, the layout of the music in simple symmetrical sections and the effective contrast between the brusque opening theme and the broad second theme.[2]

For ceremonial music on the grand scale, we turn to the *Triumphal March* from Giuseppe Verdi's opera, AïDA. Here is the perfect setting for pomp and pageantry as trumpets and drums roar a welcome

---

[2] The smooth, connected style that we heard in the second theme, where every tone melted into the next, is known as *legato*, in contrast to *staccato*, a short, sharp, and disconnected manner of playing the notes.

to the victorious Radames, general of the Egyptians, and his army at the gates of Thebes. Note particularly the effect of the rich massive chords at the opening, the brilliant tone color of the brass in the second theme, and the imposing effect of the melody supported by a full running accompaniment in the final section.[3]

Music figures no less prominently in ceremonies of a more personal character. The *Wedding March* from Wagner's LOHENGRIN has become part of the heritage of all nations. Listen to this in the *Bridal Chorus* version, as it contains beautiful choral writing.

The steady duple meter (a meter divisible by two) has nobility and breadth. When played in the correct tempo, this music is an exalted, fiery processional, instead of the languid, drawn-out distortion that too often is heard at weddings.[4]

As universal in scope is the somber music that accompanies the

---

[3] For supplementary processional music of similar character, listen to the majestic *War March of the Priests* from Mendelssohn's ATHALIE, the *Grand March* from Wagner's TANNHÄUSER (Entrance of the Knights), or the *Coronation March* from Giacomo Meyerbeer's LE PROPHÈTE.

[4] Different in mood is the gay and fanciful *Wedding March* from Mendelssohn's MIDSUMMER NIGHT'S DREAM that so well captures the spirit of Shakespeare's fantasy. Other examples of this type of ceremonial music that you should be acquainted with are the *Norwegian Bridal Procession* of Grieg, and the *Bridal Cortege* from Nicholas Rimsky-Korsakoff's fairy opera COQ D'OR.

rites for the dead. Chopin's magnificent *Funeral March* is known all over the world.

How eloquently the solemn opening chords create the atmosphere of grief! The music surges with despair. Then, as if emotion had worn itself out, comes the benign legato melody of the middle part, a song of resignation and tenderness. But the surcease is brief and we are plunged back again into the darkly quivering chords of the opening. Here indeed music says all the things that language would, but cannot.

From the structural standpoint, it is hardly necessary .to call attention to the A-B-A form, contrast between the chord theme and the legato melody of the middle part, and the spacious quadruple meter.[5]

ADDITIONAL SUGGESTIONS FOR LISTENING

As in the case of the dance, the diverse moods of ceremonial music found expression, on a more abstract plane, in the symphonies of the great composers. One of the noblest of all funeral marches is the slow movement from Beethoven's THIRD SYMPHONY, the *Eroica*. The simple, marchlike theme, announced by the violins, has that quality of intense feeling and sublimity of expression which is truly Beethovenian. The movement sweeps on in lonely grandeur until we come to the second theme, which is rich in courage and humanity. The themes are worked out in rich symphonic style, steadily mounting in intensity. Then the sorrowful first theme re-enters. If the Chopin *Funeral March* is an outpouring of grief for an individual, the slow movement of the *Eroica* is a lamentation for all mankind.

[5] The essential listening for this chapter includes: *Marche Militaire* by Schubert, *Pomp and Circumstance* by Elgar, *Stars and Stripes Forever* by Sousa, *Polonaise Militaire* by Chopin, *Triumphal March* from AÏDA by Verdi, *Wedding March* by Wagner, and the *Funeral March* by Chopin. The other works mentioned may be considered optional.

The mood of the triumphal march has been sublimated, with memorable effect, in the third movement of Tchaikovsky's SIXTH SYMPHONY, the *Pathetique*. The violins and woodwinds bustle about in the mazes of a complex orchestral web. There are traces of dancelike gaiety, which float across the scene for an instant and disappear. Presently a march tune in four-four time enters unobtrusively on the oboe:

The music gathers strength, the theme is passed from one instrument to the other; it grows steadily from its modest beginnings, becomes a swift, driving force. Now it achieves its full splendor, bursting forth from the brass in shattering clarion call, a feverish march movement that sweeps all obstacles before it, a veritable tornado of clashing cymbals and drums.

Melody and Harmony

If rhythm is the heartbeat of music, melody is its soul. It is the melody that projects much of the emotional message of the music to the usual listener; it is the melody that he will most likely remember, and sing or whistle with all the joy of recollection. True, in modern sophisticated dance music the rhythm seems at times to overshadow the melody. True also that, in contemporary music, long, lyrical melody no longer plays quite so important a part as it did in the music of the Classic and Romantic periods. Despite all this, as far as most music lovers are concerned, nothing quite equals the power of melody to captivate the human heart. Actually, there is no need to contrast or separate rhythm and melody, since the two most often exist together in the music. As we sing the melody, we are at the same time responding to its rhythm. If we change the rhythm, the effect of the melody is changed as well.

Melody may be defined as a succession of musical tones arranged in a meaningful pattern. We do not "get" the melody until we have grasped the meaning of the pattern. We saw, in the case of rhythm, that haphazard or isolated beats bear no special significance for us. It is only when these beats are arranged in definite, easily recognizable patterns that they evoke in us an emotional response. So, too, with melody. A single tone tells us little. It is only when one tone leads to another, and still another, when each takes on a definite relation to the pattern as a whole, that a melody assumes fullest significance. The tones rise and fall, communicating meanings to us that far transcend the power of words, and can only be expressed through and by themselves.

In this process, everything depends upon the ease with which the listener grasps the connection of the tones, the meaningfulness of the pattern. Folk songs and popular tunes usually present no great problem. The pattern more often than not is so simple and obvious that everybody gets it after the first or second hearing. Other melodies may be more sophisticated; they demand more expertness on the part of the listener. Still others are like those forbidding individuals whom one has to meet again and again before they will open up and reveal their true characters. How often it happens that, through repeated hearings, we grasp the significance of a melodic pattern which in the beginning altogether eluded us! As we continue to listen to great music, we broaden our experience in grasping tonal relationships, we become more and more sensitive to their implications, until a melody of Brahms or Debussy may come to be as lucid and comprehensible as one by Stephen Foster.

We have called melody the soul of music. Harmony is its body, its substance. The harmony supports the melody and serves as a background for it. Sometimes the two are as one. Harmony, in its simplest form, consists of chords; these are clusters of tones sounded simultaneously within the rhythmic pattern, and providing an accompaniment for the melody—the "um-pah-pah" that the left hand sounds while the right hand plays the tune, or that the banjo player thrums on his instrument while he sings. Notice, in the following example—the first phrase of *Long, Long Ago*—how the cluster effect of the chords and the curvilinear quality of the melody are indicated in the two staves of adapted piano music:

Just as in a painting the background harmonizes with and brings out the figures, sometimes even revealing them in a new light, so harmony colors and enriches the melody.

Various chords have distinctive personalities of their own. Some, sweetly harmonious, give an effect of rest and fulfillment. Others are harshly dissonant, clangorous, restlessly seeking completion. There are chords softly sensuous and caressing—how well Wagner knew their secret!—or grim with foreboding, or feverish and unstable. For the moment, suffice it to say that harmony not only adds support and third dimension to melody, but also, through its chords, reinforces the rhythm. We saw at the beginning of this section that in our system of music melody does not exist without rhythm. Nor does it exist without harmony, either actual or implied. Even when we whistle or sing only the melodic line, we may "hear" the harmonic background in our imagination.

Like melody, rhythm, tone color, and form, harmony has a special contribution to make to the total musical effect. In a love song, where the melody holds the center of the stage, the harmony is likely to remain discreetly in the background. In the dance, where rhythm is important, the harmony comes to the fore as thumping chords. In religious music, the swelling harmonies of organ and choir attain prime importance in creating the lofty, devotional mood.

Chapter III

MUSIC AND RELIGION

OF ALL the ceremonies in human society, those concerned with religious worship are the most profound. They express the depths of man's noblest and sublimest emotions. Above all else, religious worship is a universal expression of man's devotion to the ideals he envisages in his fellow men and his God.

From time immemorial art has been the handmaiden of religion, shedding all its luster upon the rites through which men worship. Architecture contributed the majestic cathedral with its vaulted arches soaring gracefully heavenward. The greatest painters and sculptors vied with one another to decorate the altarpieces and chapels. Master craftsmen gave their best in stained glass, in chalices of gold, in tapestries and vestments. In this atmosphere of splendor, a solemn ritual developed, designed to induce in the worshipper a mood of religious exaltation and to turn his thoughts to the fundamental problems of his spiritual life. It is hardly necessary to add that, in this union of the arts, music occupied a very important place. Indeed, because of its power over the hearts of men, music became one of the indispensable components of the divine service. And some of the most sublime measures ever written were inspired by religious feeling. Music serves either to create a mood or to be expressive of a mood that already exists.

Perhaps the most universal expression of the religious emotion is to be found in the hymn, which has become as much a part of our cultural heritage as the folk song. Since hymns were intended for performance by the entire congregation, they had to be tunes that could be easily remembered and easily sung; they had to function within a limited vocal range, to avoid rhythmic complexities and wide skips, to reflect faithfully the devotional spirit of the poetry, and to follow the metrical cadence of the words in so direct a fashion that the congregation would stay together in the singing. One has only to recall *A Mighty Fortress Is Our God, Christ Lay in the Bonds of*

Death, Jesus Joy of Man's Desiring, or *Lead Kindly Light* and *Onward Christian Soldiers* to realize that the restrictions we have enumerated did not hamper the form, but on the contrary aided it. What emerged was a body of enduring melody, profoundly expressive, that summed up the hopes and visions of many generations of men. Of the hymns just mentioned, it is suggested that you listen now to *A Mighty Fortress Is Our God,* which served as a battle hymn of the Reformation.[1]

Notice that the melody proceeds in short units and then pauses, as though to draw breath. We call these melodic units *phrases,* and the stopping places are the *cadences.* It goes without saying that when words are set to music the melody is molded, as it were, to the metrical patterns of the verse, so that both become indissoluble parts of a greater whole. Notice, too, that the rhythm moves in regular pulses, and that the chords supporting the hymn are simple but sonorous and full-bodied, as befits music of steadfastness and solemn purpose. Let us consider several types of chants and hymns.

Of remote antiquity are the Hebrew chants, a living art in the synagogue handed down from one generation to the next for well over 2,000 years. Naturally, these melodies underwent many changes as they assimilated various foreign elements. From its birthplace in the Orient, the Hebrew chant has retained some characteristics akin to those of the religious song of the Arabic world; but, at the same time, through the constant interchange between Greek and Hebrew culture at the beginning of the Christian era, it undoubtedly assimilated many elements of Greek music. To these were added, centuries later, the influences stemming from close contact with Western European culture. Listen to the *Kaddish* (Chant for the Dead), a particularly impressive example of Hebrew religious song. Better known is *Kol Nidrei,* the traditional melody that the Jews of Spain sang during the terrors of the Inquisition in the reign of Ferdinand and Isabella, and that has become part of the solemn service for the Day of Atonement.

The Christian service, which owes much to Hebrew and Greek cultures, naturally combined the heritage of both in its early liturgical chants. These religious songlike expressions evidenced themselves in

---

[1] Or use the *Doxology* on page 396. Essential listening for this chapter includes: *A Mighty Fortress Is Our God;* Jewish Chant *Kaddish; Kyrie, Gloria,* or *Tenebrae factae sunt* from Gregorian Chants; *Sanctus* and *Gloria* from Pope Marcellus Mass by Palestrina; Chorale: *Jesu, Joy of Man's Desiring,* by Bach; *Credo, Crucifixus, Et Resurrexit,* and *Sanctus* from Bach's B-MINOR MASS—reduce to the Sanctus only if necessary. Other works mentioned are optional.

many styles and directions until codified in the latter part of the sixth century under the official egis of Pope Gregory the Great (540-604), and they remained the predominant form and style of European sacred music throughout the Middle Ages; yes, they have continued quite unchanged right into our own day and are still a regular part of church services of the Roman faith (and others too) the world over. The Gregorian chants, as we now identify them, are, like those of ancient Greek and Hebrew styles, of a pure vocal line without harmonic accompaniment and are usually sung in unison. In the words of one of the greatest authorities on the chant, Dom Andre Mocquereau, ". . . it appeals to what is highest in the soul; its beauty, its nobility, come from the fact that it borrows nothing, or as little as possible, from the world of the senses."

The Gregorian chant is based upon a melodic and rhythmic system quite different from the church tunes of our own time. Listen to some characteristic examples—the *Kyrie* and *Gloria* from the *Ordinary of the Mass*, or the *Tenebrae factae sunt*, which describes the death of Christ on the Cross.[2] This music has about it a strange quality of otherworldness, of timelessness, of spirituality. (Note the apparently unmetrical and asymmetrical character of these old chants.)

From approximately 1200 to 1700, composers of Western Europe experimented with combining two or more voices, or melodic lines, simultaneously. From these early beginnings an art style, that was both religious and secular, grew and reigned supreme in Western Europe for centuries. Some contemporary composers find inspiration in this old style. The art of combining several independent voice lines into a whole is called the art of *polyphony* (from the Greek *poly*, "many," and *phonē*, "sound"). Polyphonic music, or as it is often called, contrapuntal music, is distinguished from the prevailing style of more recent times, *homophonic*, or monodic music, in which an individual melody stands out from its harmonic, or supporting, background. (See also page 395.)

A long line of composers explored the manifold possibilities of combining many voices and developed an amazing technique that could weave as many as thirty or more vocal parts into an intricate polyphonic composition. One of the greatest of these masters of church music in the polyphonic style was Giovanni Pierluigi Palestrina (1524-1594), who, in the period of the Counter-Reformation,

---

[2] The reader is advised to listen to the records of Gregorian chants prepared by the monks of the Abbey of Saint-Pierre de Solesmes and issued by Victor as *Masterpiece Album M-87*.

A MEDIEVAL MANUSCRIPT

brought this type of music to its highest perfection. It is with good reason that the period of Palestrina and of his great contemporary, Orlando Lassus (1532-1594), has gone down in music history as the "golden age of choral music."

Now listen to the *Sanctus* and *Gloria* from the MASS FOR POPE MARCELLUS, by Palestrina. Note how smoothly the vocal texture flows along, how beautifully the different voices are blended and contrasted. There is in the music of Palestrina the note of true religious fervor, of contemplation and purity, that marks it as one of the high points in the history of religious art.

In the early sixteenth century Luther, in carrying through his religious reforms, substituted for the intricate polyphonic church music that could be performed only by a choir of highly trained singers, simple hymn tunes with texts in the vernacular that the whole congregation was able to sing—the *chorales*. In the course of two centuries a rich chorale literature sprang from the very roots of the religious life of the nation. This was Bach's heritage. Upon it he reared the structure of his art. The spirit of the chorale permeates his church cantatas, chorale preludes, hymns and sacred songs, and receives its ultimate expression in the ST. JOHN and ST. MATTHEW PASSIONS.

By a *cantata* is meant a choral work of comparatively modest dimensions, either sacred—in which case it is generally intended as part of the church service—or secular, as a short lyric drama or story adapted to music but not intended to be acted. Bach, as Cantor of St. Thomas' Church, wrote cantatas for each Sunday of the church year, besides works for festivals and special occasions. The cantata was generally named after the chorale upon which it was based, and consisted of several sections for solo voices, with ensemble numbers and choruses interspersed, accompanied by organ and groups of instruments. The form was extremely flexible, and varied with the particular resources at the disposal of the composer. Passages from the Bible and religious texts were strung together to illustrate or expand upon different aspects of the thought embodied in the chorale text. The spirit was mystical and prayerful. Bach's settings of the familiar chorale tunes, as well as his presentation of original melodies, are masterpieces of imagination, his bold harmonies and rich counterpoint revealing the beauties of the famous chorale, *Jesu Joy of Man's Desiring*, from CANTATA No. 147, with its quality of naïve joy and faith.[3]

From the *preluding* (extemporization) of the organist, when he

---

[3] It is earnestly suggested that the listener hear *both* the original choral form of the chorale and the instrumental version.

announced to the congregation the chorale to be sung, arose the art of the instrumental chorale prelude, in which the tune of the hymn to be sung served as the basis for the improvisation.[4]

Most imposing of Bach's religious works, in grandeur and scale of conception, are the PASSION ACCORDING TO ST. MATTHEW, which we shall consider later, and the B-MINOR MASS. Although the Mass was written to the Latin text of the Catholic service—Bach sent the *Kyrie* and *Gloria* to the Catholic Elector of Saxony, whom he hoped to make his patron—the music is quite Lutheran in outlook and spirit. Indeed, some of the material was borrowed by Bach from his earlier Protestant masses and cantatas. In addition, the use of an orchestral accompaniment makes the *Mass* impractical to perform during the regular church service. It is, in reality, a festival piece.

The B-MINOR MASS represents the apex of the polyphonic tradition which had nurtured generations of church composers, and which had received such polished expression two centuries before in the music of Palestrina. Yet, beside the "seraphic harmonies" of the Roman master so close in spirit to the smiling madonnas of Raphael, the B-MINOR MASS appears stern and rugged, a song of strength attained through suffering and grief. The sorrow of Christ, the soul tormented and longing for union with God, salvation and life eternal —those were the issues that fired the imagination of Bach to the crowning glory of his art. Listen to the soaring phrases of the *Credo*, the mournful *Crucifixus*, in which the reiterated descent of the bass and the motive of grief in the strings give a vivid tone painting of Christ's suffering on the cross, the joyous and hopeful *Et Resurrexit*, and the massive polyphonic architecture of the *Sanctus*. The music throughout is an eloquent expression of deep religious feeling and conviction. (Reduce to the *Sanctus* if time is limited.)

---

[4] See Chapter XXVII, for fuller exposition of chorale prelude.

MADONNA DELLA SEDIA *Raphael*

ADDITIONAL SUGGESTIONS FOR LISTENING [5]

So profound an impulse as the religious naturally made itself felt in many works of the great composers that were not intended for use with any actual church service. Although Richard Wagner (1813-1883) wrote for the opera house, certainly the *Prelude* to LOHENGRIN, depicting the descent of the Holy Grail from Heaven, breathes a spirit of devotion and faith. Celestial harmonies steal upon the air from out the highest register of the strings. Gradually the music descends, growing ever richer in color; the crescendo builds unerringly toward an overpowering climax; now the Grail theme is intoned in all the sonorities of the brass, as though to envelop the worshipper in its splendor. Then the music withdraws and fades away.

Religious legend receives an even more mystical expression in Wagner's *Prelude* to his last work, the festival drama, PARSIFAL. Here the motives symbolize the Last Supper of Christ and the Apostles, the Lance that pierced the side of the Saviour, the Good Friday Spell, the Grail theme based upon the *Dresden Amen*, and the powerful Faith theme. Wagner believed that art could have as purifying an influence on the souls of men as religion, and that the music drama could achieve the same spirituality as the rites of a church. The *Prelude* to PARSIFAL is a convincing example of his attempts in this direction.

Among symphonic movements, the *Finale* of Mendelssohn's "REFORMATION" SYMPHONY builds up to a stirring climax on the Lutheran hymn *A Mighty Fortress Is Our God*. Mendelssohn was the composer who rescued Bach from the neglect into which the old master had fallen in the half century after his death. It was fitting that in this FIFTH "REFORMATION" SYMPHONY Mendelssohn should have returned to the chorale which had been so vital an inspiration to the composer whom he admired above all others.

And certainly one of the most eloquent expressions of the religious spirit—using the term in its broadest sense—in all music is to be found in the exalted setting of Schiller's "Ode to Joy" in the *Finale* of Beethoven's last symphony, the *Ninth:*

Praise to Joy, the God-descended Daughter of Elysium!
Ray of mirth and rapture blended, Goddess, to thy shrine we come . . .
O ye millions, I embrace ye, with a kiss for all the world.
Brothers, o'er yon starry sphere surely dwells a loving Father.
O ye millions, kneel before Him; World, dost feel thy Maker near?
Seek Him o'er yon starry sphere, o'er the stars enthroned, adore Him! [6]

---

[5] Further discussion of religious music may be found in Chapter VIII.

[6] The English translation generally used in performances in this country is by Natalia Macfarren, published by Novello and Company Ltd., London (New York: the H. W. Gray Company, agents). Printed by permission.

Volume and Speed as Elements in Emotional Expression: Dynamics and Tempo

We have seen how the composer uses rhythm, melody, and harmony to achieve his musical effects. Closely associated with these is *dynamics* (from the Greek *dynamis*, "power" or "strength"), the element of power and volume in music, of softness or loudness of tone. From the whisper of the muted violin or of a single voice to the thunderous jubilation of the *Et Resurrexit* chorus of the B-MINOR MASS, music is capable of innumerable gradations, each producing a different emotional effect. Sorrow, joy, mystery, triumph—every emotion expressed in music calls for its appropriate dynamic scheme. Needless to say, the effect of the other musical elements is interwoven with the dynamics in closest degree. If we were to play the *Triumphal March* from AÏDA in a subdued tone, the entire effect would be changed, even if melody, harmony, and rhythm remained the same.

The broader emotional implications of loudness and softness are fairly obvious. A mood of triumph, power, or jubilation generally calls for brilliant sonority and volume. Sadness, dreamy lyricism, or introspection usually calls for subtle shadings within a more subdued range of volume. The emotional meaning of the music automatically imposes the proper dynamic scheme.

In ordinary speech, the word *dynamic* pertains to energy, accent, and action. It is evident that in an art such as music, which moves forward steadily through time, the driving force and energy behind that forward movement are of paramount importance. For this reason rhythm, which regulates the forward flow of the music, is so basic a factor in music. But rhythm depends upon the recurrence of accent; and accent depends upon playing certain beats louder than others. Thus, rhythm is the most potent application of the principle of dynamics in music.

Dynamics enters into the general emotional projection of the mood in a larger sense. Music, like the motion pictures, exists as a series of impressions following each other in rapid sequence. Such an art must make the listener feel that it is headed somewhere, and should carry him along on the current. Otherwise he will lose interest. Music impinges upon the listener a ceaseless alternation between movement and rest. Between the points of rest, the movement must be inexorable, compelling. We shall see in subsequent chapters how melody, harmony, rhythm, and form all contribute to this supremely important forward drive. Dynamics plays here an exceedingly important part. The music undulates forward between a succession of high points or climaxes. After each peak there is a relaxing of emotional intensity, and a gradual building-up to the next. (Graphically this movement resembles the rising and falling line of a series of mountain peaks.) Dynamics helps to regulate this steady undulation. The music accumulates force in a gradual *crescendo*. It reaches the peak. Then there is a gradual *decrescendo,* or lessening of volume, until we begin to approach the next climax.

In subtler fashion, dynamics enters into the composition as a means of highlighting or shading the musical line. By varying the volume of sound, the composer achieves an effect analogous to what the painter achieves through the brush. The musical canvas at times is painted in broad vigorous strokes, at others, the composer turns to vague outlines and subtle shadings. Through changes in dynamics, the composer is able to highlight certain parts of his composition, and to relegate others to relative obscurity; to achieve, in other words, a tonal equivalent of perspective and depth. Dynamics thereby becomes a potent factor in the total artistic scheme of musical composition.

It is plain that dynamics exists in two aspects: first, as a number of distinct levels of tonal volume; and second, as a series of nuances, or changes from one volume to another while the music is playing, that are part of the very life stream of the music. We have already met the two terms that indicate the nuances—*crescendo* and *decrescendo.* One cannot listen to a piece of music of any length without encountering either one or the other. The principal dynamic indications, going from soft to loud—that is, arranged in a *crescendo*—are:

> *pianissimo (pp):* very soft
> *piano (p):* soft
> *mezzo piano (mp):* medium soft
> *mezzo forte (mf):* medium loud
> *forte (f):* loud
> *fortissimo (ff):* very loud

Closely associated with dynamics is the element of *tempo*, or speed in music. This, too, has a part to play in the total effect. A light-hearted dance requires a brisk tempo. A stately march goes at a moderate rate of speed. A song of sorrow is slow. Changes in mood require corresponding changes in tempo. The principal nuances are *accelerando,* a faster tempo that, with its resemblance to a quickened pulse, produces an effect of emotional intensification upon the listener; and *ritardando,* a retarding or slowing up, that suggests a slackening of emotion.

The reader should take care at this point to distinguish between *meter* and *tempo. Meter* refers to the time measurement, specifically to the number of beats in the measure—duple, triple, quadruple, sextuple, and so forth. *Tempo* refers to the speed at which the meter is counted. Thus, a fast waltz and a stately minuet are both in triple meter; Chopin's *Funeral March* and the *Battle Hymn of the Republic* are both in quadruple meter. In fine, both meter and tempo are involved in regulating the forward movement of the music.

Tempo is subtly connected with dynamics in building up the climax. If the music, as it grows louder, also increases in speed, there will be marked accumulation of forward driving power. We shall frequently meet the two associated in the brilliant climax at the end of a piece, as in the *Finale* of Mendelssohn's "ITALIAN" SYMPHONY. Conversely, the *ritardando* is frequently used in conjunction with the *decrescendo* to produce the fadeout or dying-away effect so often met with at the end of a composition, as at the end of the *Prelude* to LOHENGRIN.

A climactic effect of another kind is achieved by having the *crescendo* accompanied by a marked broadening out in tempo, giving an effect of great dignity and strength. The climactic entrance of the final theme in the *Triumphal March* from AÏDA illustrates this. Also, the final climax in Tchaikovsky's OVERTURE 1812 and in Franz Liszt's LES PRÉLUDES show how effective a *crescendo-ritardando* can be.

The principal tempo indications, going from slow to fast—that is, arranged in an *accelerando*—are:

> *largo:* broad and stately
> *adagio* or *lento:* slow
> *andante:* fairly slow
> *andantino:* a little faster than *andante*
> *moderato:* moderately fast
> *allegretto:* fairly fast
> *allegro:* fast
> *vivace:* lively
> *presto:* very fast[7]

[7] One of the most scholarly expositions in the English language on the functions of the elements of expression in the art of music is the book *On the Elements of Expression in Music* by Professor Donald N. Ferguson, published by the University of Minnesota, Minneapolis, Minn., 1944.

Chapter IV

MUSIC, WORK AND PLAY: THE FOLK SONG

LONG before music became an art practiced by trained composers and performers, song and dance flourished among the people as a vital, expressive folk art. In all the corners of the earth tunes sprang up, some to accompany dances, others to express every shade of personal emotion; and from these humble sources a magnificent literature grew that, together with folk tales, myths, and sagas, constitutes an enduring monument to the inexhaustible creativeness of the human race.

Folk song is, in the truest sense, a product of the national group from which it springs. A singer or fiddler in some hamlet makes up a song. His neighbors like it and sing it over and over, changing a phrase here, adding a verse there. In the course of time, the song spreads to the neighboring village and through the entire countryside. It is polished by many talents, passed down from one generation to the next, until it becomes a crystallization of the emotions of the entire group, expressing its innermost feelings, its profoundest aspirations and insights, and at the same time capturing the essential spirit of its national song and speech, the very contour of its fields and valleys.

In a broader sense, however, folk song transcends national boundaries. It is the musical equivalent of the folk tale; it has that quality of simplicity and universality that sums up human experience in a few strokes, as do the myth and legend. The folk song springs out of man's primal need to give personal expression to his feelings—his devotion to home and fatherland, his rapture in love, his longing for the beloved, his sadness at parting and death. It addresses itself straight to the heart, in a language that all mankind understands.

We may well begin our listening with a romantic folk song, in many versions, both in England and in parts of our own country, *Barbara Allen*.[1] The poem, taken from an ancient ballad found in

---

[1] Essential listening for this chapter includes: *Barbara Allen, Marlborough, Home on the Range, John Henry, Drink to Me Only*, and *Comin' Through the Rye*. All other works mentioned are to be optional.

Percy's Reliques, relates how Jemmy Grove lay dying for love of Barbara Allen, and how she, hard-hearted, repulsed him until it was too late. The melody is a North Country tune, one of the most beautiful of English airs. In his *Studies in Modern Music*, the eminent critic W. H. Hadow calls it a perfect example of the power of simplicity, "with each strain more beautiful than the one before, till it culminates in the perfect sweetness and pathos of its final cadence." The short melody is repeated with each stanza, a type of song construction that is called *strophic*.

The melodic symmetry is reinforced by the recurrence, at the end of every other line of poetry, of a distinctive rhythmic pattern used on the words "dwell-in'," "swell-in'," and "Allen": a short note on the beat (an eighth note) followed by a longer note off the beat (a quarter note). This rhythmic figure was probably associated with a little hopping step off-the-beat in the country dances of North England. In Scotland this off-the-beat, or syncopated, rhythm became even more pronounced, the first note being shortened to a sixteenth note in value, and it has appeared so frequently in native folk tunes that it has become known as the "Scotch Snap." (Another good example of its use is *Comin' Through the Rye*, which is heard later in this chapter.) Here is the English version of *Barbara Allen:*[2]

The following jolly drinking song well exemplifies the changes in fortune that a song may undergo through the centuries; and, even more important, it shows how easily a melody may transcend the bar-

---

[2] Note the simple, symmetrical structure of this song, very obvious and easy to grasp at first hearing, yet, most pleasing. The repetitions only seem to intensify the effectiveness of the "story-telling"—one of the basic reasons for folk songs.

riers of language and race. The melody appeared, according to good authority, first in the Holy Land during the period of the Crusades as the *Chanson de Mambron,* in praise of a French knight who lost his life near Jerusalem. It became so firmly rooted in the Orient that it is sung today in Egypt and Arabia and is mistakenly considered to be an old Egyptian folk tune. The "Mambron" in the title changed to "Malbrooke," and the song ultimately became the popular French *Malbrooke s'en va-t-en Guerre,* sung in England as *Marlborough Is Going to the War,* and for a long time supposed to have referred to the famous Duke. The song had disappeared for some time when Marie Antoinette heard a nursemaid sing it to the Dauphin. She took it up, the melody became enormously popular in Paris, was a favorite tune of Napoleon, and was used by Beethoven in his "BATTLE" SYMPHONY, written to commemorate Wellington's victory at Vittoria. After all these transformations, the pious lay of the medieval Crusader ended, in England and America, as the indispensable ditty of carousal.

A glance, however cursory, at the rich panorama of American folk song reveals the most varied influences. Subsidiary to the English are traces of Scottish, Irish, and Welsh folk-song idioms. Along the Northern border the French-Canadian influence predominates; in the Southwest, there is a strong Spanish tradition; in the Louisiana region, Spanish, French, and Negro influences blend in the Creole songs. In addition, there are the folk-song idioms of the various national groups—German, Bohemian, Hungarian, Italian, Jewish, Scandinavian, Negro, and Indian, all flowing together in a veritable melting pot of song.

The actual work song, or recreational song about work, plays a smaller though not less important part in American folklore. From the Northwest come lumberjack and shantyboy tunes, such as *The Logger's Boast* and *Driving Saw-Logs on the Plover.* From the Appalachian and Southern region come hillbilly tunes, and such famous songs as *The Ground Hog* and *High Up on Old Smoky.* From songs and ballads of the railroad, we have the saga of *Casey Jones, The Train That Never Pulled In,* and *Mama Have You Heard the News.* Cow-

THE FORGE   *Goya*

boy songs are distinctive: the day-herding songs with loud refrains, sometimes based on cattle calls, to keep the herds moving; and the night-herding songs, with soft and soothing "dogie" refrains. *The Old Chisholm Trail, Git Along Little Dogie, Goodbye, Old Paint, Bury Me Not on the Lone Prairie*—these are simple tunes, varying in mood from the sentimental to the adventuresome, with easy-going, graceful rhythms. Typical of these traditional cowboy songs is *Home on the Range,* which we shall now hear.

Notice the simple structural design of *Home on the Range,* the unifying effect of repetition, the refreshing character of the first part of the "refrain" where there is a contrasting change of melody and rhythm, and, finally, the feeling of completeness and unity brought about by the recurrence of the first phrase—with a closing cadence, of course.

Among work songs, *John Henry,* who pitted his strength against the steam hammer, is the very essence of American folklore.[3] The melody, consisting of only four tones (D-F sharp-A-B), is a rare example of economy of tones. Note the interesting variety of rhythmic designs, no two measures being exactly alike. Yet in spite of this emphasis on variety, a definite feeling of unity and coherence exists, due, in large measure, to the character of the melodic scale structure. There is in this song a strong descriptive element; note the hammering strokes and the downward tendency of the melody, here and there, as though the rail spike were being driven home with each stroke of the sledge hammer swung by the mighty John Henry.

Close in spirit to folk songs are folk dances, practically all of which display the same general characteristics we noted in the chapter on

---

[3] See *America Sings,* by Carl Carmer, with music by Edwin John Stringham and illustrations by Betty Carmer (New York: Alfred A. Knopf, 1942.)

music and dance—simple, catchy tunes, symmetrical phrase structure, and vigorous rhythms. The boundary between song and dance, in this case, is indeed a tenuous one. Many folk dances were sung long before they were played. Conversely, many folk songs were first danced. One might say that in many instances the two continued hand in hand. Both from Old-World and native sources a rich store of American folk dances has accrued: Virginia reels, square dances, Morris dances, country dances, and the like. Typical are such tunes as *Mississippi Sawyer, Arkansas Traveller, Irish Washerwoman, Turkey in the Straw, Pop Goes the Weasel,* and *Polly Put the Kettle On.*

Cap-tain said to big, old John Hen-ry, "That old drill keeps a-com-ing a--round. Take that steam drill out and start it on that job, Let it whop, let it whop that steel on down, Let it whop, let it whop that steel on down."

Every nation has a more or less comparable body of folk music, responsive to the language and folkways of the particular group, with a characteristic flavor wholly indigenous to the soil out of which it grew. These songs and dances have served as a source of inspiration to the great composers and constitute one of the treasures of the nation, revealing eloquently its characteristic mode of thinking and feeling in music.

One qualification, however, may be added here: there are not many unique and exclusive characteristics in the so-called national strains of folk music in any country. It would be difficult indeed to point to any one characteristic and label it as exclusively American, for example; but there are generally a sufficient number of distinctive traits in a people's music to justify some kind of nationalistic designation. Only where a people have been really isolated and removed from extraneous influences can there be truly unique features in their musical idiom. Such national isolation in culture is very uncommon. More likely than not, alongside the characteristic national tunes will be found others with mixed antecedents betraying all sorts of outside influences that might easily belong to any one of several nations.[4]

Of the various national idioms, however, the English seem to be closest to our own. The melodies are usually forthright and without superfluous accent, conforming to the simple patterns of English speech. Many songs are based on, or make use of, the old Church Modes (See article "Mode" in Groves' *Dictionary of Music and Musicians*) and are four or five hundred years old. In the Hornpipe, Maypole, and Morris dances, vigorous four-four and six-eight meters abound. The balanced and symmetrical structure of the English folk song is well exemplified by the old tune which has become associated with Ben Jonson's lovely lyric, "Drink to Me Only With Thine Eyes, which is illustrated below and offered as the next subject for study.

Notice that each phrase, or unit, of this song consists of four measures, with a pause or cadence at the end of each. (This cadence consists of a melodic or harmonic formula imparting a feeling of a slight, partial, or complete close—quite as grammatical punctuation.)

[4] Apropos of *national* versus *borrowed* musical characteristics, it might be pointed out that some Kentucky and Appalachian tunes are more truly in the early English manner of the sixteenth and seventeenth centuries than are the same tunes to be found today in England itself. They have been preserved in their original state by comparatively isolated mountain folk; in England, later influences crept in.

THE TOMB OF GIULIANO DE' MEDICI   *Michelangelo*

The first phrase is repeated, as though to take root firmly in the hearer's mind. The third phrase is somewhat new and different and provides the necessary contrast; and the fourth phrase returns to the original and opening phrase, to bring about a feeling of balance and unification. This may be diagrammed as follows, by giving each phrase a letter: A (A repeated)-B-A. This three-part form (sometimes called *ternary*) is a favorite type of construction to be found in some of our best-known songs. In fact, it is the most common and basic of all musical structures, and is found in instrumental as well as in vocal music. Elaborated and developed, it is the basis for many of the larger and more pretentious musical forms used in chamber music, the symphony, the overture, the suite, as well as in works for solo instruments. But more of this matter in subsequent chapters. It is enough for the moment that this three-part structure be noticed, and that the reader recognize, also, that this A-B-A structure is a basic one in all the fine arts, for it best satisfies our aesthetic desire for balanced variety within unity—a result of securing a well-balanced disposition of the internal elements of compositional design, whether it be a painting, a sculpture, a poem, a sermon, a dance ensemble, a novel, or a piece of music. With these ideas in mind, study the picture of the "Tomb of Giulano de' Medici" by Michelangelo on page 35; also note the play of binary and ternary elements within the scheme as a whole.

This is a truly graceful and dignified song, with its "dipping and bowing" eighth-note figure found in the first beat of so many measures, as though this were once a court dance.

We have already pointed out the rhythmic figure peculiarly known as the "Scotch Snap." This was, according to some authorities, originally characteristic of an old national dance, the Strathspey, but later found its way into all kinds of folk tunes with astonishing frequency. Notice, for example, how often the figure of the "snap" occurs in the next song we shall study, *Comin' Through the Rye*. (The words are by Robert Burns). We have indicated these figures with a star. (See page 37.)

ADDITIONAL SUGGESTIONS FOR LISTENING[5]

The poet Thomas Moore played an important part in creating the folk songs of Ireland, most familiar among which are: *The Harp that Once Through Tara's Halls, Believe Me if All Those Endearing Young Charms,* and *The Last Rose of Summer.* Other Irish folk songs are popu-

---

[5] To be used as fully as desired or as time will permit.

lar in this country, especially *The Wearing of the Green* and *Londonderry Air*.

German folk song has much in common with English: regular formations, forthright melodies, simple lyricism, homely sentiment, and not a great deal of ornamentation. The songs are often sentimental and of much emotional fervor, yet there is something solid and foursquare about them. Some of this "solidity" comes from the fact that German folk tunes restrict themselves, as a rule, to the tones that belong to the scale of the moment. Also, German folk tunes are usually in simple rhythmic patterns, in which vigorous duple and triple meters predominate; a favorite type is the *Landler*, the peasant dance in three-four time that was the ancestor of our waltz. *Ach du lieber Augustin* is such a landler.

The folk songs and folk dances of the German people have had a great influence on the composers of that nation. We saw in the chapter "Music and Religion" how Bach was indebted to the chorale and what effect that form and style had on his music. In a similar way, the national heritage echoes through the works of Haydn, Mozart, Beethoven, Schubert, Schumann, Mendelssohn, and Brahms, to name only a few, all of whom either used folk songs outright in their works, or translated the spirit and idiom of them in their compositions. Some of the German traditional airs are almost as well known in this country as in Germany; for example: *Der Tannenbaum* (the melody of our own *Maryland, My Maryland*), *Die Lorelei*, and the student song, *Gaudeamus Igitur*. Brahms used this last song in his ACADEMIC OVERTURE.

French folk songs have the cool, limpid quality associated with the Gallic spirit—generally speaking, of course. Many of the songs are of great antiquity and bear marks of the influence of the troubadours and trouvères of the twelfth and thirteenth centuries. Many of the children's songs are well known in this country; among them we might mention: *Sur le pont d'Avignon, Il Etait un Bergère, Ah! que Vous Dirai-je, Maman*, and the two most popular songs of the Revolution, the *Carmagnole* and *Ça Ira*.

Italian songs, so often gay and impetuous, reflect the fiery temperament of the Southerner, the passionate abandon to the mood of the moment. Neapolitan street songs, Venetian boat songs, Sicilian serenades—these stem from an intensely musical people for whom song is as natural, almost, as speech. *Santa Lucia* has attained much popularity in America, and it is a good example of the Neapolitan folk style.

Spanish folk songs reflect the dance rhythms of the various provinces—*sequidillas, jotas, boleros, sevillanas,* and the like. Outstanding are the passionate flamenco songs, the idiom of the Spanish Gypsy, a rhapsodical, ornate vocal melody which bears the character of an improvisation. Such a song is *Saetas,* one of the flamenco songs used in Holy Week festivals. The rapturous incantation of the voice over the steady beating of the drums and the blare of cornets releases a flood of emotion as only the greatest of music is able to do.

Russian music is extremely variegated, including all the strains of a territory that occupies one sixth of the earth—Greek, Slav, Tartar, Norse, Gypsy, German, Mongolian, the tribal songs of the Caucasus, and the melancholy tunes of the Siberian Steppes. Cossack dance songs are extremely rhythmic and vigorous, as are the Ukrainian peasant tunes.

Many currents meet in the richly imaginative folk music of Central, Northern, and Southeastern Europe—Scandinavian, Slavonic, Gypsy, Magyar, Czech, Teutonic, Croat, Bulgar, and Turkish. Those farther east and south across the Mediterranean Sea are without the scope of this book. One cannot leave this array of nationalistic and racial expressions without further comment upon the Gypsy influences in Southeastern Europe. Their rhapsodical improvisations have become a real part of western music. These highly ornate melodies of the Gypsy fiddlers and singers, passing abruptly from one mood to the next, with their capricious rhythms and emotional fervor, seem strange in comparison with our more staid English and American folk songs; but with a few repeated hearings, we can learn to embrace them into our liking, if we will. In fact, if one has the time and the proper phonograph recordings, a pleasant and profitable excursion might well be made into these more or less exotic musical expressions. It has been well said, "I care not who makes the laws if I can make the songs."

Chapter V

THE COMPOSED FOLK SONG:
ARCHITECTURE OF MUSIC[1]

BETWEEN the folk song and the so-called "art song" stands what is known, somewhat paradoxically, as the composed folk song. Certain composers are so thoroughly imbued with the spirit of their people and with their native musical idioms that their own original creations become so beloved and so generally used among the people that they achieve the status of traditional folk song. Dvořák, Sibelius, and Grieg, to name but a few, have often been charged with using actual traditional folk-song material, and they have had to refute such charges with the statement that the melodies were their own—a high compliment indeed to these composers when one comes to analyze the situation!

The composed folk song, being the product of a single creative personality, allows for wider ranges of subject emotion and aesthetic perfection than does the traditional folk song. Although well within the universality of the folk style, it will nonetheless bear the mark of a more personal approach to life and to the tenets of art. Then too, since the creator of the composed folk song may be a musician of considerable background and training, there may be a smoothness of style, a subtlety of effect in his compositions which would normally not be present, at least not to such a great degree, in the true folk art.

It may be said, therefore, that the composed folk song crystallizes within the span of a single career and through the medium of a single personality what it might take generations of spontaneous growth to achieve. In any case, the composed folk songs of a nation are as much a part of its national lore as the pure folk songs, in that they are actually used as such by the people. Indeed, it is entirely possible that had the composers of such songs as *O Sole Mio*, or *La Paloma*, or *My Old*

---

[1] Essential listening for this chapter includes: *Lullaby* by Brahms, *The Birch Tree*, Russian folk song, and *Finale* of Tchaikovsky's FOURTH SYMPHONY (in part, to show use of *The Birch Tree* song). Other works mentioned may be considered supplementary and optional listening.

Kentucky Home lived in a somewhat earlier age, they might have been numbered among the vast forgotten company of gifted village singers and players who had some part, however small, in the creation of the immortal literature known as traditional folk music—just as we now do not know the architects who actually conceived the original designs of most of the great Gothic cathedrals of Europe.

One of the first names that comes to mind, in connection with the composed folk songs of our own country, is that of Stephen Foster (1826-1864), whose songs have in the truest sense become part and soul of the heritage of the people of the United States. Foster's songs actually represent the essence of the American folk idiom in music. His was a fresh and untutored genius, which touched the hearts of his countrymen as no other composer's creations have done. Some of his songs, such as *Old Black Joe, Swanee River, My Old Kentucky Home, Massa's in de Cold, Cold Ground, Jeanie with the Light Brown Hair,* to name but a few, are deeply loved and sung throughout our country and beyond. And how much poorer the English-speaking peoples, especially those of America, would be without the immortal song by Sir Henry Bishop, *Home Sweet Home,* the words of which were penned by the New Yorker, John Howard Payne (1792-1852).

In this category may also be mentioned a number of national anthems which, through long association, have become symbols of patriotic emotion. Here the intimate folk style is superseded by a vigorous martial tune which the nation as a whole is able and eager to accept. Typical of these anthems are *The Star-Spangled Banner,* an old English song known as *To Anacreon in Heaven,* to which Francis Scott Key adapted his poem; *America,* or *God Save the King,* an old English song attributed to one of a number of composers; the *Battle Hymn of the Republic,* a hymn tune for which Julia Ward Howe wrote the words we now use; Rouget de Lisle's *Marseillaise,* written overnight in the heated atmosphere of the French Revolution; *Rule Britannia,* by Thomas Arne; and the hymn of the old Austrian Empire, *God Preserve Our Gracious Emperor,* by Joseph Haydn, one of the few national anthems composed by a great master.

As we might expect, the nineteenth-century composer's approach to folk song was more romantic than that of contemporary musicians. Often the simple folk idiom was dressed up with all the tricks of the composer's craftsmanship. Characteristic among such are the HUN-GARIAN RHAPSODIES of Franz Liszt, in which the native tunes (it must be said that he was more prone to use Gypsy than "pure" Hungarian melodies) were treated in a dramatic and brilliantly technical manner often bordering on the bombastic. Some of these virtuoso piano pieces have received a new lease of life in brilliant orchestral arrangements. Try, sometime, listening to his Second, Sixth, or Twelfth Hungarian Rhapsody, and note how a highly charged romantic composer can treat his folk material.

Many of the great composers betray a startling closeness to their native soil. Many melodies of Schubert and Brahms, for example, evince the characteristics of true German folk song. Brahms carried the folk spirit into some of his original songs so successfully that two of them, at least, have become virtual folk songs—the universally loved *Lullaby*, and the delightful *Vergebliches Standchen* (Futile Serenade), with its irresistible lilting tune.

The *Lullaby* by Brahms possesses a number of characteristics that we are prone to associate with the folk-song genre. Its simple and straightforward internal structure consists of four phrases, each of four measures in length, with a salient cadence at the close of each; the sincere and deep feeling is presented with simplicity and economy of means; and the unity, contrast, and symmetry are secured in an inevitable yet unpretentious manner. Let us study it; but first let us listen to it.

We might express simply the structural formula of the melodic pattern thus: four phrases (marked "a," "b," "c," and "d," or two basic periods marked "I" and "II"—often called the *Binary*, or two-part, form). Note the melodic and rhythmic figures that are repeated more or less identically, and observe the process of building a work out of small units. Note the unifying effect of such a simple method of construction. Now put all this technical matter to the background of your mind and listen to the music with the idea of enjoying it to the full. The same basic plan of study might well apply to all our efforts.

It would take far more pages than we have at our disposal simply to enumerate other worthy instances of the uses many great composers have made of the folk song in their larger works; and the same is true of the composed folk song and the original folk-songlike themes composers sometimes create. The listener will enjoy discovering such instances rather than having them pointed out for inspection. It is enough, we believe, merely to indicate the general principles involved and typical examples of such principles. Thus, the listener is

THE VISITATION WITH TWO SAINTS   *Piero di Cosimo*

Observe that this picture is divided into two balanced parts. Note also the wavelike contour described by the heads of the four figures. The first characteristic corresponds to the two balanced periods of the musical form known as two-part or binary, while the graphic curve is analogous to the rising and falling tonic-dominant key relationship that exists in the true binary musical structure. It is almost needless to add that these objective facts are very secondary to the subjective and aesthetic considerations.

in possession of a "tool" that will enable him to pursue this subject further.

As a further challenge, listen to the *Finale* of Tchaikovsky's FOURTH SYMPHONY. In this work, the composer uses the following Russian folk song known as *The Birch Tree*, with its curious phrase structure of three (not four) measures each, with a cadence at the end of each measure, and a repetitious design that is very simple and almost primitive:

Compare that traditional folk song with the following version of it that Tchaikovsky evolved. Note the regular two-measure figure, four-measure phrase, and the repetitions that are more exact than are those in the original folk song:

Upon this tune and a contrasting theme is built a mighty symphonic development. The movement advances precipitously. Powerful fanfares in the brasses pronounce the ominous Fate motive, heard at the onset of the first movement. The work builds up, the gay opening theme returns, and the mood of triumph is powerfully reaffirmed. The movement closes in a blaze of color and animation.

The Architecture of Music: Form and Structure[2]

We have seen in our earlier discussion on rhythm and melody that the essential element of both is pattern or design, and that through the discernment of such a pattern, the listener perceives that there is a meaning and inter-relationship of the small parts, first to each other and then to the whole. This desire to achieve design and order out of chaos, to balance unity with diversity, receives its ultimate expression in that basic element of the art of music known as *form*.

Form results from the attempt of the artist to achieve the most effective arrangement and balance of the material and the most coherent relation between the parts and the whole. Actually, the urge to secure unity and variety, symmetry, balance, contrast, and climax is not limited to art. It appears in one guise or another in all the activities of life, whether in the laying out of a garden, the setting of a table, or the embroidering of a dress. Children playing in the sand lay out elaborate structures in symmetrical patterns. Dancers go through elaborate sequences in movement that are coherent, balanced patterns. Both in the spatial arts—painting, sculpture, architecture— and in the sequential or time arts—poetry, drama, motion pictures, music—the material must not only say something significant to the beholder, it must say it to him in a coherent and intelligible—more, in an alive and interesting—way. This need to be coherent, intelligible, and interesting will lead the artist to seek the most appropriate, the one inevitable, form for his content.

If an artist is overflowing with something worth saying, the form in which it can best be said will come out of the materials themselves. Conversely, if he has nothing significant to say, no amount of perfection of form will breathe life and meaning into his art work. Whether he is dealing with word patterns or tone patterns, with shape and line and color, or with great architectural masses, he will mold his materials to the form that they themselves demand. The content will lead him to a certain form.

However, we cannot look upon form as purely functional, a con-

---

[2] The following exposition of certain aspects of the creative artist's craft, as with all such technical and academic matters discussed *throughout this book*, is presented for its own extra-musical, scholarly, and interest-arousing values. It is not given with a mistaken notion that it is indispensable to the aesthetic appreciation of music. A good general rule to bear in mind is that all matters ABOUT MUSIC are just that and no more; and that the real appreciation OF MUSIC is quite a different matter. Further, that technical and academic knowledge is neither essential to nor a substitute for the listening appreciative process.

venient means to an end. The pillars of the Parthenon had not only to help support the edifice; but they also had to become important contributors to the general beauty of the building. We cannot think of form as a thing in itself, a convenient mold into which the artist pours his meaning. The artist wishes his content to be clear and easily grasped. He wants to keep his audience interested in what he is saying. The artist desires his message to have a powerful, unified effect, and yet at the same time to have novelty, suspense, variety, climax. Also, being an artist, he must have beauty of outline in the external shape of his message. If he has felt his material deeply, if he has been endowed with creative imagination, and if he has achieved mastery in his medium, the requisite forms that will best enable him to achieve all these will come to him.

The artist would have a difficult task if he had to start from "scratch." Actually, he is working in an art that has a history and a tradition. He inherits a body of techniques, the cumulative achievement of generations of artists, of centuries of trial and error, to help him solve his aesthetic problems. The principles of form are timeless; but the actual forms that enable artists to carry out those principles change from one age to the next. The artist studies the forms at hand; alters them to suit his personal needs. Sometimes he abandons them altogether and turns in a new direction, blazing a trail for those who will come after him. Thus, when viewed dynamically, forms in art are living, growing organisms, adapting themselves to the needs and tastes of each successive generation of artists—they are so many diverse manifestations, in one century or another, of that eternal quest for law and order, for harmony and coherence, that seems to be one of the immanent characteristics of the human mind.

Since the particular form employed by the artist springs out of the materials he is working with, every art develops its own principles of construction. Nevertheless, certain underlying principles seem to be common to them all. First and foremost is that of unity: the desire to organize all the components of the art work into one cohesive design, so that each part of the cathedral, the novel, the painting, or the symphony will function organically within the total framework. In this connection, Poe's celebrated dictum on the short story—"In the whole composition there should be no word written of which the tendency, direct or indirect, is not to the established design"—shows a fine insight into this basic factor in form.

Closely allied to unity is the need for symmetry and balance, which make more easily perceptible the fundamental unity of the pattern. Man seems to take great pleasure in orderly arrangement, in the repetition of familiar quantities, in balancing one side against another. It is almost as if he found refuge in the orderliness of art from the chaos, the unpredictable accidents, of life. As in the case of rhythm, he begins to expect certain things to happen in a certain order within the art pattern, and achieves a deep satisfaction, a pleasant sense of fulfillment and security, when his expectation is realized.

But security alone would soon grow wearisome, were it not enlivened with novelty and surprise within the pattern. And so the unity of the art form must be adroitly alternated with variety and contrast. From man's psychological need for both safety and adventure—seemingly irreconcilable elements—springs the basic aesthetic problem of the artist. If he were continually to introduce new material into his work, the result would be chaos. If, on the other hand, he were to continue to repeat the same motif again and again—like a child, or a member of a primitive tribe who sings a snatch of melody over and over for hours on end—he would become fearfully boring. Form results from the artist's attempt to achieve a satisfying balance between the two, from repeating enough of the old to give us a sense of pattern, while introducing enough of the new to achieve variety and sustain our interest.

In addition, the artist introduces into the material an element of suspense, of movement and growth toward a culminating point or climax. Whether it be the soaring dome in architecture, the denouement in drama, the crescendo and peak in melody, the climax carries the spectator aloft to the high point of intensity, after which the movement subsides or ends. Thus the art work takes on shape and form: a beginning, a middle, and an end.

The arrangement of the material is naturally of crucial importance in the space arts. Painting, sculpture, architecture, interior decoration—all place the utmost emphasis upon the problems of organizing space into a unified whole. One has only to look at Raphael's celebrated "School of Athens" (page 47) to see how masterfully the painter has arranged his material with an eye to formal unity and structure. The rectangular space is bound together by the curve of the arch, reinforced by the three concentric arches. These, like a reiterated climax in music, frame the central figures of Socrates and Plato. Notice how effectively the figures on either side of the two philosophers focus the movement upon them. The canvas presents a central group flanked on either side by two symmetrical groups, the balance accentuated by the two statues. Although analogies between

SCHOOL OF ATHENS
Raphael

different arts must be made only in a general way, the reader will have no difficulty in recognizing in this design an equivalent of the A-B-A structure in music. The larger rhythms of the three areas are subtly varied with all kinds of cross rhythms within the groups, and by the gentle elliptical movement between the figures in the middle distance and those in the foreground. The canvas of this most classical of the Renaissance masters presents an extraordinary example of the utmost diversity within a unified pattern, with symmetry, balance, climax, and richly variegated rhythms all contributing to the monumental effect. Note the crescendo effect of the four expanding arches.

Even more important is the problem of form in architecture, where the artist is faced with the task of organizing great expanses of mass and space into a coherent pattern. He does not begin with a definite form into which, as into a mold, he pours his conception. Rather, he considers the use to which the building will be put—whether it is to be a cathedral, a courthouse, or a villa; the materials available, whether marble, stone, or brick; the engineering problems involved. Out of this consideration grows the particular form that he will use. Notice, for example, in the Capitol at Washington, how appropriate is the serene, majestic form for a building intended as a seat of government. The magnificently climactic dome towering over the two symmetrical wings at either side is an architectural equivalent to the A-B-A structure in music. Considered in detail, without the dome, the build-

COURTESY OF THE UNIVERSITY PRINTS, NEWTON, MASS.

THE CAPITOL BUILDING IN WASHINGTON

ing presents three similar façades—the repetition of an idea—which are brought out dramatically by means of the steps, the pillars, and the cornice, alternating with two sections—the contrast—which are fairly well in the background. Here is a kind of A-B-A-B-A structure, which is precisely what we shall soon discover the classical rondo form to be. As in the painting of Raphael, we have unity and variety, symmetry, balance, climax, and diversified rhythms, expressed in appropriate architectural values.

These values, which depend on space measurements in the plastic arts, are translated into time measurements in the sequential or time arts. In the dance, the performer takes four steps in one direction followed by four in another. In poetry, the stanzas are symmetrical in length—the very word *length* being equally applicable to time and space—and the lines are symmetrical in the number and arrangement of the metrical pulses. The *rondo*, with its subtle reiteration of a unifying element, is one of the most effective lyric forms in poetry. Notice, in Jean Froissart's "Rondel" how the reiterated phrase takes on new meaning with each repetition, at the same time giving strength to the delicate pattern. We have here an A-B-A-C-A pattern, with the repetition of the first two lines in the middle of the poem and at the end:

> Love, love, what wilt thou with this heart of mine?
> Naught see I fixed or sure in thee!
> I do not know thee,—nor what deeds are thine:
> Love, love, what wilt thou with this heart of mine?
> Naught see I fixed or sure in thee!
>
> Shall I be mute, or vows with prayers combine?
> Ye who are blessed in loving, tell it me:
> Love, love, what wilt thou with this heart of mine?
> Naught see I fixed or sure in thee! [3]

At this point, we should listen to Beethoven's *Rondino* as arranged by Fritz Kreisler for violin and piano. We should like to leave the discovery of the internal structure to the listener, and we shall do so with one admonition: watch for the recurrent theme and the episodes that alternate with that theme, then compare the form you have dis-

---

[3] Translated by H. W. Longfellow. A rondeaux proper generally contains 13 or 14 lines.

covered with the general design of Froissart's rondeau. Bear in mind that the composer may have as many alternations as he deems necessary.

So, too, the other literary arts—the novel and the drama, as well as the cinema—have their problems of organization and structure, of tempo and transition, climax and denouement. One need only watch a well-directed movie as it unfolds from its leisurely beginning, gradually accelerating its pace, piling up suspense in a steady crescendo, yet adhering to the firmest kind of unity up to the inexorable climax, to realize how all-pervading are the basic elements of design and structure, tempo and dynamics, no matter what the particular art form or medium may be.

If these compositional values are of such importance in the static arts, where the spectator may linger at will over every detail of the painting, sculpture, the building, or the printed space, how much more important they are in an art where all is flow and movement, where the landscape rushes past before the listener has had a chance to grasp the details, where the tone lives but for an instant before dissolving in air, where unity and coherence of form are perceived mainly in retrospect—or in anticipation. Indeed, no sooner has the listener become aware of one tone than another is on its way. It took composers centuries of groping, of trial and error, to develop the techniques of form as we now know them; but they gradually learned how to achieve in an art that exists as a rapid succession of impressions in time all the solidity and orderly arrangement of structure in space. Through mastery of form they succeeded in creating extensive works that, although they have their being only in the momentary billowing of the air, nevertheless communicate to the listener that sense of organic growth and towering strength found in the most imposing edifice—veritable cathedrals in tone, enduring monuments to the matchless resourcefulness and power of man's imagination.

In the folk songs that we have heard, one observed that the phrases were combined in several variants of the unity-and-variety, or A-B-A, pattern. In subsequent chapters we shall discover the many variations of this and other patterns in the most familiar forms, analyzing both their external structure—the relation of the individual sections to each other and to the composition as a whole—as well as the internal structure of the units within the section.

Chapter VI

MUSIC AS PERSONAL EXPRESSION:
THE ART SONG; "SENTENCE" STRUCTURE
IN MUSIC[1]

THE same diversity of mood and immediate emotional appeal that we noticed in folk song animates its city cousin, the art song. Here, too, we meet with every shade of human feeling projected through beautiful melody and through the most personal of all musical instruments, the human voice. But whereas the folk song more often breathes of the soil and is racy with the life and humor of the peasantry, the art song usually has its being in urban culture and is the flower of a carefully nurtured tradition. Thus, for the simple universality of the folk song, the art song substitutes a more individualized idiom, the expression of a definite creative personality, subtly evocative in mood and atmosphere—an art form that has enlisted the talents of the most distinguished composers.

Although the two categories of song have flourished side by side since the days of the troubadours—we saw how such masters of art song as Schubert and Brahms captured the folk spirit in some of their works—some important points of difference between them exist. The art song is generally set to a high order of lyric poetry, instead of to a simple folk rhyme. Whereas the folk song is strophic in construction—that is, the tune is repeated over and over for successive stanzas—the art song, as often as not, follows the poem throughout, interpreting each new phase and nuance of the verse. This type of song is known as *durchkomponiert*, or "composed throughout," and it naturally captures the mood of the various stanzas more intimately

---

[1] Essential listening for this chapter includes: *Serenade* by Schubert, *Der Erlkönig* by Schubert, *Ich Grolle Nicht* by Schumann, *Minnelied* by Brahms, *Ich Liebe Dich* by Grieg, *The Flea* by Moussorgsky, and *The Sea* by MacDowell; for Part II, "Sentence Structure in Music," use *London Bridge Is Falling Down, The Farmer in the Dell* and Foster's *Swanee River*. All others are supplementary and optional.

than does the strophic type of song. (There are many strophic art songs, too, but by and large the through-composed type has predominated, particularly since the middle of the nineteenth century.)

The art song depends for its success on the perfect fusion of text and music. In some of our great songs this union is so complete that it is practically impossible for us now to conceive of the one existing without the other. Having picked a text with an emotional or poetic content that invites musical setting, the composer uses all the resources of his art to bring out every nuance, every hidden implication of the words. In this task all the elements of music that we have hitherto discussed play their parts. The rhythm not only conforms to, but also accentuates the meter of the poetry. The curve of the melody traces the rise and fall of emotion in the text. The important words and syllables are brought out by the musical accent. The harmonic background in the accompaniment provides a sympathetic commentary, ranging from lightness and gaiety to somber drama. Timbre, too, is brought into play: the bright tinkling melody given to the brilliant soprano differs from the heroic ballad assigned to the baritone or the romantic love song of the tenor and lyric soprano. The themes alternate and reappear according to a formal scheme that matches the form of the poem. Tempo and dynamics underscore the mood, changing with each shade of meaning. Finally, all these factors combine to build up musically the emotional climax of the poetry. What emerges is a miniature tone poem, lyric or dramatic, that captures the innermost spirit of the poem.

The history of the art song goes back about eight hundred years to the works of the courtly Troubadours and Trouvères, and of their German counterparts, the Minnesingers (love singers) and the Master Singers who are so vividly satirized in Wagner's opera. The madrigals and airs of the Renaissance, cultivated in Italy, France, Germany, and England, were followed by a rich literature throughout the seventeenth and eighteenth centuries. The masters of the Baroque and Classical periods left a number of songs that are still part of the repertory. *If Music Be the Food of Love,* by England's great composer Henry Purcell (1658-1695), Haydn's *My Mother Bids Me Bind My Hair,* Mozart's *The Violet,* as well as a number of songs by the Italian masters, such as the frequently performed *Come Raggio di Sol* (As a Ray of Sunlight) by Antonio Caldara (1670-1736), and *Vittoria, Mio Core* (Victoria, My Love) by Giacomo Carissimi (1605-1674), are outstanding examples.

Yet, despite the excellence of these songs of the masters, when we say "art song" to a music lover he immediately thinks of the early nineteenth century and of the lyricism that welled out of the early Romantic Period through the transcendent genius of the greatest of song composers, Franz Schubert, who wrote well over five hundred. He was the first of a great line of writers who established the art song as one of the most fascinating forms in music, capturing the essence of the poem and translating it into its tonal equivalent with an almost clairvoyant insight. Although he left a legacy of first importance in every branch of music—symphony, chamber music, piano sonata, religious choral work—to the millions of his admirers, the composer of the *Serenade, Hark Hark the Lark, The Linden Tree, Death and the Maiden*, remains first and foremost the inspired master of song.

In Schubert, the time, the place, and the man came together in more than fortuitous fashion. To begin with, a group of German lyric poets, headed by Goethe, had raised aloft the banner of Romanticism and created a new literary form, the intimate lyric of mood and emotion in which language was so surcharged with feeling as to cry for fulfillment in music. Then, too, the art of music as a whole was beginning to move ever closer to literature, a development that can be noticed throughout the whole of the nineteenth century. The short piece, lyrical in style and emotional in mood, was ready to take its place beside the large structural forms of the Classical Period. The piano had been sufficiently perfected to become a flexible, highly imaginative assistant to the voice. When all these influences had blossomed, there appeared the master who was able to bring them all to fruition in an art form so distinctive, so indissolubly associated with himself and his successors, that even today, when the art song has for decades been reproduced with the utmost felicity by French, Italian, Russian, English, and American composers, we still frequently call it, as Schubert did, the *Lied*.

Although the moods reflected in the art song are as diversified as those of the folk song, that of romantic love naturally holds first place. We may begin our listening study with one of the greatest of love songs, Schubert's *Serenade*. Over an accompaniment of simple chords there unfolds a melody so expressive, so attuned to the most intimate inflections of the human voice, that it conveys its message even if one does not understand the German in which it is usually sung. Here, the mood of tender longing, so characteristic of the early romantic movement in Germany, finds expression:

Softly goes my song's entreaty
   Thro' the night to thee,
In the silent woods I wait thee,
   Come, my love, to me.

The whispering tree-tops shield us
   From the light of the moon,
Fear no intruding foot-steps coming,
   Fear no spying eye.

Hark! the nightingales are singing,
   Ah, they plead with thee!
With their notes so sweet, so ringing,
   They would plead with me.

Well they know a lover's longing,
   Know the pain of love,
With their silver-toned voices
   Tender hearts they move.

Ah, let thine, as well, grow tender,
   Sweetheart, why so coy?
Anxious, fevered, I wait thee,
   Come and bring me joy! [2]

We have had occasion, frequently, in discussing the folk song, to point out the regular construction of four measures in a phrase and four phrases (or two periods) in the melody. You will find an analogous construction in these verses—four lines in a stanza, four feet in a line (alternating with lines of three feet. When set to music, these shorter lines are filled out, so that they become equal in length to the others). Schubert has skillfully avoided an excessively four-square construction, first, by introducing short interludes in the accompaniment; second, by repeating certain lines of poetry, especially in the later stanzas.

Notice the characteristic introduction of the piano accompaniment; the interplay between the regular phrases of the voice part and the piano interludes; the effective repetition of the melody to other words, in strophic style; the intensification of mood, building up to the wonderful climax in the last stanza, with the accompaniment subtly imitating the vocal line; and the rounding off of the design in a

---

[2] English version (except the second verse) by Henry G. Chapman, copyright 1911 by G. Schirmer, Inc. Copyright renewed 1939 by G. Schirmer, Inc. Quoted by permission of the publisher. Free and literal translation of second verse by the present author.

gentle subsiding of emotion, dying away in the tender piano postlude.

If the *Serenade*, written to verses by Rellstab, represents the lyric genius of Schubert, his setting of Goethe's narrative poem "Der Erlkönig" (The Erlking) reveals his dramatic powers. The song was composed in 1815, when he was but eighteen years old, and is considered by many the greatest lied ever written. Schubert's friend Spaun told how he and another companion went one afternoon to call on Schubert. They found him enthusiastically reading Goethe's dramatic ballad aloud. He walked up and down the room, book in hand, then sat down and, as fast as he could write, put the song on paper practically in its finished form.

Nothing is more characteristic of the first period of German romanticism than the somber mood of this ballad, with its commingling of the supernatural and the strangely picturesque. Our second required listening in this chapter is, then, the immortal ballad-art song, *The Erlking*, by Franz Schubert:

Who rides so late through night and wind?
It is the father and his child.
He holds the boy in his arms,
He clasps him firmly, he keeps him warm.

"My son, why do you hide your face in fear?"
"See you not, father, the Erlking?
The Erlking with his crown and train."
"My son, that is but the mist trailing down."

"Thou lovely child, come with me!
And I'll play lovely games with thee,
Where many gay flowers lie in the field,
And my mother has many garments of gold."

"Father! Father! don't you hear
What the Erlking is softly promising me?"
"Be calm, my child, have no fear,
That is but the wind moaning through the leaves."

"Won't you go with me?
My daughters will wait upon you,
They will play in the evening
And they will sing and dance."

"Father! Father! don't you see
The Erlking's daughters in that dark place?"
"My child, I see it quite clearly—
Those are but the hoary willows so gray."

"I love thee, thy beautiful face arouses me,
And comest thou not freely, I shall use force!"
"My father, my father, he clasps me now,
His icy grasp hurts me!"

The father shudders, he rides on faster,
Clasping in his arms the ailing child.
He reaches home in dread and anguish—
In his arms the child lay dead! [3]

The octaves in galloping triplets with which the accompaniment opens, the ominous figure in the bass, at once set the atmosphere and the mood of the drama. The three protagonists—father, son, and seductive Erlking—are clearly differentiated through changes in tempo, in vocal line, and in tonal register. (By *register* we mean the general location in regard to high or low; the "lie" of the music.) Thus, the father's tones are conspicuously lower than those of the child, while the Erlking sings a soft alluring strain, as if from another world. The cries of the child are abrupt and harrowing; the father's reassurance is sonorous, giving an impression of strength; the Erlking sings sirenlike in a broad, suave melody. As the father rides on in terror, we hear the galloping figure of the opening, leading to the dread climax. The final line is declaimed, with a dramatic pause before the two words at the end, "lay dead," followed by two simple chords. The effect is very impressive.

To get an inkling of Schubert's achievement in song, one should hear several of the masterpieces that music lovers the world over have come to treasure almost as a personal possession. *Hark Hark the Lark*, written at one sitting on the back of a bill of fare, at a beer garden, after he had glanced through a volume of Shakespeare; *Ave Maria*, to the words from Walter Scott's *Lady of the Lake*; the dramatic masterpieces *Death and the Maiden, The Wanderer, The Phantom Double*; the folk-songlike *Heidenröslein* (Hedge-Rose); *Who Is Sylvia?; My Peace Thou Art; The Post; The Linden Tree*—each has become so integral a part of our song inheritance that it is almost inconceivable to think of the art without them. (See reproduction of manuscript of *Hedge-Rose* on page 57.)

Schubert's successor in the art song was Robert Schumann, one of the most original and striking figures among the Romantics. Schumann possessed unusual dramatic power and a deep sensitivity to

---

[3] English version (except the fifth verse), by Arthur Westbrook. Copyright by Oliver Ditson Company, 1931. Quoted by permission of the publishers.

COURTESY OF THE JUILLIARD SCHOOL OF MUSIC, NEW YORK

FROM THE ORIGINAL MS. OF THE SONG "HEIDENRÖSLEIN"

57

poetry, which he projected into his songs by a melodic line and harmonies much more complicated, as a rule, than those of Schubert. He was not nearly so fertile, but his choicest works must be accounted as among the glories of literature of the lied.

For Schumann, the lyrics of Heinrich Heine provided the same inspiration that those of Goethe, Schiller, and the earlier Romantic poets of Germany had for Schubert. Unlike his predecessor, who set to music all kinds of poetry, good, bad, and indifferent—Schumann remarked of him that he could set even a placard to music—Schumann needed a really beautiful poem to be inspired to musical creation. As a result, the poetry in Schumann's songs is far more worthy of the music than is that in some of Schubert's songs.

Ich Grolle Nicht (I'll Not Complain), set to an exceedingly intense lyric of Heine, is one of the most powerful of Schumann's songs. The famous critic and scholar, H. T. Finck, has said that the best traits of Schumann's songs are united in this one, the third of our listening study:

> I'll not complain, even though my heart be breaking.
> O love for ever lost! O love for ever lost!
> I'll not complain, I'll not complain.
>
> Even tho' you shine with the splendor of a diamond,
> No rays of it brighten your dark heart.
> But I know full well I'll not complain,
> Even if my heart is breaking.
>
> I saw thee in my dream,
> And saw the night within thy heart's abyss,
> And saw the snake that on thy heart doth gnaw,
> How all forlorn thou art, my love, I saw.
> I'll not complain, I'll not complain. [4]

The brooding chords under the vocal line, with their acrid dissonances, communicate the emotion of the rejected lover. Very gradually the music builds up to a climax on the line, "And saw the snake that on thy heart doth gnaw." For emotional projection, this song composed in 1840 remains one of the best of its type in the full-blown German Romanticism.

Next in the dynasty of the masters of the lied was Johannes Brahms, who united with the utmost lyricism a quality of inner fervor

---

[4] English version (except the second verse) by Arthur Westbrook. Copyright by Oliver Ditson Company, 1931. Quoted by permission of the publishers.

and introspection that has given his songs a high place in the literature.
Brahms' songs have passion and intensity, a distinctive coloring in the
vocal line and in the intricate piano background, which stamp them
as unmistakably his.

There is brooding melancholy in such songs as *May Night* and
Death Is Like a Cool Still Night; contemplation and gentleness in
In Summer Fields; and fervid lyricism pervading the slow movements
of his symphonies are matched in such a song as *Minnelied* (Love
Song). The flowing accompaniment that serves as the introduction
in the *Minnelied*—Brahms directed it to be played "with much tenderness, but not too slowly"—leads into a vocal melody of deep feeling
and the intimate quality of inwardness that is so peculiarly his own.
Note the gloomy and despondent low-pedal point (a sustained or reiterated tone) in the bass of the piano throughout the verse beginning with "But for thee all joy were dead." The eminent authority
on the lied, H. T. Finck, whom we have quoted before, has said that
the *Minnelied* is the most inspired, spontaneous, and delightful of
Brahms' vocal works. The words of our fourth study song follow:

> Sweeter sounds the song of birds
>   When she roams the meadows,
> When she comes with step so light
>   'Mid the woodland shadows.
>
> Brighter is the blooming Spring,
>   Greener are its bowers,
> When her tender fingers touch
>   Their countless flowers.
>
> But for thee all joy were dead,
>   All earth's brightness faded.
> E'en the glow of evening sky
>   Were for me o'ershaded.
>
> Dearest sov'reign of my heart,
>   Never leave me, never,
> Bloom sweet blossoms of thy love,
>   In my soul forever.[5]

Notice the richness of the chords in the piano part and the symmetrical structure of the voice part, and how both the melody and

---

[5] Translation (except the second verse) by Arthur Westbrook. Copyright, 1931,
by Oliver Ditson Company. Quoted by permission of the publishers. The second
verse is a literal translation by the present author.

the piano accompaniment interpret and highly intensify the spirit and mood of the poem—a perfect wedding of the two arts! Each of the four stanzas is given to two four-measure phrases. Each stanza is separated from the next by a brief piano interlude. The first, second, and fourth phrases are similar in contour, the third is contrasting, outlining the phrase-period pattern we met so frequently in the folk song—A,A:B,A. The last line of the poem is repeated, bringing us to the peak of the melody and the climax of the emotion. It has often been pointed out that in Brahms profundity of emotion and intricacy of texture go hand in hand with the simplest structural formations. In the tender *Minnelied* we have a good example of this.

German Romanticism, in the second half of the nineteenth century, strongly influenced composers throughout the entire musical world; and even such ardent nationalists as Grieg, Tchaikovsky, and our own Edward MacDowell (1861-1908) came under its spell. In their songs they combined the lyricism of the lied with their own national idiom. A number of Grieg's songs, among them the beloved *Solvejg's Song*, are completely nationalistic in style and content; but one of the most famous, *Ich Liebe Dich* (I Love You), written when he was twenty-one and very much under the influence of Schumann, is in the great tradition of the lied. Like Schumann, who turned to song in the year of his marriage to Clara Wieck, Grieg wrote *Ich Liebe Dich* as an outpouring of his love for his cousin Nina Hagerup, whom he later married. In a letter to the American critic, Henry Finck, he said, "My best songs were composed for her; they embody my personal feelings, and I could no more have stopped expressing them in songs than I could have stopped breathing." The sincerity of the songs, and the gentle lyricism which is so much a part of Grieg's musical personality, have established him as one of the most popular composers of song. This is our fifth listening study.

Grieg wrote the music of *Ich Liebe Dich* to the lyrics of Hans Christian Andersen; but the German words are almost always used. The lyrics follow:

My thought of thoughts, my very inmost being,
Thou only art my heart's felicity!
I love thee more than all else under heaven,
I love but thee, I love but thee,
I love but thee thro' all eternity!

For thee alone my thoughts are turning,
My heart is happy only for thee!

Where ever God wills that I go,
I love but thee, I love but thee,
I love thee only thro' all eternity! [6]

It is not without reason that this has become one of the most popular of love songs. It has the spirit of a live and passionately expressive emotion, tuneful throughout and as spontaneous as the declaration itself. It also contains an excellent example of a climax. Unfolding itself in a gentle curve, it begins to rise in emotional intensity on the words "I love but thee," and increases, with each repetition, to the peak on the line, "I love but thee thro' all eternity!" The melody is then repeated for the second stanza.

Of Tchaikovsky's 107 songs, unquestionably the most popular, and certainly one of the finest among them, is his setting of Goethe's *Nur Wer Die Sehnsucht Kennt* (None But the Lonely Heart), which he wrote in his twenty-ninth year, the same year that produced the ROMEO AND JULIET OVERTURE. (See Chapter XII.) He succeeded in capturing the essence of Goethe's poem. The song has come to be regarded as a characteristic expression of the melancholy that pervades so many of this composer's works, and that reaches its culmination in his last work, the PATHETIQUE SYMPHONY.

None but the lonely heart
Can know my sadness;
Alone and parted far
From joy and gladness.

Heav'n's boundless arch I see
Spread out above me.
Ah! what a distance drear
To one who loves me!

[The first stanza is repeated here.]

My senses fail,
A burning fire devours me.
None but the lonely heart
Can know my sadness. [7]

Both the choice of Goethe's lyrics and the manner in which they are handled stamp this song in the tradition of the lied, shot through

---

[6] Translation (except the second verse) by Auber Forestier. Copyright, 1936, by Oliver Ditson Company. Quoted by permission of the publishers. The second verse is a literal translation by the present author.

[7] Translation by Arthur Westbrook. Copyright by Oliver Ditson Company.

with the same quality of *sehnsucht* that permeated so much of the German Romantic poetry of the early nineteenth century. The highly emotional vocal line, with the downward leap in the first two measures, projects a mood of lassitude and despair. The melody undulates in a broad curve, a true outpouring of feeling, until it works up to the climax. Notice how masterfully the emotion is carried to its peak in the accompaniment, after the voice has stopped, on the last line of the third stanza (that is to say, the first stanza repeated as third). After a dramatic pause, the voice droops in despair, while the piano mournfully intones the original melody. The intertwining of both parts is faultless and is achieved with rare eloquence.

Much more truly Russian in style are the songs of Tchaikovsky's countryman, Modeste Moussorgsky, one of the most original creative spirits in nineteenth-century music. In his works we find a potent, highly personal idiom, dramatic and intense, but altogether free from the influence of the German lied. The composer seeks to discover the exact musical equivalent of the words, sometimes with an almost brutal realism. As Moussorgsky himself wrote to the critic Stassoff: "Life wherever it shows itself, truth no matter how bitter, courage and frankness above all, point blank—that's my object, the thing I hope to achieve."

For our sixth listening study, we present Moussorgsky's famous *Song of the Flea*, which is spoken by Mephistopheles in Goethe's *Faust*.[8] He used the text as a means for expressing his hatred and contempt for the sham and favoritism of the Russian court:

> Once upon a time there was a king
>   Who had a big flea;
>   A flea? A flea!
> Whom he loved
>   As if 't were his own son.
>   The flea? Ha, ha, ha, ha, ha!
>   The flea! Ha, ha, ha, ha, ha!
>   The flea!
>
> The king called his tailor,
>   The tailor came.
> "Make clothes for my pet,
>   And trousers too!"
>   Trousers? Ha, ha, ha, ha, ha!
>   The flea? Ha, ha, ha, ha, ha!
>   The flea! Ha, ha, ha, ha, ha!
>   Yes, trousers!

---

[8] *Faust*, Part I, Scene in Auerbach's cellar.

In silks and satins
   He was now arrayed,
With ribbons across his chest,
   And a star.
      The flea? Ha, ha, ha, ha, ha!
      The flea!

He became Minister of State,
   And received many decorations;
And all his relatives
   Were most important at court.
      Ha, ha!

And the courtiers and their ladies
   Were plagued by fleas,
The queen and maids of honor
   Had quite a time of it!

Not one of them dared scratch
   Or kill the pests.
Yet we ordinary folks are free
To scratch whene'er we like, and kill
   As soon as one bites us!
      Ha, ha, ha, ha, ha, ha, ha,
      Ha, ha, ha, ha, ha, ha, ha!

In view of his nationalism and the poetic quality of his lyric gift, Edward MacDowell has frequently been held up as the American counterpart of Grieg. Both men spent the formative periods of their careers in Germany, and both adapted the lied to the requirements of their native milieu. Although much less prolific a song writer than Grieg, MacDowell infused his works with the same richness of atmosphere and mood. They have all the melodic charm that has made his piano pieces so popular. *The Sea, The Swan Bent Low, Thy Beaming Eyes,* and *To the Sea* are among the best known. Notice, in *The Sea,* written in 1892 to the verses of William Dean Howells, how the six-eight time gives a gently flowing effect. MacDowell marked it "Broadly, with rhythmic swing." The rich chords limn the emotion of the poem:

One sails away to sea, to sea,
One stands on the shore and cries;
The ship goes down the world, and the light
And the light on the sullen water dies.

The whispering shell is mute,
And after is evil cheer;
She will stand on the shore and cry in vain,
Many and many a year.

But the stately wide-winged ship lies wrecked,
Lies wrecked on the unknown deep;
Far under, dead in his coral bed,
The lover lies asleep.

This is the seventh, and last, essential listening in this section of the chapter.

ADDITIONAL SUGGESTIONS FOR LISTENING

Among the German composers who continued in the tradition of the lied, special mention must be made of Robert Franz (1815-1892), Hugo Wolf (1860-1903), and Richard Strauss (1864-　). Franz never achieved great popularity in this country, but his melodies—among the best known are *Für Musik* (For Music), *Gute Nacht* (Good Night), and *Im Herbst* (In Autumn)—have an elusive lyric charm. Wolf, by far the most important song writer of the late nineteenth century, and an artist of highly individual gifts, achieved within the limited framework of the song a kind of miniature Wagnerian music drama. He was strongly influenced by Wagner in his harmonic idiom. With him, the piano part became a most complex web, out of which the vocal line emerged, with an extraordinary combination of emotional power, psychological acumen, and imaginative tone painting. Try listening to his *Anakreon's Grab* (Anacreon's Grave), *Auch Kleine Dinge* (Even Little Things), *Verborgenheit* (Secrecy), or *Zur Ruh, zur Ruh!* (To Rest, to Rest!). They stand among the great songs.

Richard Strauss, phenomenally successful in symphonic music and opera (See Chapter 18), has also enriched the song repertory with a number of compositions that have achieved world-wide fame. *Ständchen* (Serenade), *Traum durch die Dämmerung* (Dream in the Twilight), *Zueignung* (Devotion), and *Allerseelen* (All Souls Day) are among the works that have stamped him a contemporary master of the lied.

In France, the principal composers during the height of the Romantic Period—Hector Berlioz, Charles Gounod, Camille Saint-Saëns, Georges Bizet, and Jules Massenet—devoted their best efforts to either opera or instrumental music. It was not until the latter part of the century, when a group of French composers made a concerted attempt to break away from German influence and found a true national style, that the French art song came into its own. The leader in this movement was César Franck (1822-1890). Although he wrote few songs, they occupy a high place in the repertory, chief among them being *(La) Procession*, *Nocturne*, and *(Le) Mariage des Roses*. His followers were Gabriel Fauré

(1845-1924), best known for such songs as *L'Automne* and *Clair de Lune* (Moonlight); and Henri Duparc (1848-1933), composer of the exquisite *L'Invitation au Voyage* and *Extase*. Although Duparc wrote only a few songs, they are among the finest in French literature.

But the most distinctive song composer of France, and the one who influenced the form most profoundly, was Claude Debussy (1862-1918), master of Impressionism (see Chapter XXVIII), that tenuous cool and fluid style to which European music turned for respite after the overemotionalism of the Wagnerian music drama. Debussy subordinated his vocal line to the poetic declamation of the verse—he set to music the great French poets, François Villon, Baudelaire, Mallarmé, and Verlaine—with the result that melody as such disappeared from his songs. Instead there developed a vocal line of the most exquisite subtlety, demanding from the performer the utmost sensitivity to nuance, while the piano let float a background of wavering harmonies. When performed by two artists who understand the style, these songs produce an effect of sheer magic. A fine introduction to this idiom is afforded by the setting of Verlaine's *Mandoline*, in which the tinkling chords give the atmosphere of the "gallants who go serenading and fair dames who to them listen," as their shadows

> Whirl ecstatic where the moonlight
> Falls in rose and silver splendor;
> A mandolin softly tinkling
> Answers the wind, gay and tender.[7a]

Here, and in such songs as *Harmonie du Soir* (Evening Harmonies), *Receuillement* (Meditation), and *La Mort des Amants* (Death of the Lovers) is to be found that exquisite sensibility and suggestiveness that we shall meet again and again when we study the works of the Impressionists.

In America, the song has always been a favorite form, running the gamut from the sentimental, popular kind to the highest type of art song. At one extreme are songs such as Carrie Jacobs Bond's *Just a Song at Twilight* and James Molloy's *Love's Old Sweet Song*, which have sold millions of copies. Then there is the romantic art song, such as Charles Wakefield Cadman's *At Dawning* and *From the Land of the Sky-Blue Water*, or Thurlow Lieurance's *By the Waters of Minnetonka*, which combine a charming lyricism with popular melodic appeal. Typical of this genre are such extremely successful works as *Love Went A-Riding*, by Edward Bridges; Ethelbert Nevin's *The Rosary; Trees*, the setting by Oscar Rasbach of Joyce Kilmer's poem; Richard Hageman's setting of Rabindranath Tagore's *Do Not Go, My Love*, and Ernest Charles' *When I Have Sung My Songs*. In the tradition of French Impressionism are such works as *By a Lonely Forest Pathway* by Charles Griffes (1884-1920), the gifted young American whose career was cut short by an untimely death, and the exquisite songs of Charles Alden Carpenter (1876-   ), *When I Bring You Colored Toys*, the *Serenade*, and *On a Screen*.

[7a] Translation by Bliss Carman. Copyright, Boston Music Co. Reprinted by permission.

Sentence Structure in Music: Phrase, Period, and Cadence

The reader may have noticed, in the songs we just heard, that there were definite breaks or pauses in the musical thought where the singer paused to draw breath. These naturally corresponded to the breaks in poetic thought at the end of the verse or sentence. In reading or speaking, we all pause an instant, almost automatically, at the end of the thought, which is generally marked by a comma—or half stop—at the end of a phrase or clause, and by a period—full stop— at the end of a sentence.

It is apparent, from our discussion on musical architecture, that, although music may at first sight appear to us to be a continuous flow without shape or form, it is in reality built of well-defined structural units or sections—the equivalent, we might say, of paragraphs or stanzas in writing. In many of the compositions we have listened to thus far, these sections or paragraphs were fairly easy to recognize, since often a new theme appeared in each section and dominated the scene until followed by another theme in the next section. We saw also that these sections appeared and reappeared in conformity with general aesthetic principles of construction—symmetry, balance, contrast, climax—which obtained not only in music but also in poetry, painting, sculpture, and architecture.

The paragraph in literature is further subdivided into sentences, clauses, and phrases, as is also the stanza. So, too, the musical section is subdivided into definite groupings of thought, known to the reader as phrases and periods. These groupings have to be set off with punctuation, otherwise they could not function effectively as recognizable units. The first phrase generally ends with a half stop or comma, known in music as the incomplete or semicadence, which gives the impression that more is to follow. In many folk songs two phrases make a musical sentence, or period, which ends with a full stop, an authentic or full cadence. The word comes from the Latin *cadere*, "to fall," since the pause was indicated, in song as in speech, by a downward inflection of the voice.

The upward and downward inflection of the two types of cadence, and the relation of the two phrases in the period, are well illustrated in a simple musical sentence such as the tune of *London Bridge*. (See page 67.)

We have here two four-measure phrases which stand in a kind of question-answer relation. The first, ending with an upward inflection

Lon-don Bridge is fall-ing down, fall-ing down, fall-ing down,

Lon-don Bridge is fall-ing down, my fair Lad-y.

on the semicadence, is answered by the second, ending with a downward inflection on the full cadence. A similar relation is observable in the two phrases that comprise the period in *The Farmer in the Dell:*

The far-mer in the dell. - The far-mer in the dell.

Heigh-ho the Mer-ry - Oh! the far-mer in the dell.

Phrasing in both speech and song sprang up from an interplay of two factors: first, an inherent need of the human mind for logical organization in grouping its thoughts; second, the number of words or tones that could be conveniently carried on one breath. We phrase, or pause for breath, not only when we speak but also when we read silently or write. Phrasing is just as important for the instrumental player as it is for the singer, even though certain instrumental performers are not restricted by breathing and could go on playing indefinitely. In singing, we stop at the end of the thought which, we noticed, comes simultaneously in both words and music. In playing an instrument, the phrasing has to be brought out just as carefully; and the wind instruments are akin to the singer as regards breath. If a pianist or violinist does not phrase properly he will be unable to indicate clearly the outlines of the musical structure. Incorrect phrasing in music is equivalent to running sentences together in speech or writing. It is symptomatic of confused thinking.

There is no fixed length for the phrase. Many folk songs, especially those that date back to the Middle Ages, when our system of "measured music" was not yet as prevalent as it became in later centuries, have quite irregular phrase lengths. The rhapsodical outpourings of the Hungarian Gypsy or of the flamenco are apt to be very irregular in phrase structure. We noticed a three-measure phrase in *The Birch Tree* (page 43). Nonetheless, the music of Western Europe was strongly influenced, as we have seen, by folk-dance rhythms. And as soon as dance becomes a factor in music, we find a tendency to clearly defined, regular phrase structure. Also, the simple meters of poetry played their part in calling forth a regular phrase structure. Although we find innumerable exceptions and variants, the four-measure phrase, organized in a period of eight measures or in a double period of sixteen, seems to have been most attractive to folk and art musicians alike, in their search for simple, symmetrical patterns. Many of our best-loved tunes are built on a four-measure phrase structure.

Let us examine Stephen Foster's *Swanee River* for phrase, period, and cadence structure. The verse consists of four lines in two sentences:

Way down upon the Swanee River, far far away,
Dere's wha my heart is turning ever, dere's wha de old folks stay.
All de world is sad and dreary, ev'rywhere I roam,
Oh! darkies, how my heart grows weary, far from de old folks at home.

The first and third lines end in a comma (semicadence); the second and fourth in a period (full cadence). Each line is set to a four-measure phrase. (Notice the following musical example.)

It is apparent that we have here two musical periods, each equivalent to a sentence (two lines) of verse. Notice too that, of the four phrases, the second repeats the melody of the first, the third introduces contrasting material, and the fourth returns to the old phrase. Thus, we have here unity, variety, symmetry, and contrast achieved through that serviceable pattern, A-A:B-A.

Notice particularly, in the Foster song, that each of the four cadences occupies a full measure, giving a definite sense of pause. The break in the thought is indicated by the rest. The semicadence in the first line, an upward inflection on the word *away*, is balanced by the full cadence at the end of the second line, the downward inflection on *de old folks stay*. Similarly, the half pause at the end of the third line on *I roam* is answered by the full stop at the end of the fourth line, the final cadence on *at home*. Thus, we have a question-answer formation in the first two phrases, and a similar formation in the last two.

Chapter VII

THE OPERA

1. Operetta and Light Opera[1]

LOOKING back upon the study we have made so far of vocal music, it becomes apparent that a song is an independent and self-contained work of art. Whether the song be a "traditional" or a "composed" folk song, an art song or a lied, the words and the music, between them, contain all there is to say for the moment, and only a singer is necessary to interpret and reveal the content. The listener has but to hear and react to the performance of the song itself to obtain the complete experience.

It is but a logical and easy step, now, to consider songs, for one or more singers, that require the addition of something outside themselves; that are an integral part of a more extended story, action, and environment. Let us think of the type of song that involves the action and participation of others, that is incomplete without the co-operation of the other arts—painting, drama, costuming, dancing, acting, and so on. Such a song is only a small portion of the whole, and thus a number of songs are required in succession for the unfolding of the drama of which each is a part; and as the moods and situations of the performers change, so must the songs change in the development of the story.

Such a type might well be considered an operatic song; and so a number of them in sequence and involving a number of persons might well be an opera—after a fashion, a simple type of opera. If the tale were a tragic one and ·sung and acted throughout (or almost), it might well be called a "grand" opera; if, on the other hand, there were spoken dialogue and action between the songs, and the plot of a cheerful, romantic, and even humorous nature, it might well be an *operetta* or a "light" opera. Thus the song, or *aria*, as we should now call it, is to be considered in the environment of a number of arts and

---

[1] Listening Study for this chapter is in Part II: excerpts from the opera CARMEN.

a number of persons, all joined in concerted action to tell a story—and we have a simple and general recipe for an elementary and hypothetical opera.

The combination of these different elements into one unified entertainment seems to answer some deep human need, for we find it persisting throughout history under all sorts of conditions. The Greeks and the Romans had elaborate dramatic performances with song and dance; the Middle Ages and Renaissance saw the emergence of various types of musical plays, sacred and secular. Nor is the genre confined to Western European civilization. We find dramatic spectacles with song and dance, some of great antiquity, in India, China, Japan, Java, and Persia, some obviously inspired by the spiritual and dramatic contents of the religious ritual, others quite secular, romantic, or humorous, and of high artistic order. Even primitive cultures have song-and-dance cycles, highly symbolic in character, that display in rudimentary form the elements of the musical-dramatic genre.

Of the various types of musical play that flourish in our culture, the comic opera, or operetta, is one of the most engaging. The comic opera (known in Italy as *opera buffa*, in France as *opéra bouffe*, and in Germany as *Singspiel*, or *song-play*) is a play in which songs and dances are interspersed with spoken dialogue, and which contains highly diverting situations that combine fantasy, romance, warm human sentiment, and racy, topical humor. This popular kind of opera is distinct from grand opera (which is sung throughout), is of a lofty nature, generally tragic in mood, and may be far removed, as far as plot and characters go, from the environment in which it is presented. The relation between comic opera or operetta and grand opera may be compared to that between popular song and art song. Where grand opera is formal in character, *opera buffa*, *opéra bouffe*, and *Singspiel* are delightfully informal. Where grand opera demands a lavish expenditure for soloists, chorus, ballet and orchestra, scenery and costumes, comic opera is fairly accessible to the common man. Where grand opera is aristocratic and cosmopolitan, subsidized in its early stages by kings and nobles, comic opera is plebeian and close to the soil, a worthy descendant of the song-and-dance plays presented at village fairs and in the market place by the itinerant musicians, jugglers, tumblers, and actors of the Middle Ages. Where grand opera, as often as not, deals with mythical or historical personages, comic opera bases itself on the personal experiences and interests of the audience, presenting them with rich satire and drollery. As happened with popular music and art music throughout the history of the art, the two genres flourished side by side and interacted on each other. In the eighteenth century, short comic operas were presented as *interludes* or *intermezzos* between the acts of grand opera. The popular opera took over some of the techniques and style characteristics evolved in grand opera. In return, whenever grand opera threatened to become excessively formalized and stilted, it found new life and vitality in the spirit of the folk opera.

The American stage has developed its own genre, the *musical comedy*, in which youth, beauty, and romance are intermingled with comedy, spectacular scenic effects, and a dancing chorus. Allied to this form is the *musical revue*, which presents the same elements either in a series of separate scenes and skits, or held together by the merest thread of plot or continuity. With the advent of the "talkies" came the motion-picture operettas, some of which presented song, dance, romance, and comedy in an even more lavish manner than was possible for the Broadway stage. All these types, with their appealing love songs sung by hero and heroine against a most romantic background, the rollicking antics and misadventures of the comedian, and the invariable happy ending, offer, through a combination of all the theater arts with music, an irresistible type of entertainment which transports the spectator, in most compelling fashion, to the world of the imagination.

Since the essence of theater is make-believe, we accept without question the convention whereby a character in an operetta suddenly switches from speech to song; pours out his feelings in a lyrical number, while the action pauses; and, after the applause has died down, resumes his role in the play. True, we know that he would never behave like this in real life. Yet in some mysterious way the music creates a reality and value of its own, lifting the action to the plane of pure emotion; and it is on this plane that we respond. When Shakespeare presents to us the jealousy of Othello or the anguish of Lear in the iambic pentameters of blank verse, we are aware that people do not express themselves in this fashion in everyday existence. Through the use of lofty and impassioned verse, the dramatist has lifted us into a world more intense, more "real" than the actual world, a realm of pure imagination in which our awareness of life is immeasurably heightened.

In the same way, when a character in a musical play sings of his love and longing for the heroine, even though he seems to violate every canon of realism, he communicates to us, as he could never have done through mere speech, the essence of romantic emotion. The music has added a new dimension, a new meaning, to the emotional impact of the drama. "It is better to invent reality than to copy it!" said Giuseppe Verdi, one of the great opera composers. There could be no better comment on both the poetic and the music drama.

The *romantic operetta*, or *light opera*,[2] which came into prominence all over Europe in the second half of the nineteenth century, has been cultivated with great success in America, and has enjoyed phenomenal popularity on our stage. The roster of gifted operetta composers includes such names as Victor Herbert (1859-1924), Reginald DeKoven (1859-1920), and later Rudolf Friml (1881-   ), Sigmund Romberg (1887-   ), and Jerome Kern (1885-1945). These men developed a style of smoothly flowing, sentimental melody of wide popular appeal, most appropriate to the picturesquely romantic plots of their operettas. Many of these musical plays are no longer given on the stage; but one or two songs from each seem to hold on year after year with astonishing vitality. Some even, as in the case of *Oh Promise Me* from DeKoven's ROBIN HOOD, and *Ol' Man River* from Kern's SHOW BOAT, are well on the way to becoming part of our stock of composed folk songs. A number have survived as favorite love songs: the *Indian Love Call* from Friml's ROSE-MARIE; *Will You Remember?* from Romberg's MAYTIME; the *Song of Love* —based on the second theme from the first movement of Schubert's UNFINISHED SYMPHONY—from BLOSSOM TIME, the musical romance of that composer's life; *Kiss Me Again* from Herbert's MLLE. MODISTE, as well as the *Gypsy Love Song* from his FORTUNE TELLER; and *Smoke Gets in Your Eyes* from Kern's ROBERTA.

In his short career George Gershwin (1898-1937) made an outstanding contribution to the tradition of American operetta. His gifts found apt expression in his "folk opera" PORGY AND BESS, a setting of DuBose Heyward's play. Technically, the work is on the borderline between operetta and opera, since some of the dialogue is spoken and some of it sung. The classification is immaterial. In PORGY AND BESS the conventions of the drama with music are invested with the color and life of folk tale and folk speech. The result is a work of vivid imagination and effective as "good theater." Listen to the following excerpts, which have become popular: the lullaby *Summer-*

---

[2] It is recommended that the specific songs mentioned in Part I, "Operetta and Light Opera," be considered as suggested and supplementary rather than assigned listening, and be indulged in as far as taste and time will allow. The "musts" for listening are in Part II of this chapter.

time; A Woman Is a Sometime Thing; Porgy's I Got Plenty o' Nut-tin', and his love song, *Bess, You Is My Woman Now;* Sporting Life's edifying sermon, *It Ain't Necessarily So;* the *Requiem;* and Porgy's final song, *Where Is My Bess?*

In England the comic opera reached its apogee in one of the most amazing collaborations in dramatico-musical history, that between William S. Gilbert and Arthur Sullivan, which began in 1875 and lasted for over twenty years. Out of it came a type of operetta so original and distinctive that it has become something of a cult for hundreds of thousands of "Savoyards" throughout the English-speaking world. (The Savoy operas were so named after the theater in which they first made their unparalleled success.) Here were fantasy and romance, whimsy and social satire, keyed to the rapierlike wit and astonishing verbal dexterity of Gilbert, and set off by the sparkling tunes of Sullivan.

The distinctive flavor of the Savoy operas is amply demonstrated in what has remained, in this country, the most popular of the series, THE MIKADO. A wonderful satire is leveled here against the English bureaucracy, through the symbolic figures of Ko-Ko, Lord High Executioner, and Pooh-Bah, Lord High Everything Else. In addition there are the lovers Nanki-Poo and Yum-Yum, the formidable Katisha, an elderly Lady in love with Nanki-Poo, and the Mikado, who humanely desires to "let the punishment fit the crime." It is futile to attempt to describe, in mere prose, the plot of a Gilbert and Sullivan operetta. Like *Alice in Wonderland*, it exists in a world of its own within which, through the magic of the verses and the music, it makes perfectly good sense. To transplant it out of that fantasy world is little short of fatal. See it on the actual stage if possible; if not, hear it through carefully selected records—and exercise your imagination a great deal.

Opera buffa

The spirit of comedy through music, which found such felicitous expression in the late nineteenth century, had reached its perfection of form and style a century earlier in the *opera buffa* of the Classical Period. This genre depended for its charm on a situation often extravagantly comical, keyed in the mood of the eighteenth-century comedy of manners; a light, playful style of music, and that pure vocal line that was the glory of the Classical masters; an ebullient ensemble number at the finale of each act; and the personality of the *buffo*, the chief comic character. Generally baritone or bass, the buffo not only was one of the protagonists in the play but, in the fashion of a master of ceremonies, he informally harangued the audience from the footlights, taking them into his confidence—as the Gilbert characters do—commenting slyly, in almost improvisational manner, on life, love, and politics, and keeping them in gales of laughter with his couplets: the living embodiment, in short, of the spirit of the *commedia dell 'arte*. Between the arias, duets, and ensemble numbers, the action was carried on by a *secco* (dry recitation), a rapid-fire interchange of question and retort carried on in a manner bordering on speech, in which the musical line was subservient, in shape and rhythm, to the words, and supported by the flimsiest accompaniment of chords on the harpsichord. (These, in modern productions, are played by the orchestra.) Among the outstanding examples of this type are LA SERVA PADRONA (The Maid-Mistress), by the short-lived Giovanni Pergolesi (1710-1736), which was revived in recent years at the Metropolitan Opera House; IL MATRIMONIO SEGRETO (The Secret Marriage) by Domenico Cimarosa (1749-1801), the delightful overture of which is still frequently performed; and the BARBER OF SEVILLE by Gioacchino Rossini (1792-1868), which, for over a century, has remained a favorite with opera audiences. But the supreme example of opera buffa is Mozart's MARRIAGE OF FIGARO, in which the spirit of eighteenth-century comedy is clothed in music eternally young and radiant that for sheer loveliness has never been equaled.

Incidentally, both the Rossini and Mozart operas are based on the satirical comedies of Beaumarchais (1732-1799), THE MARRIAGE OF FIGARO being the sequel to THE BARBER OF SEVILLE. Beaumarchais, who was a musician as well as a dramatist, intended the BARBER as a comic opera, with music by him based on the songs and dances he had heard in Spain. When the work was refused by the *Opéra Comique*, he submitted it, as a "comedy in prose interspersed with songs," to the *Comédie Française*, where it was produced.

ADDITIONAL SUGGESTIONS FOR LISTENING

For excerpts from the MARRIAGE OF FIGARO, listen to the *Overture*, a delectable tidbit of musical merriment which, although it does not use any of the themes of the opera itself, fully captures the spirit of what is to follow; the aria of Cherubino in the first act, *Non so più cosa son* (I Know Not What I Am Doing), in which he pours out his love for the Countess; the Countess' aria in the second act, *Porgi amor* (Love, Thou Pure Impulse), in which she begs the God of Love either to bring her husband back to her or to let her find release from grief in death; the wonderful *Voi che sapete* (You Who Know, Tell Me), in which Cherubino expresses all his youthful ardor; the song of the Countess in Act III, *Dove Sono* (They Are Over), in which she looks back with longing to her former days of happiness; and Susanna's beautiful *Deh vieni, non tardar* (Oh Come, Do Not Delay), in the final act. Here is sparkling vocal melody, spontaneous and flowing, pure in form and luminous of texture. The listener might wish to include in his supplementary listening the vivacious and humorous aria from Rossini's THE BARBER OF SEVILLE, *Largo al factotum* (Room for the Factotum), sung by the leading male character, Figaro.

II. Grand Opera

In the operetta, we found, the plot is carried on through spoken dialogue which, at the lyrical moments, reverts to song. In the opera, the dialogue too is sung, in the free and flexible musical declamation or song-speech known as *recitative*, which gives way, at the lyrical high points, to the arias, the songs or airs. This procedure gives us a dramatic work set to music from beginning to end.

In view of what we have said about the theater as a world of fantasy, and about the function of music or poetry in heightening the emotional intensity of the dramatic situation, it need not surprise us that generations of theater-goers throughout the world have accepted the conventions of the play that is sung instead of spoken. Indeed, for over three hundred years the opera has been one of the most popular forms of entertainment in Western European culture.

This acceptance of musico-dramatic art goes back much farther than is commonly supposed. We have already pointed out (in Chapter III) the role of music in religious ritual. It should be remembered that the formal theater, whether in ancient Greek or medieval European civilization, probably sprang out of the spirit and dramatic elements of religious ceremonial. From the beginning of the Catholic Church, the supreme drama of Christendom—the life and death of Christ—has been presented within a framework of words and music. The ceremonial Mass of the Church became the supreme music drama of Europe. Magnificent vestments, sacred vessels, incense, an elaborate ritual, and music by the greatest composers, known and unknown, against a scenic background furnished by the finest artists in painting, sculpture, and architecture—all combined in a most imposing spectacle. In the later Middle Ages there sprang up the *Mystery* and *Miracle plays*, containing basic elements of both opera and poetic drama. Based on incidents in Scripture or in the lives of the saints, these plays were originally given either inside the church or in the open space before it, with such realistic props as calves, donkeys, and other Biblical animals, and used spoken dialogue as well as song. It can readily be supposed that such episodes as the lament of the mothers over the slaying of the Innocents or the repentance of Magdalene lent themselves to effective musical treatment. Thus, for centuries before the actual development of the opera, music had become an integral part of the most engrossing symbolic drama known to European man.

On the other hand, no less important elements of the opera came from secular sources. Dance, pantomime, scenic splendor, and certain musical characteristics were derived from the masques and spectacles which throughout the feudal period predominated at the entertainments of the princely courts. Musical declamation stemmed out of the experiments of a group of Florentine noblemen who, spurred on by the spirit of the Italian Renaissance, sought to revive the lost musical-dramatic art of ancient Greek tragedy. By the year 1600, all these elements were ready to be united, awaiting only the touch of the creative artists who would fuse them into a new art form. This fusion was accomplished, in the early stages, by Jacopo Peri (c. 1561-c. 1633) and Giulio Caccini (c. 1588-c. 1615), and brought to completion by the first great master of operatic style, Claudio Monteverde (1567-1643) who, at about the same time that Shakespeare was carrying the poetic drama to a higher level than it had ever before attained, opened new vistas of dramatic expressiveness for music in the theater.

We are so accustomed to the naturalistic drama of today that we think of opera and drama as poles apart. Actually, not only do poetic drama and music drama go back to the same origin in the medieval religious plays, but they also had many elements in common during long periods of their development. The so-called realistic drama of our contemporary theater, which presents to us characters and situations familiar to us from our everyday milieu, is, strictly speaking, a comparatively recent innovation, having come into its own only a little over a half century ago, with the plays of Ibsen and Shaw. The theater of the past, of Shakespeare and Marlowe, of Corneille and Racine, of Calderon and Lope de Vega, of Schiller and Lessing—it goes without saying, of Sophocles and Aeschylus—was a theater of poetry and lofty declamation, of pageantry, musical interludes, songs, choruses, and stately dances. (One has but to examine the stage directions in Shakespeare's plays to realize the extent of this "operatic" element.) It is from this emotional-musical speech that musical declamation arose in the theater of antiquity, returning two thousand years later to the theater of the Renaissance. As the two genres developed, the literary element was subordinated to the musical in the opera, while the poetic element was subordinated to the realistic in the drama, with the result that we encounter them today as completely contrasting types of theater. But this should not blind us to their common ancestry.

In the music drama, a number of elements come together within the musical framework: poetic mood, dramatic action, vocal and orchestral music, singing and dancing, solos, ensembles and choruses, scenery, and costumes and pageantry all held together. The basic problem in operatic aesthetics is the need to fuse all these elements into a harmonious whole. The fundamental differences between the several operatic styles, in all periods, have sprung from the various ways in which this synthesis is accomplished, from the emphasizing of one or another, or several, of the different ingredients. Even the style of individual composers may be analyzed from this point of view.

The Italians, throughout the whole of operatic history, have been enamored of the voice, and developed in their lyric theater a style of *bel canto*, or beautiful singing, that has, in the opinion of many musicians, never been surpassed. Italian opera, consequently, is primarily vocal opera, depending for its appeal on the power and beauty of the human voice, to which all the other factors are subordinated. This preoccupation led, on the one hand, to showy exhibition pieces calling for prodigious technique on the part of the singer, and as often as not having very little to do with the mood of the drama out of which they were supposed to have sprung, and on the other, to the development of a style of flowing, sensuous vocal melody that is the glory of the Italian school. The tendency to subordinate drama to voice was pushed so far that in the classical opera of the eighteenth century the plot became little more than a meaningless, artificial framework for the brilliant arias and ensemble numbers of the chief performers. This was the so-called "prima donna opera," which was really little more than a vocal concert in costume.

By the beginning of the nineteenth century, the Italian opera had already begun to return to the dramatic principles with which it had started out. The start was made in the works of the three great masters of brilliant vocal melody who flourished in the first half of the century, the earliest composers of Italian opera whose works are still performed today: Rossini, whose masterpiece, THE BARBER OF SEV-

SCENE FROM THE OPERA "AÏDA" *Verdi*

ILLE we mentioned earlier in the chapter; Gaetano Donizetti (1797-1848), known to us for his setting of Walter Scott's tragic story of "Lucy of Lammermoor" (LUCIA DI LAMMERMOOR), as well as the delightful comic operas DAUGHTER OF THE REGIMENT, DON PASQUALE, and ELIXIR OF LOVE; and Vincenzo Bellini (1801-1835), composer of NORMA. Their successor was Giuseppe Verdi (1813-1901), a great dramatic composer, who brought the Italian operatic style to its peak. He perfected a type of melody that was not only attractive to the ear and admirably shaped to the contours of the singer's voice, but essentially dramatic melody: that is, it sprang logically out of the situation on the stage, out of the personalities, the moods and inner conflicts, of the characters. The famous works of his middle period, RIGOLETTO, LA TRAVIATA and LA FORZA DEL DESTINO (The Force of Destiny), and the three masterpieces of his maturity—AÏDA, OTELLO and FALSTAFF—represent a superb fusion of the great *bel canto* tradition with dramatic truth and musical expressiveness.[4]

The French, on the other hand, loved not only the voice but also logic, literature, elegant diction—and the ballet. They insisted on understanding what the singers were singing. Consequently, pure vocal line could not gain complete ascendancy over dramatic coherence. Their composers stood in close contact with their literary men. As a result, the principles of French classical drama had some influence on operatic procedure. At the court of the Bourbons poetic drama, music, and the dance attained a greater homogeneity of style than anywhere else in Europe.

Opera in France had its roots in the elaborate ballet spectacles and masques performed at the entertainments of the nobility. It was an Italian, Jean Baptiste Lully (1632-1687), who introduced the new Florentine music drama to the court of Louis XIV and who, by adapting it to the tastes and needs of the French genius, became known to history as the "father of French opera." His successor in the period of Louis XV was Jean Philippe Rameau (1683-1764), a friend of Voltaire, several of whose librettos he set to music. Rameau was a theorist as well as a composer, author of several important treatises on harmony. He was, besides, a trenchant critic who carried

---

[4] His successors followed in his footsteps, adapting the Italian vocal style to the exigencies of modern dramatic realism. Chief among them were Giacomo Puccini (1858-1924), composer of LA BOHÈME, TOSCA, and MADAME BUTTERFLY; Ruggiero Leoncavallo (1858-1919), known chiefly for the ever-popular I PAGLIACCI (The Clowns); and Pietro Mascagni (1863-1945), who wrote CAVALLERIA RUSTICANA (Rustic Chivalry). Although less gifted than the master, they and their confrères all had a flair for vocal-dramatic music that was the essence of their Italian heritage.

on extensive polemics with Diderot, Jean Jacques Rousseau, and d'Alembert on the esthetics of the opera.

In the reign of Louis XVI, it was a foreigner again who guided the destinies of French opera—the German, Christophe Willibald Gluck (1714-1787). Gluck, who achieved his greatest triumphs in Paris, under the patronage of his one-time pupil Marie Antoinette, attempted to lead the eighteenth-century opera back to the principles of sound dramaturgy, which had been espoused by Monteverde and the Florentine founders of the music drama. For this he is remembered as one of the reformers of the opera. His famous preface to his opera ALCESTE formulates his artistic creed and gives a clue to the significance of his reforms:

When I undertook to set this poem it was my intention to avoid all those abuses which had crept into Italian opera through the mistaken vanity of singers and the unwise compliance of composers, and which had rendered it wearisome and ridiculous instead of being, as it once was, the most beautiful and imposing spectacle of modern times. I endeavored to reduce music to its proper function, that of seconding poetry by enforcing the expression of the sentiment and the interest of the situations without interrupting the action or weakening it by superfluous ornament. . . . I also thought that my first and chief care as a composer was to aim at a noble simplicity; and there is no rule of composition which I have not thought it my duty to sacrifice in order to favor truthfulness of emotion and produce the proper effect.

The first half of the nineteenth century saw the triumph in Paris of grand opera, a type of heroic drama set in a background of orchestral and scenic splendor. Despite the intensity of its tragic moments and the lofty plane of the action, this genre strikes us today as being somewhat bombastic and pompous. In this period French grand opera reached its peak in the works of the German, Giacomo Meyerbeer (1791-1864), and the Italian, Gasparo Spontini (1774-1851), composer of LA VESTALE. Meyerbeer's works, enormously popular throughout the nineteenth century, are gradually disappearing from the repertory, although we still hear the *Coronation March* from LE PROPHÈTE, the aria *O Paradiso* from L'AFRICAINE, and that wonderful show piece for the coloratura soprano, the *Shadow Song* from DINORAH.

The reader will have noticed that, until this point, French grand opera was largely the work of Italians or Germans who adapted the international Italian opera style to Parisian tastes. Yet, side by side with this type of opera, there flourished the truly native *opéra comique.* Out of the combination of the two there came into being, about the middle of the nineteenth century, what we consider today the distinctive French contribution to opera, the *drame lyrique* or lyric drama, as typically French in its conception and execution as the opera of Verdi and Puccini is Italian. In the French lyric drama we have convincing dramatic situations; a type of musical declamation that grows out of the inflections of the French language; a certain literary quality in the libretto; and a sweet lyricism that is quite distinct from the dramatic melody of the Italians. The most popular of these French works are Charles Gounod's FAUST (1859), based on an episode from Goethe's drama, although completely Gallicized; Jules Massenet's MANON (1884), a setting of the appealing novel of Abbé Prevost; Camille Saint-Saëns' Biblical opera, SAMSON ET DELILAH (1877); and the finest of the French operas, Georges Bizet's CARMEN (1875), a masterful setting of Prosper Mérimée's exciting story. To these may be added two more recent works, Gustave Charpentier's LOUISE (1900), an opera of modern working-class life in Paris; and Debussy's memorable setting of Maeterlinck's symbolist drama PELLÉAS AND MÉLISANDE, the quintessence of the French spirit in modern music drama.

Just as the Italians emphasized vocal melody, and the French, musical declamation, the Germans tended to use the orchestra as the foundation of their music drama. With Richard Wagner this tendency became so pronounced that we may with justice speak of his works as symphonic operas. Yet already the first great composer of German opera, Mozart, had used his orchestra for dramatic characterization and theatrical effect as it had never been used before. When Napoleon asked Grétry the difference between the style of Mozart and that of Cimarosa, he replied: "Sire, Cimarosa puts his statue on the stage and the pedestal in the orchestra; Mozart puts his statue in the orchestra and the pedestal on the stage." We believe today that in Mozart statue and pedestal are one; but the remark provides some insight into the reactions of his contemporaries.

It must be remembered that Mozart was one of the outstanding symphonic composers of all time. He was heir alike to the Italian tradition of *bel canto* and the German instrumental style. The combination of the two produced, in DON GIOVANNI, a work that is coming more and more to be rated as one of the great music dramas, in which orchestra and voice fuse in a perfect unity, and in which the symphonic background interprets with the utmost psychological penetration and power every nuance of the action and characterization unfolding on the stage. In the Italian *opera buffa* tradition he produced the MARRIAGE OF FIGARO; and in the style of the native comic opera, the *Singspiel*, he wrote, three months before his death, the fairy opera, THE MAGIC FLUTE. With these works, as far as present-day audiences are concerned, German opera begins.

Carl Maria von Weber (1786-1826), generally called "the father of German romantic opera," is today chiefly remembered for the overtures to his three operas, FREISCHÜTZ, OBERON, and EURYANTHE. In him we find the beginnings of that ardent nationalism, the glorification of German folklore and myth, of German forest and mountain and river, which reached its culmination in the music drama of Richard Wagner (1813-1883). Outside of Germany, where his operas still hold the stage, Weber is considered of importance in operatic history mainly as having prepared the way for his illustrious successor.

Wagner, particularly in the music dramas of his mature period— TRISTAN AND ISOLDE, the cycle of THE RING OF THE NIBELUNG, and his comic masterpiece DIE MEISTERSINGER (The Master Singers)— represents the peak of German operatic style in the same way that Verdi does the Italian, Bizet and Debussy the French. In Wagner's works the chief protagonist, and the mainspring of the action, is the orchestra. The orchestra reminisces and warns of things to come; it comments on the action as did the chorus in Greek tragedy; it weaves a symphonic web that encases actors and audience alike. Out of this seething harmony rises the vocal line, which is declaimed by the singers in a kind of *sprechstimme,* or speaking song, geared to the German tongue as intimately as is Debussy's declamation to the French. This form Wagner, in his later works, called "endless melody," to distinguish it from the aria, the molded and "set" tune of Italian opera. At high lyrical moments, the "endless melody" gives way to what might be considered equivalent to arias; yet these are always but strands in the rich symphonic texture. There are no pauses at the end of the songs to allow for applause; no ballets or *divertissements,* choruses, or ensemble numbers save those that are an integral part of the dramatic action.

Wagner believed that the poetic drama was worthy of the same reverence as a religious ceremonial. His life work represents an attempt, carried through with singular devotion to what he considered his mission, to purge the lyric theater of the triviality into which it had fallen, and to restore it to the place of honor it had occupied among the Greeks. One of the most original figures in the history of art, he inaugurated a revolution in musical thinking comparable to that effected by his contemporary Darwin in the domain of scientific thought. (He has been called by so trenchant a critic as H. L. Mencken "one of the greatest geniuses in the history of man.") Yet, despite the elaborate aesthetic theory that he built up in his philosophical works—his prose writings fill twelve volumes—by making the orchestra more important than the voice in his dramas, he laid himself open to the charge of having misunderstood the fundamental nature of opera. (In any case, his theoretical writings do not always offer a trustworthy guide to what he achieved in his operas, for his practice often differed widely from his theory.) Excerpts from his music dramas are played continually at symphony concerts, where they sound effective without the voices—in the opinion of some, even more so. This means, in effect, that the voices are not indispensable to this type of performance, a condition that would be unthinkable in Italian or French opera. Whatever the merits of the controversy, the Wagnerian dramas remain with us, despite their many faults, as extended vocal-symphonic tone poems with passages of sweeping power and beauty; and the great moments in them rank unquestionably with the enduring achievements of musical-dramatic art.

As might be expected, German opera is somewhat slower in pace than is either Italian or French opera. The action is less externalized, and the music is less likely (especially in the later Wagner) to be a series of set-pieces, or arias. Rather, there is likely to be a continuous flow of song—either one song going imperceptibly into another, or assuming the half-lyric and half-declamatory style that Wagner used in his late music dramas. In the early Wagnerian operas, and those of his contemporaries, one finds the Italian traditions well established.

We have already referred to the *Prelude to Act I* of LOHENGRIN (See page 24) as an example of religious sentiment in music. (The function of the prelude to an act is to create in the audience the proper receptivity for the unfolding of the drama.) The motive reappears in the first act, in Elsa's great aria known as *Elsa's Dream*, in which the falsely accused Princess describes a vision that appeared to her of a knight in shining armor come to do battle in her behalf. The shimmering theme originally heard in the *Prelude* accompanies her recital in the aria, indicating that the deliverer of whom she dreamed is a knight of the Holy Grail. Then, softly, in the brass, we hear a chivalric motive that well describes the brave knight who is on his way to help her—the orchestra assuming the function of a commentator.

The *Prelude to the Third Act* of LOHENGRIN is an outburst of jubilation to celebrate the marriage of the Swan Knight of the Grail and Elsa. The tumultuous theme in the trombones sets a mood of festivity, which gives way, in the middle section, to tender lyricism and meditation; then the exuberance returns. At the very end, in the concert version, we hear the ominous theme of doubt, which is to prove Elsa's undoing—she had promised Lohengrin that she would never inquire into his identity. Then, softly, in the brass, we hear repeated the chivalric motive describing the brave knight.

If LOHENGRIN represents the German Romantic opera of Wagner's first period, TRISTAN AND ISOLDE belongs to the fully developed music drama of his maturity. Here, certainly, is a great paean of love between man and woman; love as seen by nineteenth-century Romanticism—love as escape, ecstasy, oblivion. The essence of this mood is captured in the magnificent duet in the second act, *Hymn to the Night* (O Descend Upon Us, Night of Love), sung by the two lovers in the garden of Isolde's palace. Never did dramatic music more eloquently capture the mood of rapture, of sheer sensuous beauty, the power of romantic passion, of wonder and ecstasy—and sustain it to such length!

We shall return to Wagner as a symphonic composer in a later chapter. (See page 234.) Suffice now to point out several other favorite excerpts from his operas that should be heard when time permits—and inclination directs. Among those selections, we name: *Song to the Evening Star*, the *Pilgrims' Chorus*, and Elisabeth's aria, *Dich teure Halle* (Oh! Hall of Song), from Wagner's opera TANNHÄUSER; the *Prize Song* from DIE MEISTERSINGER; Siegmund's *Love Song* from DIE WALKÜRE; Senta's *Ballad* and the *Spinning Chorus* from THE FLYING DUTCHMAN; and Isolde's hymn to love and death, the *Liebestod*, from the final scene of TRISTAN. Acquaintance with these will, we feel sure, lead the listener to others.

The opera "Carmen," by Georges Bizet (1838-1875)

The opera we have chosen for the essential listening project for this chapter is generally conceded to be one of the two or three most popular operas of the standard repertory, though its première in Paris in 1875 was a failure. Thus the listener has a likely chance of hearing

SCENE FROM THE OPERA "CARMEN"

Bizet

it either on the stage or over the radio, or both. CARMEN is filled with beautiful *recitatives*,[5] arias, and ballet tunes that are captivating on the first hearing.[6]

The underlying drama, based on the novel by Prosper Mérimée, is much more real and probable than that met in most operas; the general tempo of the opera is moving, vivacious, full of effective action, and tragically gripping from the brief overture, or prelude, to the fall of the final curtain, with hardly a dull moment in the entire work. It is a brilliant piece of operatic writing, with vocal parts that are so well conceived that they almost sing themselves; and the orchestration is so expertly executed that it stamps Bizet a master of that craft. There is in CARMEN musical characterization of a very high order, and a dramatic insight into the persons of the cast as people of real life and not merely stage appurtenances.

If the story of the opera is gone over carefully beforehand and held well in mind, the selections that we have indicated for listening will give a good idea of the continuity of the whole, and we hope will create a desire to see and hear a real stage presentation—for nothing can take the place of that. A large number of good recordings are available to choose from, all the way from separate pieces to a judicious and well-executed condensation of the opera as a whole. Only the listener's interest and available time can determine the limitations. In the author's opinion, no other opera adapts itself more naturally to a "record" performance than does CARMEN.

The characters of the opera are, in order of appearance:

Morales, an officer: *baritone*
Micaela, a peasant girl: *soprano*
Don José, a corporal of dragoons: *tenor*
Zuniga, captain of dragoons: *bass*
Carmen, a cigarette girl and Gypsy: *mezzo-soprano*

---

[5] A *recitative* is a kind of vocal declamation, free of the restrictions of regular and fixed rhythm, form, meter, or regularity of lyrical song, so as to follow more faithfully the accents and inflections of emotionalized speech, or rapidly changing moods in action. This "glorified speech" type of singing usually parallels the function of the monologue, dialogue, and speech accompanying action in the ordinary drama. The recitative usually precedes the lyrical and more static set-piece, the aria, throughout the opera; the arias being, more often than not, in the familiar three-part, or ternary, form.

[6] It should be noted here that Micaela's aria in Act III was "lifted" from GRISELIDIS, and the ballet scenes in Act III and IV were from ARLÉSIENNE and THE PEARLFISHER—a practice common enough among operatic composers. Also, it is interesting to note that when Bizet composed CARMEN he wrote it in *opera comique* style with the dialogue spoken; these dialogues were replaced with recitatives, singing parts, composed by Ernest Guiraud (Paris, 1837-1892), thus transforming the work into a more truly "grand opera" type.

Gypsies, friends of Carmen, Frasquita, *soprano;* Mercedes, *contralto*
Escamillo, a toreador: *baritone*
Smugglers, El Remendado: *tenor;* El Dancairo; *baritone*
Inkeeper, guide, officers, dragoons, Gypsies, boys, cigarette girls, smugglers, etc.
Time: About 1820
Place: Seville and near-by mountains

The brilliant *Prelude* to Act I introduces us to the music from the final scene before the bull ring at Seville—music of riotous color and animation. Then we hear the famous *Toreador Song* theme, and just before the curtain rises, the ominous Fate motive, which will appear again and again in various guises throughout the work, as the characters are swept to their doom. The Fate motive follows:

"Fate Motif."

ACT I

The curtain rises, disclosing a guardhouse to the left, the cigarette factory to the right, an overhead bridge to the rear, and an open square to the fore. Through the crowd, which has assembled to watch the changing of the guard in the square at Seville, darts the flirtatious Carmen, looking for the young and handsome corporal, Don José.

She sings of love, as he understands it, to the seductive rhythms of an "Habañera":

> Ah! love is like a wild wood bird,
> None may hope to tame his wings. . . .
> Often, deaf to threats and prayers alike,
> You refuse ardent homage,
> While the one who coldly slights you,
> You pick for a master. . . .
> If you love me, beware!
> If I love you, beware too!

Here, as in the music to come, we have not only a melody that is superb in its own right, but what is more—and this makes it great dramatic music—the melody reveals the essence of the character and of the situation. As the Gypsy sways hither and yon, circling about the simple, quiet soldier who has caught her eye, finally throwing him a rose, we have the beginning of that interplay of personality which is the essence of good theater. Don José finally repulses Carmen, saying that he loves Micaela. The bell calls the girls back to work and José is left alone. Micaela appears with a letter from his mother, and he sings while she goes off stage. José sings (reading):

Tell him that his moth-er is lone-ly, pray-ing all the day for her son.

Presently a commotion is heard coming from the factory; the girls crowd upon the stage and report that Carmen has stabbed another girl in a fight. José is sent to arrest her. When apprehended, Carmen is tied to a chair for temporary safekeeping, until the Captain, Zuniga, can arrive. However, she continues to flirt with José and sings the captivating "sequidilla," *Near the Walls of Seville*, in which she promises to meet him at the inn if he will let her go free.

Near to   the   wall   of   Se - vil - - - - - la.

There   lives   my   friend   Lil - las   Pas - tia,

The guards return to lead Carmen away, and in the scuffle that ensues, she makes her escape. Of course José is held to blame, arrested and led away to the guardhouse. (End of Act I.)

ACT II

The vivid and atmospheric introduction to Act II brings us the rhythmic music of the Dragoons of Alcala; then the curtain rises on the scene of the inn of Lillas Pastia outside Seville, where Carmen has gone to join a band of smugglers from the mountains. As she watches the dancers, she sings the gay *Gypsy Song* in praise of the wild, carefree Gypsy life:

The ting-ling of the zith-er bars, And with the cas-ta -nets are sound - ing.

When the sound of gay guitars floats on the air,
The Gypsies spring forth in a merry dance,
Tambourines beat in time with the music,
And every voice repeats a merry song. . . .

The rhythm of the song, the curve of the melody, and the mysterious effect of plucked strings unite with the clicking of castanets in music that grows ever faster, ever more abandoned.

The shouting of the crowd announces the arrival of Escamillo, the popular toreador. In the famous *Toreador Song*, in which he

glowingly describes the life of the bull ring as one of swift action, reckless courage, applause, and love, we have another melody that not only is irresistible as pure melody, but one that paints the personality, the mood, and the manner of Escamillo in a sure and graphic fashion.

Don José arrives, looking for Carmen; he has just been released from his prison in the guardhouse. Fascinated by the Gypsy, Carmen, he overstays his leave. When she chides him for his eagerness to return to the barracks, he takes from underneath his coat the flower that she tossed to him in the first act, and gives vent to his feelings in the impassioned *Flower Song:*

I kept the flower you gave to me
Even amid the prison walls;
Although faded, for me it still retained
Its sweet perfume.
Night and day I inhaled its lovely odor
And wildly called to you—in vain. . . .
Hoping only, beloved, to see you once again!

He is torn between his love and his deep desire to return to his duty; but the issue is decided by Fate. His superior officer, Zuniga, who has flirted with Carmen at the beginning of the act, returns to the inn. A fight breaks out between the two men, who are separated by the Gypsies. For José the life of a soldier—and of a law-abiding citizen—is over. He has no choice but to join Carmen and the smugglers.

ACT III

The *Intermezzo* that introduces Act III is of exquisite simplicity. A graceful shepherd tune played by the woodwinds and harp serves as a charming interlude in the mounting tensions. The curtain rises on the gathering place of the smugglers in the heights of the mountains; the *March of the Smugglers* gives a vivid tone picture of their stealthy movements as they clamber over the rocks to their camp.

Don José is tormented by remorse and jealousy; he quarrels with Carmen. She joins the Gypsy girls who are telling their fortunes with cards. Shuffling the deck, she draws the ace of spades. *Death— Always death!* she sings as the orchestra repeats the Fate motif a dozen times—a real dramatic stroke.

The smugglers leave on an expedition; the mountain pass is deserted. Micaela, Don José's sweetheart before his fatal infatuation with Carmen, arrives to look for her faithless lover. Micaela's aria —a prayer for Heaven's protection—is a superb example of the French equivalent of Italian dramatic melody. Here, too, we note Bizet's genius at delineating character and dramatic situation through the aria.

Following her prayer, Micaela spies José high above her on a cliff. She hails him, but he does not hear. Only a shot is heard, fired by José at Escamillo who has come to take Carmen. A duel takes place between the two rivals; but it is stopped by Carmen herself. Micaela is discovered hiding near by and is brought to José. She tells him that his mother is dying and pleads with him to return to the city with her. Of course Carmen urges him to leave, and as he exits, José threatens with, "We shall meet again!"; but Carmen is far too engrossed in listening to the Toreador's song that comes from the distance. The cards are flung to the winds, and as the curtain falls, Carmen's defiant laughing at Fate is heard above the hurried music of the orchestra.

ACT IV

The *Aragonaise* heard at the onset of this act provides a gay, tumultuous, and impassioned accompaniment for the colorful ballet.

The scene is at the entrance of the arena at Seville. Here is the hustle and bustle of gay pageantry in the square, just before the time set for the opening of the bullfight. The bullfighters march by in a jolly procession. A shout goes up on the entrance of the crowd's favorite, Escamillo, with Carmen at his side in the carriage. He takes affectionate leave of her to enter the ring. The crowd follows the procession into the entrance of the arena.

Just as Don José appears, the Fate motif is heard sounding from the orchestra and a sinister mood fills the scene. In the tragic final scene we see Carmen, in turn defiant, cruel, contemptuous of José, at last confessing that she loves Escamillo and has finished with the soldier. The drama mounts steadily to the climax where José draws his dagger and plunges it into Carmen. The Fate motif thunders forth from the orchestra. The crowd returns, as the shouts of "Bravo" to the victorious Escamillo come from the arena, mingled with the *Toreador Song*. José throws himself beside the lifeless form of the Gypsy and sobs, "O my Carmen, my adored Carmen!"—and the curtain falls.

ADDITIONAL SUGGESTIONS FOR LISTENING

Another of the three most popular operas in the standard repertory is unquestionably Verdi's spectacular AïDA, and we suggest the following numbers, which are readily obtainable in very good recordings:

ACT. I: *Celesta Aïda* (Heavenly Aïda), sung by Rhadames, tenor; *Ritorna Vincitor* (Return Victorious), sung by Aïda, soprano. ACT II: the opening *Balabili Dance* ballet music, the ballet from Scene 2, and the March of Victory. ACT III: *O cieli azzurri* (O Sky of Azure Hue), sung by Aïda; *Pur ti riveggo mia dolce Aïda* (Again I See Thee, My Own Aïda), sung by Rhadames. ACT IV: *O terra addio* (Farewell, Oh Earth), duet sung by Rhadames and Aïda as the final curtain falls upon their impending death together in the sealed tomb. AïDA is often chosen to open an operatic season because of its spectacular and colorful pageantry, the large number of participants possible, the many opportunities for very impressive scenes on the stage—to say nothing of the countless, beautiful arias, the superb choral writing throughout, and the timely and graceful ballets. As for potential scenic effects, Aïda has few equals. It is an excellent "first" for anyone who has never heard and seen an opera. This is Italian opera at its peak, composed by a master of the stage and traditional vocal styles, one who defies equality of comparison—yes, even with Wagner, in many respects.

Continuing our brief discussion of Italian opera at this point, it is fitting to follow Verdi by another of his countrymen who has, in many ways, departed from the older traditions and has taken up the more realistic type of thought and expression. We have in mind Giacomo Puccini (1858-1924), and mention first among his works his popular setting of Henri Murger's sketches of the life of young artists in Paris, LA BOHÉME (Première, Turin, 1896). Characteristic of Puccini's rich vocal line and appealing lyricism is the music of the love scene between Rudolph and Mimi in the first act: Rudolph's vibrant aria, *Che gelida manina* (Your Tiny Hand Is Frozen); Mimi's reply, *Mi chiamano Mimi* (My Name Is Mimi); and the love duet *O soave fanciulla* (Oh Lovely Maiden). From Puccini's other works, the stirring aria from the second act of MADAME BUTTERFLY, *Un bel di vedremo* (Some Day He'll Come), in which the little Geisha affirms her belief that her American lover will return to her; Tosca's impassioned plea to Scarpia in the second act of LA TOSCA, *Vissi d'arte* (I've Lived for Art and Love), and Mario's song before his execution, in the third act, *E lucevan le stelle* (The Stars Were Shining) are favorites.

From the two outstanding examples of *verismo*, or dramatic realism, in Italian operas, Leoncavallo's PAGLIACCI and Mascagni's CAVALLERIA RUSTICANA, a number of excerpts have achieved great fame. From the first comes one of the most intense of operatic arias, Canio's anguished outcry that he must go on with his clowning before the audience while his heart is breaking with grief, *Vesti la giubba* (On With the Play):

> Put on your smock, smear your face with powder—
> The people pay you; they must have their fun.
> Even though Harlequin take your Colombine from you,
> Laugh loud, Pagliaccio,
> Hide your grief and play your part.
> Laugh, Pagliaccio, for your love that is destroyed,
> Laugh for the pain that is breaking your heart!

From CAVALLERIA RUSTICANA, the *Intermezzo;* the *Brindisi* or Drinking Song; and the *Siciliana*, the serenade of Turiddu in which he expresses his love for Lola (Thy Lips Like Crimson Berries), are most popular.

From the French lyric drama, a group of representative excerpts would include Delilah's seductive song, *Mon coeur s'ouvre a ta voix* (My Heart at Thy Sweet Voice), from the second act of Saint-Saëns' SAMSON AND

DELILAH; the *Jewel Song* (*Air des Bijoux*) in which Marguerite expresses
her delight at Faust's gift, from the third act of Gounod's classic, as well
as the *Soldiers' Chorus* and the *Serenade of Mephistopheles* from Act IV,
and the celebrated waltz, *Ainsi que la brise legère*, from the scene of the
Fair in Act II; Juliet's *Waltz Song* from Gounod's ROMEO AND JULIET;
Manon's farewell to the little table at which she and Des Grieux have
been so happy, *Adieu, notre petite table*, from the second act of Mas-
senet's MANON, as well as Des Grieux' aria later in the act, *Le Rêve* (The
Dream), in which he describes the home he plans to share with her; from
Massenet's THAÏS, the courtesan's passionate invocation to her mirror,
Dis-moi que je serais belle eternellement (Tell Me That I Shall Always
Be Beautiful!), and the *Meditation*, symbolical of Thaïs' conversion, as
famous an instrumental interlude as the *Intermezzo* from CAVALLERIA
RUSTICANA; and the rapturous aria of Louise, *Depuis le jour* (Ever Since
the Day), in which she expresses her happiness at being with her lover
Julien, from the third act of Charpentier's opera, LOUISE.

The finest example of Russian operatic style unquestionably is Moussorgsky's BORIS GODUNOFF, one of the few Russian operas that have attained a permanent place in our repertory. Listen to the two excerpts
from the magnificent final scene, the Farewell of Boris, *Farewell, My
Son, I Am Dying*, and the Death of Boris, *Hark 'Tis the Passing Bell!*
Boris, who had gained the throne by causing the rightful heir, Dmitri, to
be assassinated, realizes that he has reached his end. He asks his nobles
to withdraw, and remains alone with his son. With great feeling he bids
the child rule justly, and protect his sister Xenia; he hopes the boy will
never learn how his father came to the throne. Laying his hands on his
son's head, he calls down Heaven's blessing upon him. Bells toll mournfully while the voices of the people outside the Kremlin rise in prayer
for their Czar. The choral writing here, as in the Coronation Scene, is of
surpassing beauty: with Moussorgsky, the emotional base of national
opera lay in the chorus, the folk. The music, which depicts the anguish
of the sick and tormented Czar, rises to a climax of great power, with
something of the grim realism that we found in Moussorgsky's songs. A
procession of priests files into the royal apartment, followed by the
nobles. Boris, in his final struggle with death, points to his son: "Behold
your Czar!" and falls back dead, the word "Mercy!" upon his lips.

Throughout the later nineteenth century German opera was wholly
dominated by the Wagnerian music drama. A new note was introduced
by Richard Strauss who, with the orchestral wizardry that was his heritage from the master, combined the lyricism and freshness of the lied,
together with the sophistication and sensuous charm of French influences.
The result was an idiom creating three works that made operatic history
in the first decade of the twentieth century—the brilliant setting of Oscar
Wilde's SALOMÉ; the stark and terrifying ELEKTRA, to the libretto of
Hugo von Hoffmansthal; and the captivating comedy of eighteenth-century Vienna, DER ROSENKAVALIER (The Cavalier of the Rose). For the
full flavor of Strauss' style, listen to the *Dance of the Seven Veils* from
SALOMÉ, and the Princess' delirious exultation as she receives the head of

the Prophet on a silver charger, *I Have Kissed Thy Lips, O Jokaanan*. The more wholesome side of Strauss' genius animates his immortal comedy. Listen to the enchanting waltzes; the resigned and world-wise *Soliloquy* of the Marschallin in the first act, as she realizes that soon her charms will fade, and she will no longer hold her youthful lover; the ecstatic *Presentation of the Rose* in the second act, when Octavian meets Sophie and forgets the Marschallin; the great trio in Act III, when the Marschallin unites the youthful lovers and graciously accepts her inevitable defeat; and the final duet of Sophie and Octavian, Mozartian in its limpid beauty and simplicity.

We have refrained from mentioning many of the larger ensembles to be found in opera, for they are likely to be quite unsatisfactory in records —they must be actually heard and seen on the stage to be fully effective, for dramatic action, the setting and the function of the ensemble are likely to be of prime importance. However, two very popular ensembles (not choruses) are pointed out here, as illustrating how the composer, by weaving together several threads of song, is able to pour out the emotions of several of his characters simultaneously, the voices joining in a single tonal web of power and effectiveness, though the individual emotions of the participating characters might differ widely.

Perhaps the most famous of ensemble numbers is the *Sextette* from Donizetti's LUCIA DI LAMMERMOOR. Although the broadly flowing melody is known to all the world, it requires some knowledge of the opera to realize how well the music expresses the dramatic situation in the play, and how adroitly each of the six voices reveals the conflicting emotions of the individual character. The *Sextette* is sung in the second act, when Edgar returns to the castle of his enemy, Lord Henry, to find that his beloved Lucy—sister of Lord Henry—has just married another. Edgar is swept by rage and hatred of Henry, yet realizes that he still loves Lucy; Henry, who has engineered the marriage for his own ends, fears for the success of his project; Lucy, who was led to believe by her brother that Edgar was faithless, is overcome with grief and shame when she realizes that she has wronged her lover; Raymond, the kindly chaplain, prays that Heaven will protect Lucy; Lord Arthur, the man whom Lucy has just married, is utterly bewildered; and Alice, Lucy's companion, shares her mistress' sorrow. The individual voices soar and intermingle in a rich harmonic pattern that constitutes one of the great moments in opera.

Equally effective is the *Quartet* from RIGOLETTO, one of the finest of Verdi's many ensemble pieces. Rigoletto, the hunchbacked court jester, attempts to cure his daughter of her love for the profligate Duke, who wooed her, won her, and has now forgotten her. He takes her to the inn where, peering through the door, she may watch the Duke making love to the barmaid Maddelena. The Duke sings a smooth amorous melody to Maddelena; the coquettish barmaid, wise in the ways of the world, retorts that she knows full well he is only trying to flatter her; Gilda, concealed in the darkness outside, pours forth the grief of her broken heart, while Rigoletto sternly vows to avenge his betrayed daughter.

Opera in this country has had, and is having, a difficult time to overcome the readiness of American audiences to bask in the Italian, French, and German heritage. Also, it has had to shake off the Old-World operatic traditions concerning essential characteristics, and it has been trying to work out native idioms of expressions. Then, too, the opportunities for hearing operas written by native composers are not many, and, consequently, the inspiration, encouragement, and tuition that would normally be derived from such performances are absent. However, a relatively small number of American composers have devoted their efforts in behalf of native opera. Among the outstanding composers and their works, obtainable in records, are:[7] Charles Wakefield Cadman's SHANEWIS (it is interesting to note that Cadman's Indian opera was the first American work to be performed for two consecutive seasons by the Metropolitan Opera Company); Louis Gruenberg's THE EMPEROR JONES; Howard Hanson's MERRY MOUNT; Deems Taylor's THE KING'S HENCHMAN and PETER IBBETSON; Richard Hageman's CAPONSACCHI; Victor Herbert's NATOMA; Gian-Carlo Menotti's AMELIA GOES TO THE BALL; and it is hoped that Vittorio Giannini's SCARLET LETTER will have been recorded by the time this book is published.

---

[7] According to the latest edition of the *Gramophone Shop Encyclopedia of Recorded Music* (New York: Simon and Schuster) at the time of writing.

Chapter VIII

THE ORATORIO

IN OUR introductory paragraph to the preceding chapter, we suggested the construction of a simple, hypothetical opera through the use of a series of songs having a common theme, or story, then the acting of them on a stage with the usual trappings. To carry the idea still further, we suggest that if those solo songs, ensembles, and choruses were built around a religious subject and the whole were sung, without actions, in a concert hall or a church instead of the theater, we might have a fair representation of the basic idea of an oratorio. So the humble song of our early chapters assumes still greater importance. As a matter of fact, much of what has been said in the preceding chapter applies equally well in this; so let us discuss the immediate subject more precisely.[1]

We think of the oratorio as a dramatic poem, generally of a sacred or spiritual character, which is sung throughout by soloists and chorus to the accompaniment of an orchestra. It is distinguished from the mass and church cantata in that it is intended for concert or festival performance rather than as part of a regular religious service, and from the opera in that—at any rate in modern times—it is presented without scenery, costumes, and action. Its style and character make it ideally suited for performance by church choirs and choral societies.

Today the oratorio is considered as a type altogether distinct from the opera, although, from what we said in the preceding section about the origins of the music drama, it should be apparent that the two were derived from common sources. From the twelfth to the sixteenth centuries—a period that saw the brilliant flourishing, all over Europe, of the Miracle and Mystery plays—there developed in Italy, France, Germany, and England a species of musical drama based on incidents in the Old and New Testaments and the lives of the saints. These were intended to reinforce, on a popular basis and with strong emotional appeal, the teachings of the church, and were generally per-

[1] For essential listening, see section on THE MESSIAH, page 102.

formed under the supervision of the clergy, with scenery, acting, costumes, and all kinds of vivid dramatic effects. Often performers traveled from town to town in wagons, giving performances in public squares, palace courtyards or in the market place—a practice that may be seen in the episode of the strolling players in HAMLET, or in the "play within a play" in Leoncavallo's PAGLIACCI.

COURTESY OF THE UNIVERSITY PRINTS, NEWTON, MASS.

MILAN CATHEDRAL   (*From a photograph*)

This rare example of pure Gothic in marble, with its hundreds of pinnacles soaring toward the sky and whose exterior is adorned with more than 4,000 statues amidst incredibly delicate lacework carved in stone, was begun in 1386. To our day it remains one of the most beautiful works of man erected as an expression of homage to the divinity. Such great artists as Brunelleschi, Leonardo da Vinci, Pellegrini, and countless others lent their genius to its glorious realization.

Toward the end of the fifteenth century, at about the same time that the poets and musicians at the court of Florence were experimenting with the type of musical dramatic declamation that ultimately led to the opera, St. Philip Neri, founder of the congregation of the Oratorians at Rome, encouraged the performance of sacred musical dramatic allegories as a means of religious instruction. Since these performances were given in the oratory of his church, the sacred drama with music soon became known as *oratorio*, while the secular drama with music took the title of *opera*. At this point opera and oratorio differed from each other mainly in the choice of subject, for both used all the resources of the musical dramatic theater. In 1600 Emilio del Cavalieri (*c.* 1550-1602) presented in Rome an elaborate allegory of the struggle between body and mind, LA RAPPRESENT-AZIONE DI ANIMA E DI CORPO, a spiritual opera in the tradition of the Mystery and Miracle plays that is erroneously set forth, in histories of music, as the first oratorio. Since secular and sacred music drama were arising simultaneously from a common ancestry, it is difficult to mark clearly the first separation of their paths. For additional matter on the historical background, the reader is referred to a number of texts on musicology available in most libraries.

Opera and oratorio thenceforth developed side by side, borrowing from each other, and often crossing over into each other's territory. Thus, in our own time Saint-Saëns' Biblical opera SAMSON ET DELILAH has been performed in concert, without the trappings of the opera house, as an oratorio. Similarly, Mendelssohn's oratorio ELIJAH received a memorable performance in America with scenery, costumes, and acting. The two genres have, however, steadily gone farther and farther apart in character, style, and outlook. With opera we associate swift dramatic action, tense emotional climaxes, ardent romanticism, sensuous melody, and brilliant effect. With oratorio we connect vast harmonies, sublime choruses, lyricism of an introspective nature, and spiritual exaltation. Where opera remained a dynamic form, oratorio became increasingly static and contemplative. The last trace of dramatic action disappeared from the oratorio with the introduction of a narrator, whose function it was to relate the connecting incidents in the sacred play, instead of having them acted out. Above all, while the opera continued to rely for its emotional effect on the inner conflicts of individuals, the oratorio depended increasingly for its majestic effects on the chorus.

George Frideric Handel (1685-1759)

Interestingly enough, the composer who is considered to have played the decisive role in the oratorio as we know it today, George Frideric Handel, spent the greater part of his career in writing operas. For well on to twenty-five years, the great Saxon guided the destinies of opera in London. It was only when his audience began to tire of the conventional, artificial Italian opera of the period and turned with avidity to the freshness and charm of Gay's BEGGAR'S OPERA that

Handel, sensing a competition he could no longer meet, turned his inexhaustible energies to the oratorio. With Handel the oratorio took on new life and color; the chorus became the chief protagonist of the drama, much as the orchestra did, a century later, in the Wagnerian music drama. His great oratorios—THE MESSIAH, SAUL, ISRAEL IN EGYPT, JUDAS MACCABAEUS, JEPHTHA—are in effect choral tragedies, in which the lives and destinies of the individual heroes take on meaning and direction from the dynamic force embodied in the chorus. Master of a spacious architecture, of bold dramatic effect, of vivid musical characterization and of a variegated style of writing, Handel poured all the riches of his imagination into these works, which so perfectly hit off the taste of English Protestantism. For a century after his death, they completely dominated the musical life of his adopted land.

Handel and his great contemporary, Bach, represent the peak of that era in music which is known as the *Baroque*.[2] We shall have more to say of the Baroque in a later chapter. Suffice it for the present to point out that this term is used, in painting, sculpture, architecture, and music, to indicate the spirit of bold design and vigorous execution, of sweeping lines, richly imaginative ornamentation, imposing dimensions and dramatic effects, that characterized European art in the seventeenth and early eighteenth centuries. The Baroque was the counterpart, in the realm of art, of the spirit that pervaded the age: a spirit of bold questing for new horizons, of restless questioning of accepted norms, of exuberant self-confidence and achievement, and of intellectual inquiry throughout the period, in the far-flung religious and dynastic struggles, in the vigorous colonization of the New World, and in the steady, forward movement of the *bourgeoisie*—the "burgesses," the merchants and industrialists—as they consolidated their power in their five-hundred-year-old struggle against the feudal agricultural aristocracy. This was a dynamic, rapidly changing world, demanding pomp and external splendor, opulent façades riotous with ornament, magnificent curves and stairways and candelabra: a style that found its perfect expression in the palaces of the absolute monarchs of the seventeenth century, in the bold and teeming canvases of a Rubens or a Caravaggio. It is the spirit of this world that is immortalized, in music, by the sweeping recitatives, arias, and ensembles, above all by the grandiose, stirring choruses of the Handelian oratorio.

[2] For extended discussion on the *Baroque*, see page 399.

Handel's oratorio: "The Messiah"

We know of no better introduction to the oratorio style at its best than the study of Handel's immortal work in that form, THE MESSIAH, which he wrote in twenty-three days, in the early fall (Aug. 22 to Sept. 14) of 1741. The work consists of a series of recitatives, arias, choruses, and orchestral numbers arranged in three parts—analogous to the acts of an opera. There is an overture and an instrumental interlude in the first part, the latter known as the *Pastoral*

GEORGE FRIDERIC HANDEL   *From a rare old print.*

Symphony. The text is made up of appropriate verses from the Bible, some direct quotations, others adapted to Handel's needs by the librettist, Charles Jennens. The first part prophesies and anticipates the coming of Christ; the second speaks of His sufferings and death; and the third tells of His resurrection. In order to make the work more acceptable for use during the Christmas season, a large part of sections two and three are omitted.

Therefore, to enable the listener to follow the vagaries of concert as well as recorded performances of THE MESSIAH, we present here the complete outline of the arias and choruses.[2] But for practical reasons, we have indicated with one star (*) those numbers we should like to use as minimum essential listening for this chapter. A further abridged series is reluctantly proposed for still greater limitations of time. These are indicated with two stars (**) before the title. (Other choices than these are possible.)

Part the First:

    1. Overture.
* ** 2. Recitative (Tenor), "Comfort ye my people."
* ** 3. Aria (Tenor), "Every valley shall be exalted."
  * 4. Chorus, "And the glory of the Lord."
    5. Recit. (Bass), "Thus saith the Lord."
    6. Aria (Bass), "But who may abide the day of His coming?"
    7. Chorus, "And He shall purify."
    8. Recit. (Alto), "Behold, a virgin shall conceive."
    9. Aria (Alto) and Chorus, "O Thou that tellest good tidings."
 *10. Recit. (Bass), "For, behold, darkness shall cover the earth."
 *11. Aria (Bass), "The people that walked in darkness."
* **12. Chorus, "For unto us a child is born."
 *13. Pastoral Symphony.
* **14. Recit. (Soprano), "There were shepherds abiding in the
      field."
     Recit. (Soprano), "And lo! the angel of the Lord."
  15. Recit. (Soprano), "And the angel said unto them."
  16. Recit. (Soprano), "And suddenly there was with the angel."
 *17. Chorus, "Glory to God."
 *18. Aria (Soprano), "Rejoice greatly, O daughter of Zion."
  19. Recit. (Alto), "Then shall the eyes of the blind be opened."
* **20. Aria (Alto), "He shall feed His flock like a shepherd."
 *21. Chorus, "His yoke is easy, and His burden is light."

Part the Second:

 *22. Chorus, "Behold the Lamb of God."
* **23. Aria (Alto), "He was despised."

---

[2] As shown in the Schirmer Edition, edited and revised according to Handel's original score by T. Tertius Noble.

* **24. Chorus, "Surely He hath borne our griefs."
   25. Chorus, "And with His stripes we are healed."
   26. Chorus, "All we like sheep have gone astray."
   27. Recit. (Tenor), "All they that see Him, laugh Him to scorn."
   28. Chorus, "He trusted in God that He would deliver Him."
*29. Recit. (Tenor), "Thy rebuke hath broken His heart."
*30. Aria (Tenor), "Behold, and see if there be any sorrow."
   31. Recit. (Tenor), "He was cut off out of the land of the living."
   32. Aria (Tenor), "But Thou didst not leave His soul in hell."
   33. Chorus, "Lift up your heads, O ye gates."
   34. Recit. (Tenor), "Unto which of the angels said He."
   35. Chorus, "Let all the angels of God worship Him."
   36. Aria (Bass), "Thou art gone up on high."
   37. Chorus, "The Lord gave the word."
   38. Aria (Soprano), "How beautiful are the feet of them."
   39. Chorus, "Their sound is gone out into all lands."
* **40. Aria (Bass), "Why do the nations so furiously rage."
   41. Chorus, "Let us break their bonds asunder."
   42. Recit. (Tenor), "He that dwelleth in heaven."
   43. Aria (Tenor), "Thou shalt break them."
* **44. Chorus, "Hallelujah!"

Part the Third:

* **45. Aria (Soprano), "I know that my Redeemer liveth."
   46. Chorus, "Since by man came death."
   47. Recit. (Bass), "Behold, I tell you a mystery."
   48. Aria (Bass), "The trumpet shall sound."
   49. Recit. (Alto), "Then shall be brought to pass."
   50. Duet (Alto and Tenor), "O death, where is thy sting?"
*51. Chorus, "But thanks be to God."
   52. Aria (Soprano), "If God be for us, who can be against us?"
*53. Chorus, "Worthy is the Lamb," "Amen."

THE MESSIAH took England by storm and it was during the first London performance that the audience, carried away by the lofty sentiments, the impressive power and the noble character of the *Hallelujah Chorus*, arose in concert as though by prearranged signal. Ever since then audiences the world over express a similar respect by rising at the onset of this chorus and remaining standing until the conclusion of the section.[3]

---

[3] Of course, there is usually no applause, and the listener is cautioned to be on guard for omissions throughout, but especially in Parts II and III, and transpositions of certain numbers from Part II to Part III, in order to effect a climax at the close. The complete outline provided above should be a helpful guide.

ADDITIONAL SUGGESTIONS FOR LISTENING [4]

If Handel represents the pomp and splendor of the Baroque, Bach, as the reader will remember from our discussion of his religious music, stands for its other side—mysticism, introspection, passionate religiosity, and otherworldliness. Where Handel was at home in the glare of public life, in the atmosphere of royal courts and theaters, as artist, producer, and businessman all in one, Bach lived his life in the circle of his family, circumscribed by his duties as Cantor of St. Thomas', completely devoted to his religion and his art. Both by native temperament and mode of life he was eminently suited for the most eloquent projection, through his music, of the intense Pietism which pervaded his native Thuringia. Where Handel was fired by the dramatic conflicts in the Old Testament, Bach addressed himself almost exclusively to what was for him the supreme religious tragedy—the Passion of Christ. In the three PASSION oratorios, by Bach, according to the Gospels of St. Luke, St. Matthew, and St. John, and in the CHRISTMAS oratorio, it is the reflective lyrical note that predominates, a brooding tenderness, a grandeur of resignation and peace rather than one of action; the spirit of evangelical mysticism rather than the spectacular dramatics of Handel. Throughout, there is that mingling of profound lyricism and pathos which makes Bach, for many listeners, the *sine qua non* among composers.

Of the two masters of the Classical Period in the late eighteenth century, Mozart devoted his best efforts to actual church music rather than to festive religious drama. Haydn, who achieved a triumphal success in England toward the end of his career, on the other hand, continued in the tradition of Handel with two works well calculated to please English taste—THE CREATION, after the first part of Milton's *Paradise Lost;* and THE SEASONS, after the famous poem of James Thomson. Haydn was a devout Catholic, writing for a Protestant audience on the heels of the Enlightenment; the result was a beautiful hymn to the Creator couched in language that men of all creeds and loyalties could understand. Haydn applied well, to his own idiom, the lessons he learned from his great predecessor; in England and in this country, THE CREATION has remained second only to THE MESSIAH in popularity. The reader should also be acquainted with characteristic examples from THE CREATION, the exciting choruses *Achieved Is the Glorious Work* and *Rolling in Foaming Billows;* also, the touching *Dove Aria* for soprano.

The nineteenth century saw intense cultivation of the oratorio, even though the spirit out of which it had come into being no longer held undisputed sway over the souls of men. Neither Beethoven's MOUNT OF OLIVES nor Schubert's VICTORY SONG OF MIRIAM have retained their hold on the musical world; the genius of these composers flowed in other channels. It is in Mendelssohn who, like Handel and Haydn, met his greatest success in England, that we have a continuation of the "great choral tra-

---

[4] In this chapter, we have had to relax the policy of restricting the references to recorded works because of the scarcity of the gramophone disks. Here, even more earnestly than elsewhere, we admonish hearing actual performances, and better still, that the reader participate as a singer in the chorus.

dition." His ELIJAH and ST. PAUL have taken their places in the literature along with THE MESSIAH and THE CREATION. The cycle of German
oratorio closes with Brahms' GERMAN REQUIEM. Brahms was perhaps the
last of the great masters to express the religious emotion of the late nineteenth century with something of the profundity and passion of the
masters of the Baroque.

In France, the Catholic revival, which was part of the Romantic movement, created an atmosphere most favorable for the oratorio. The finest
examples are Liszt's CHRISTUS and ST. ELISABETH, Berlioz's sacred trilogy
THE CHILDHOOD OF CHRIST, and César Franck's THE BEATITUDES. The
oratorio has always been most popular in England, where outstanding
works are presented in all forms. Among the better known examples of
English oratorio are Charles Hubert H. Parry's JUDITH and SAUL; Charles
Villiers Stanford's THE HOLY CHILDREN and EDEN; John Stainer's GIDEON
and Edward Elgar's DREAM OF GERONTIUS, LIGHT OF LIFE, THE APOSTLES,
and THE KINGDOM. Among contemporary English composers, William
Walton has written BELSHAZZAR'S FEAST; Frederick Delius THE MASS OF
LIFE; and Gustav Holst a HYMN TO JESUS.

American composers have contributed a number of notable oratorios
to the repertory. Among the best known are John Knowles Paine's ST.
PETER; Horatio Parker's HORA NOVISSIMA and LEGEND OF ST. CHRISTO-
PHER; Edgar Stillman Kelley's PILGRIM'S PROGRESS; Charles Martin Loeffler's CANTICLE TO ST. FRANCIS; Harry Rowe Shelley's DEATH AND LIFE,
and David Stanley Smith's RHAPSODY OF ST. BERNARD.

Twentieth-century composers continued the established traditions
with such oratorios as Vincent d'Indy's LEGEND OF ST. CHRISTOPHER;
Ermanno Wolf-Ferrari's LA VETA NUOVA, based on Dante's poem; and
Pierné's CHILDREN'S CRUSADE.

Not many contemporary oratorios have as yet been made available on
records. Consequently, to gain an idea of what the modern idiom in this
form is like, one has, in most cases, to hear an actual performance. For a
contrast between the old and the new, listen to the recorded excerpts
from Honegger's oratorios: KING DAVID, *De mon coeur jaillit un cantique*
(From My Heart There Sprang a Hymn); the *Penitential Psalm;* the
Psalm, *I Was Conceived in Sin;* and the *Death of David.* This is powerful
choral music, with a quality of primitivism, if you will, and an abundance
of dissonances.

Chapter IX

MUSIC IN THE THEATER; INCIDENTAL MUSIC: THE SUITE[1]

As WE saw in our chapter on the opera, music has been used in connection with dramatic performances since ancient times. The theater of the Greeks, of the Middle Ages, of Shakespeare and Molière and Calderon, all made extensive use of music. When the songs and dances become so important as to change the character of the play, we have the several varieties of operetta and comic opera. When the music remains in the background, that is, "incidental" to the play, we have one of the most delightful genres of the art—incidental music.

Incidental music may be played before the curtain goes up (*overture*); between the acts (*entr'acte* music); between two scenes (*interlude* or *intermezzo*); or during the course of a scene. It must rise out of the salient incidents in the play; must capture and project the mood. If it is used as an integral part of a dramatic scene, it must either heighten its emotion or underscore the feelings and actions of the characters. Just as in a song the high points of the poetry and of the music must coincide, so here the music becomes part of the forward-driving momentum of the scene and helps to carry it to its climax. Because it can be so effective, incidental music as a rule is used rather sparingly and is reserved, in most cases, for high points of the play.

Often the incidental music for a play is arranged by the composer as a *suite* for concert performance and in this form becomes far more popular than the play for which it was written. Thus, thousands of people who have never seen Ibsen's poetic drama, PEER GYNT, are familiar with Grieg's PEER GYNT SUITE. In this sense, the word *suite* is used to indicate a group of movements of instrumental music, often

---

[1] Essential listening for this chapter includes: *Valse Triste* by Sibelius, *Peer Gynt Suite* by Grieg, *Midsummer Night's Dream Suite* (Overture, Nocturne, Scherzo, and Wedding March) by Mendelssohn, and MacDowell's *Indian Suite*. Others, including Taylor's *Through the Looking Glass Suite*, are supplementary and optional.

concert versions of theater or ballet music, and therefore bound together by some literary thread. In the eighteenth century, as the reader may recall from the Bach suite that we heard in the chapter on music and dance, the word denoted a group of dances in contrasting moods and meters often in the same key, or in closely related keys.

"Valse Triste" by Sibelius

A fine example of the function of incidental music is offered by the ever-popular *Valse Triste*, which Sibelius wrote for Arvid Jarnefelt's romantic drama KUOLEMA (Death). The scene portrays a young man watching at the bedside of his dying mother. It is night, and he has fallen asleep. Suddenly a strange glow and the sound of distant music pervades the room. We hear the rhythm of a slow, mournful waltz. The mother rises from her bed. Her long white garment takes on the semblance of a ball dress. She moves amid a host of pale wraiths who sway silently to the rhythm and finally falls exhausted on her bed. The music breaks off. Presently she gathers her strength and goes back to the dance. The eerie music grows ever faster, reaches its climax. There is a knock at the door. The mother utters a dreadful cry; the guests vanish; Death stands on the threshold.

It is evident that in a scene such as this the music is not in the least incidental. Actually, the scene as it was imagined in the mind of the dramatist could not be carried out without the aid of the music. Nor, obviously, would any mournful waltz do. It must be a composition that not only catches the spirit of the fantasy but that—even more important—carries it in a steady intensification of emotion to the dread climax. In addition, the music must have the indefinable quality that makes good theater; it must be vivid, forthright, not oversubtle; it must achieve its dramatic effect in a direct, concise manner. Notice how well Sibelius' piece satisfies not only the general requirements of the theater music but also the specific needs of the scene for which it was written. The sorrowful waltz theme announced by stringed instruments in a low register is a haunting melody that seems to spring right out of the dramatic situation. The contrasting second theme, gliding downward from the treble in eighth notes, is lyrical and nostalgic. Then come the ghostly staccato chords in waltz rhythm that constitute the third theme. There is an effective crescendo and a steady quickening of the pulse as the music mounts in intensity. Now the music rushes forward in a kind of delirious agitation. Suddenly comes a dramatic pause—and then the final chords, strangely calm.

"*Peer Gynt Suite*" by Grieg

No less imaginative as mood-painting is Grieg's incidental music for PEER GYNT which he arranged in two concert suites, each containing four numbers. The SUITE No. I has become quite popular. It opens with *Morning*, a serene picture of day settling over the Norwegian forest, done in Grieg's best lyrical manner. There is something cool and transparent about the music with its broadly flowing melody in six-eight time.

The second number is the dirge for the mother in the play, *Ase's Death*. The solemn chords and the heartfelt melody ascending in accents of grief communicate with proper simplicity the tone of elegiac music. The repetition of the repeated melodic figure grips one most thoroughly.

Next comes the seductive *Anitra's Dance* (performed in the play by the exotic beauty whom Peer meets on his travels). As with the *Valse Triste,* the music here is, strictly speaking, not incidental since it enters into the action of the play. The dance is in graceful three-four time. The use of muted strings, of the staccato figure in the accompaniment, and of the *pizzicato* (plucked strings) effect creates an atmosphere of subtle Oriental allure. Note particularly that when the original dance theme returns Grieg varies the effect by having the 'cellos sing a new, full-throated melody against it—in other words, a *countermelody.* The addition of a countermelody to a repeated theme is obviously a subtle and effective means by which a composer may vary his material.

The final number, *In the Hall of the Mountain King,* depicts the exciting scene when Peer, lost in the mountains, is surrounded by mischievous trolls and sprites who perform a grotesque dance around him. The piece presents an extraordinary combination of the three most striking devices for building a climax—*crescendo, accelerando,* and a steady rise in pitch. The dance opens at a fairly slow pace, softly, in the lowest register, with a bizarre staccato effect on the bassoons. From then on the simple motive is repeated again and again—somewhat in the manner of the ascending half of the *Ase's Death* pattern—each time louder, faster, and higher, building up steadily until all the sonorities of the orchestra are engaged in an overpowering climax at breakneck speed punctuated by the shattering exclamations of cymbals and drums. Here, too, the music is not incidental in any sense of the term, but captures the very essence of the scene as envisaged in the imagination of the poet-dramatist.

Suite from "Midsummer Night's Dream" by Mendelssohn

For a full century Mendelssohn's incidental music to MIDSUMMER NIGHT'S DREAM has been a favorite. The *Overture* was written in 1826, when the composer was seventeen, in the form of a piano duet. Seventeen years later, in 1843, King Frederick William IV of Prussia asked Mendelssohn to add the other numbers. Of the thirteen that he wrote, the *Overture, Nocturne, Scherzo,* and *Wedding March*—are generally heard in the concert version. Shakespeare's fairy play called forth all the delicacy and grace, the polished craftsmanship and elfin lightness, so frequently associated with Mendelssohn's music.

The *Overture* ranks as one of his best works and is truly an amazing production for a boy of seventeen. Four mysterious chords in the woodwinds introduce us to the magic world of Oberon and Titania. The violins, in high register, announce the twittering staccato theme of the woodland sprites, which grows into a joyous outburst from the entire orchestra. A romantic legato motive floats for a moment before us, faintly suggesting the lovers in the play. This suave second theme offers a perfect contrast to the staccato opening theme. Then comes the jolly *Bergomasque Dance* from the fifth act of the play, with its great downward leap in the melody, a vivid musical picture of the sprawling movements of the uncouth peasant dancers. We hear a braying-like figure in the strings reminding us of Bottom, the immortal clown, who through magic spell receives the head of a donkey—and the adoration of Titania.

The themes are developed at some length with much fantasy and zest and then return in their original form. The mysterious chords of the opening return; finally the music floats away, higher and higher, into space.

The lovely *Nocturne* comes at the end of the third act, when sleep has descended upon the bewitched Titania and her doltish lover, Bottom. The serene melody for the horn is one of the famous passages written for that instrument. Here all the mystery, the remoteness, the intangible beauty of its tone are used by Mendelssohn to paint the dream-filled loveliness of the summer night. Too often, after success and fame had come to him, Mendelssohn allowed himself to substitute the perfection of form, which he mistakenly held up to himself as the classical ideal, for warmth and depth of feeling. Here, for once, he let himself recapture the romantic fervor of his youthful vision and articulated it in accents of unmistakable sincerity. (By *nocturne* we designate either a composition that describes the romantic beauty of the night—the word is derived from the latin *nox*, "night"—or a tender, lyrical outpouring of romantic feeling, a night song such as a lover might address to the object of his affections.)

The *Scherzo*, a favorite with concert and radio audiences, is a lacy bit of playfulness that serves as a prelude to the second act of the play. The opening vaguely resembles the first theme of the overture in its use of the violin staccato in high register. (Both themes, incidentally, are in the key of E minor.) The vigorous triple meter and the abrupt accents lend a bubbling energy to the theme in the middle section, a lusty dance tune in low register. Then the music returns to the first theme; little wisps of sound dart through the air and dissolve in a silvery mist. (*Scherzo*, from the Italian word meaning "a jest," is the title of a composition usually in rapid triple meter, often of a humorous or whimsical character, either a movement of a symphony or an independent concert piece.)

The suite is brought to a close by the *Wedding March*, which we spoke of in the chapter on music and ceremonial. Its opening chords, with their commingling of stateliness and joy, have become the universal processional at the end of the marriage ceremony. Detached from its original setting in a mythical Athenian court, this music has become a part of the personal experience of all mankind. There could, perhaps, be no greater tribute to any composer.

Edward MacDowell (1861-1908)

We have previously seen that suites may be made up of contrasting dance tunes, and in this chapter we have learned that suites may be an assembly of incidental music written for plays. Now we direct attention to suites that have no connection with the ballet or dramatic performance; instead, they were composed directly for the concert program and have as their underlying element of unification a poem, a story, or a series of similar or parallel moods. A good example of the so-called concert suite, and also one of the finest examples of its kind of American genius, is MacDowell's INDIAN SUITE, where the unification is secured through the use of salient and characteristic American Indian melodies.

The composer of the universally popular WOODLAND SKETCHES, from which come *To a Wild Rose* and *To a Water Lily*, was born in New York City in 1861. After studying piano with Teresa Carreño, the famous Venezuelan pianist and teacher, he entered the Paris Conservatoire at the age of fifteen, remaining there for three years. For five years after that he studied, played, and taught in the musical centers of Germany—Stuttgart, Wiesbaden, Darmstadt, and Frankfort—coming under the influence of the leading German Romanticists, notably his teacher Raff, and Liszt. He found the artistic atmosphere of Germany so congenial to his nature and the German musical world so appreciative of his talents that for a time he considered the possibility of settling there permanently. He married his pupil, Marion Nevins, in 1884. In 1887, he returned to America, settled in Boston,

and appeared successfully as a concert pianist, introducing his two brilliant piano concertos, the second of which has remained a favorite both with virtuosi and their audiences. In 1896 he became the first professor of music at Columbia University, where he remained for eight years during which he fought unceasingly to have music recognized as a full-fledged member of the curriculum. Despite his zeal in the cause, the university authorities did not see eye to eye with him; and in 1904, after much vexation, he resigned his post. His pioneer efforts in this direction bore

PORTRAIT OF EDWARD MACDOWELL

fruit later. For the remaining years of his life he devoted himself to composing and to conducting the Mendelssohn Glee Club, which he made into one of the best male choruses in the country. He died prematurely in 1908, the victim of a cruel and tragic illness.

MacDowell remains America's first great composer in the formal sense. His lovely melodies, such as the two we mentioned, have found wide popularity among the nation at large; his more ambitious works, especially his brilliant and colorful SECOND PIANO CONCERTO, have remained in the standard repertory. He fought steadfastly for the cause of music in America, seeking to bring it to independence and

self-expression; he was the first American to command respect from
the musical circles of Europe. Like his contemporary, Henry James,
he sought to combine the best in the old tradition with the new. In
many of his works, such as the INDIAN SUITE and WOODLAND
SKETCHES, he turned to Indian themes for inspiration; although, unlike Dvořák, who was active in this country in the same decade as he,
MacDowell was not greatly influenced by Negro themes. In Mac-
Dowell, as in so many of the nineteenth-century composers, the Romantic impulse fused with the nationalistic. Like Dvořák and Grieg,
he sought to adapt the German Romantic tradition to the needs of his
native land. Like them, he is "folksy" at times; but there is a vein of
rich, tender lyricism in his work, of real poetic imagination and deep
feeling. The titles of some of his compositions are revealing: *Forgotten Fairy Tales; Moon Pictures*, after Hans Christian Andersen;
*Launcelot and Elaine; From an Old Garden; Six Idyls After Goethe;
Six Poems After Heine; The Song of Roland; Sonata Tragica; Norse
Sonata; Celtic Sonata; Fireside Tales; New England Idyls; Indian
Suite*, and the *Woodland Sketches*, which contains such numbers as
"Br'er Rabbit" and "From an Indian Lodge." To round out the picture of his nationalism, it is interesting to note that he made a practice
of writing the tempo indications for his compositions in English instead of using the "allegros" and "adagios" of conventional musical
usage—a sort of gesture of independence that some of his disciples
have adhered to.

After his tragic death in 1908, his widow transferred his estate at
Peterboro, New Hampshire, to the MacDowell Memorial Association
for use as an artists' colony. Here every summer, writers, painters,
and composers gather from all parts of the country; the name of the
composer thus continues to be a symbol for the progress of the arts in
America.

*MacDowell's Suite No. 2 for Orchestra ("Indian") in E minor, Op.
48* [2]

THE SUITE is of five numbers: *Legend, Love Song, In War Time,
Dirge*, and *Village Festival*. In the *Legend*, there is a melody of the
Iroquois tribe and a Chippewa theme; the second number is built on a
love song of the Iowa tribes; the third has a Dakota theme, as well as
some features of an Iroquois scalp dance; the fourth is a Kiowa—a
woman's song of mourning for her absent son; and the *Village Festi-*

---

[2] MacDowell themes used with permission of Associated Publishers, Inc., N. Y.

val includes a women's dance and a war song of the Iroquois tribe. The Suite is scored for piccolo, two flutes, two oboes, two clarinets, two bassoons, four horns, two trumpets, three trombones, bass tuba, a set of three kettledrums, a bass drum, cymbals, and strings.

Introduction

Horns With much dignity

Legend: Not fast; with much dignity and character. E minor, 2-2. This number is reported to have been inspired by Thomas Bailey Aldrich's Indian legend, "Miantowona." The composer, however, made no attempt to relate the incidents of the poem, but suggested, rather, the general mood and atmosphere.

Clarinets
Bassoons

pizz strings

Love Song: Not fast; tenderly, A major, 6-8. A lyrical melody introduced by the woodwinds is developed, with an answer from the strings that is followed by another melody, more determined in character, in the woodwinds.

Flute
Clarinets
Horn
Etc

In War Time: With rough vigor, almost savagely, D minor, 2-4. Two flutes, unaccompanied, announce the chief theme in unison. A secondary theme is sung by two clarinets, also in unison and unaccompanied. The material is worked out in a well-knit musical form with frequent changes of rhythm toward the end from 2-4 to 6-8 and back again.

Flute solo
mf

Dirge: Dirgelike, mournfully, in G minor, 4-4. The lamentation is sung by muted violins in unison that are then reinforced by violas, while woodwinds and muted horn sustain the harmony rooted on the tonic note G. MacDowell directs that, to create the proper effect, one of the muted horns be played offstage.

Village Festival: Swift and light, in E major, 2-4. Several themes, all of them more or less related to those in the first movement, are developed in animated dance rhythms. The general mood of a tribal festival is captured with great felicity.

ADDITIONAL SUGGESTIONS FOR LISTENING

Deems Taylor's Suite: "Through the Looking Glass"

More typical, perhaps, of the cosmopolitan East is Deems Taylor, composer, music critic, and author of books on music. In composition he is known for his incidental music for the BEGGAR ON HORSEBACK, his opera THE KING'S HENCHMAN, on a text by Edna St. Vincent Millay; his PETER IBBETSON, on a libretto adapted from the celebrated novel of du Maurier; and his ORCHESTRAL SUITE based on Lewis Carroll's sequel to *Alice in Wonderland.* Originally written for chamber orchestra, Taylor later revised the score for full orchestra. His own program notes for the first performance of the suite offer the best introduction to the music:[3]

> The Suite needs no extended analysis. It is based on Lewis Carroll's immortal nonsense fairytale: *Through the Looking-Glass and What Alice Found There,* and the five pictures it presents will, if all goes well, be readily recognizable to lovers of the book. There are four movements, the first being subdivided into two connected parts.

I. (*a*) *Dedication*

Carroll precedes the tale with a charming poetical foreword, the first stanza of which the music aims to express. It runs:

> "Child of the pure unclouded brow
>   And dreaming eyes of wonder!
> Though the time be fleet, and I and thou
>   Are half a mile asunder,
> Thy loving smile will surely hail
>   The love-gift of a fairy-tale."

[3] From the program notes of the New York Symphony Orchestra.

A simple song theme, briefly developed, leads without pause to

(b) *The Garden of Live Flowers*

Shortly after Alice had entered the looking-glass country, she came to a lovely garden in which the flowers were talking:

"O Tiger-Lily," said Alice, addressing herself to one that was waving gracefully about in the wind, "I wish you could talk."

"We can talk," said the Tiger-Lily, "when there's anybody worth talking to."

"And can all the flowers talk?"

"As well as you can," said the Tiger-Lily, "and a great deal louder."

The music reflects the brisk chatter of the swaying, bright-colored denizens of the garden.

II. *Jabberwocky*

This is the poem that so puzzled Alice, and which Humpty Dumpty finally explained to her:

" 'Twas brillig, and the slithy toves
  Did gyre and gimble in the wabe;
All mimsy were the borogoves
  And the mome raths outgrabe.

"Beware the Jabberwock, my son!
  The jaws that bite, the claws that catch!
Beware the Jubjub bird, and shun
  The fruminous Bandersnatch!

"He took his vorpal sword in hand;
  Long time the manxome foe he sought—
So rested he by the Tumtum tree,
  And stood awhile in thought.

"And, as in uffish thought he stood,
  The Jabberwock, with eyes of flame,
Came whiffling through the tulgey wood,
  And burbled as it came!

"One, two! One, two! and through and through
  The vorpal blade went snicker-snack!
He left it dead, and with its head
  He went galumphing back.

"And hast thou slain the Jabberwock?
  Come to my arms, my beamish boy!
O frabjous day! Callooh! Callay!
  He chortled in his joy.

" 'Twas brillig, and the slithy toves
  Did gyre and gimble in the wabe;
All mimsy were the borogoves,
  And the mome raths outgrabe."

The theme of that fruitful beast, the Jabberwock, is first announced (*lento*) by the full orchestra. The clarinet then begins the tale, recounting how, on a "brillig" afternoon, the "slithy toves did gyre and gimble in the wabe." Muttered imprecations by the bassoon warn us to "beware the Jabberwock, my son." A miniature march signalizes the approach of our hero, taking "his vorpal sword in hand." Trouble starts among the trombones —the Jabberwock is upon us! The battle with the monster is recounted in a short and rather repellent fugue, the double basses bringing up the subject and the hero fighting back in the interludes. Finally, his vorpal blade (really a xylophone) goes snicker-snack, and the monster, impersonated by the solo bassoon, dies a lingering and convulsive death. The hero returns, to the victorious strain of his own theme—"O frabjous day! Callooh! Callay!" The whole orchestra rejoices—the church bells are rung —alarms and excursions.

Conclusion. Once more the slithy toves perform their pleasing evolutions, undisturbed by the uneasy ghost of the late Jabberwock.

III. *Looking-Glass Insects*

The score contains this extract:

This was anything but a regular bee; in fact, it was an elephant—as Alice soon found out, though the idea quite took her breath away at first. . . .

The gnat (for that was the insect she had been talking to) was balancing itself on a twig just over her head, and fanning her with its wings. It certainly was a very large gnat: "About the size of a chicken," Alice thought.

"——then don't you like all insects?" the gnat went on, as quietly as if nothing had happened.

"I like them when they can talk," Alice said. "None of them ever talk, where I come from. . . ."

"Half-way up that bush, you'll see a Rocking-horse-fly, if you look. Look on the branch above your head, . . . and there you'll find a Snapdragon-fly. . . . Crawling at your feet, you may observe a Bread-and-butter-fly."

"And what does it live on?"

"Weak tea with cream in it."

"Supposing it couldn't find any?"

"Then it would die, of course."

"But that must happen very often," Alice remarked thoughtfully.

"It always happens," said the gnat.

Here we find the vociferous *diptera* that made such an impression upon Alice—the Bee-elephant, the Gnat, the Rocking-horse-fly, the Snapdragon-fly, and the Bread-and-butter-fly. There are several themes, but there is no use trying to decide which insect any one of them stands for.

IV. *The White Knight*

He was a toy Don Quixote, mild, chivalrous, ridiculous, and rather touching. He carried a mouse-trap on his saddle-bow, "because, if they *do* come, I don't choose to have them running about." He couldn't ride very well, but he was a gentle soul, with good intentions. There are two themes: the first a sort of instrumental prance, being the Knight's own conception of himself as a slashing, dare-devil fellow. The second is bland, mellifluous, a little sentimental—much more like the Knight as he really was. The theme starts off bravely, but falls out of the saddle before long, and has to give way to the second. The two alternate, in various guises, until the end, when the Knight rides off, with Alice waving her handkerchief—he thought it would encourage him if she did.

Music for the Cinema

In recent years a new field of musical composition has been made possible through the cinema. From very modest beginnings—for we are only a few decades away from the movie pianist and fiddler with their albums of set excerpts appropriate for storm scenes, deathbeds, "hurries," battles, love, Indians, and the like—a new type of incidental music has developed, with a technique and an idiom of its own.

The opportunity for cinema music came, naturally, with the development of sound pictures. At first the musical accompaniment consisted of excerpts from various musical works selected to fit the needs of the particular moving picture. But it soon became customary to write original scores for the better pictures. The studios, especially the artistically advanced ones in Germany and France during the twenties, soon began to engage the services of distinguished composers for these scores. Among the outstanding musical scores in the years before the war may be mentioned that of Karol Rathaus for Ufa's production of *The Brothers Karamazov*; Arthur Honegger's score for *Giono's Harvest*; William Walton's for Shaw's *Major Barbara*; Sergei Prokofieff's for *Lieutenant Kije* and *Alexander Nevsky*; and Arthur Bliss's for H. G. Wells' fantastic movie, *Shape of Things to Come*.

Hollywood has adopted the practice of commissioning a special score for each movie; and in the past decade American cinema music has made great strides forward. Among notable musical scores in the past few years have been Max Steiner's atmospheric background music for Somerset Maugham's *The Letter*; Erich Korngold's, for *Marco Polo*; Aaron Copland's, for *Of Mice and Men*; Virgil Thomson's, for *The River*; and Hans Eisler's for *The Forgotten Village*. The reader may recall how effectively the approaching tragedy in *Of Mice and Men*—the scene in the stable before the murder—is proclaimed in the music through the insistent repetition of an ominous staccato figure deep in the bass; or how the mood of mystery and suspense in *The Letter* was intensified through the recurrence again and again throughout the picture of the sinister motive heard at the beginning. In *Major Barbara*, the heroine's emotional conflict, which constitutes the climax of the film, is projected completely through the stirring symphonic interlude of Walton as Barbara walks alone toward the river. Here the music takes on an even greater importance than it would have in a play. There is hardly any external action, or acting; we see only the heroine walking slowly away; the drama is an inner one and is conveyed almost exclusively through music.

Perhaps new and as yet unanticipated musical forms and styles may come from incidental and suite compositions, as well as briefer sequences, composed directly for the films. Only the future can tell.

Additional styles of the suite will be presented in the succeeding chapters.

Chapter X

MUSIC AND BALLET

THE spontaneous dances of the folk had their counterpart in the domain of art in the highly organized dance pageants that figured prominently in religious ceremonials and in the entertainments at the royal courts. In Greek tragedy, the chorus (from *choros*, a round dance) danced as it chanted. The ballet thus lent itself simultaneously to the needs of the theater, the temple, and the palace entertainment, absorbing elements from each.

In our theater the ballet figures in two ways: first, as a spectacular interlude in drama or opera; second, as an independent art form in which dramatic action and atmosphere are conveyed to the audience through dance pantomime. In either case, the music is of paramount importance both in furnishing an accompaniment for the actual dancing and in communicating and intensifying the mood. Ballet music as a rule combines the qualities of good dance music—melodious charm, strong rhythmic appeal, simplicity of form and content— with theatrical atmosphere, the dramatic *elan* of incidental music. It represents, in short, a fine fusion of the spirit of the dance with that of the theater.

Much of the outstanding ballet music of the nineteenth century was written as part of operas, or incidental music to dramatic performances, and might or might not be an integral part of the dramatic plot and action of the moment. For instance, in an opera like Gounod's FAUST, the plot and action cease for the moment, and out of the wings from either side of the stage ballet dancers flutter onto the stage on the tips of their toes. They go through well-prepared graceful movements, singly and in ensembles, presenting the eye with a pleasing sight of charm in rhythmic motion and design—all this to music of a comparable character. Then the dancers disappear into the wings again, to reappear at a later time. Degas, the French painter, has caught the various moods and life of such ballet dancers in many of his paintings. Similar ballets are to be found in many French operas

Degas

BALLET REHEARSAL ON STAGE

from the time of Lully, and before. A popular ballet of this type is Delibes' SYLVIA.[1]

As the ballet established itself as an independent art form, it employed music in conjunction with dance, pantomime, scenery, and costume to create a distinctive type of dramatic-musical entertainment. In some cases, ballets were arranged to music already in existence. Thus, Rimsky-Korsakoff's SCHEHEREZADE (Chapter XV) and Debussy's AFTERNOON OF A FAUN (Chapter XXVIII) are two of the many famous orchestral compositions to which ballets were adapted. Often, however, the music was written specifically for the ballet. As with incidental music, the composers of these ballets frequently arranged the music into concert suites, some of which became very popular as independent compositions, preserving as they did their excitement and rhythmic verve even when removed from the glamour of the ballet theater. Thus was established a continual interplay between music and ballet, with symphonic compositions moving into the ballet theater, and ballet music becoming part of the symphonic repertory.

As to the relationship between the two arts, the reader may recall our discussion on musical architecture in Chapter V, where we pointed out that the qualities of symmetry and balance, which are space concepts in painting, sculpture, and architecture, become time concepts in music. The ballet affords a vivid example of the transformation from the one dimension to the other. The musical phrases that balance each other in time, in the music become the basis for movements that balance each other in space in the dance, producing a synchronization of the two dimensions.

To make a long story short, then, the new art form of the ballet was built upon a story with a well-defined dramatic plot, and the action, or pantomime, served as the basis of telling the story and of providing a proper and desirable vehicle for the dancers themselves in the medium of their own art. Of course, the costumes, stage settings, and, what concerns us most for the moment, the music, combined to provide the complete performance, the result being a dramatic stage performance through dancing, pantomime, and music— *sans* words of the drama and *sans* singing of the opera. Naturally, to enjoy such ballets to the full, one must know the story and the plot,

---

[1] Essential listening for this chapter includes: *Ritual Fire Dance* from EL AMOR BRUJO by Falla, PETROUCHKA by Stravinsky, SKYSCRAPERS by Carpenter, and the MOTHER GOOSE BALLET by Ravel. All other ballets mentioned in the text are to be considered supplementary and optional. If time does not permit complete performances of the required listening, select excerpts, or movements, from them accordingly.

the choreographic interpretation of these, as well as an understanding of the other arts that fuse into this art form. (Those who are especially interested in this subject will want to acquaint themselves with further information concerning the French, the Russian, and later-day ballet styles. Read John Martin on *The Dance*.)

There are many choices of this new ballet style that we might make for our first offering; but, for more or less arbitrary reasons, let us begin with EL AMOR BRUJO (Love the Magician), a "choreographic fantasy" in sixteen parts (with vocal parts also), by the eminent Spanish composer, Manuel de Falla (1876-   ). The story, based on Andalusian life, concerns a Gypsy girl whose dead lover is jealous of her friendliness with his successor. The ghost makes several attempts to break up the new affair, but is foiled by another Gypsy girl who is courageous enough to flirt with him and distract him from his plot. The thematic material, while original with Falla, is so true to the character and spirit of the people that it is often mistaken for folk music. The orchestral version for concert use was made by the composer after the first performance of the ballet in 1915, and it is frequently played in that form. Since the whole, sixteen scenes or movements, is too long for the nonce, let us hear number seven of the series, the *Ritual Fire Dance to Exorcise Evil Spirits*.

The scene is in a dark cavern in the center of which the magic fire flickers, musically depicted by the mysterious *pizzicato* (plucking the strings rather than bowing them) in the stringed instruments of the orchestra. A weird incantation sweeps through the music over a strange seductive rhythmic foundation. Abrupt chords sounded by the full orchestra punctuate the ritual dance; but the inexorable rhythm never ceases. The dance grows steadily more abandoned; the theme is now repeated in a kind of fury; and a series of savage chords, suggestive of the wild figures leaping through the air, brings the music to a close. Notice how successfully the composer has projected the atmosphere of "black magic" and strange, fantastic shapes, and how adroitly he has used orchestral timbre, or instrumental tone color, of the oboes, clarinets, 'cellos and double basses, and throbbing drums, to portray and intensify the dramatic action and to arouse the proper emotions. Of course we miss the "seeing" part of the performance.

Now let us listen to a much more complete ballet of the Russian School, provided in Igor Stravinsky's ballet-suite PETROUCHKA. But first, because the composer is an outstanding world figure in music of our own time, a brief biographical sketch.

Igor Stravinsky

Stravinsky, the son of a Russian opera singer, was born near St. Petersburg (Leningrad) in 1882 and now resides in the United States. Like Tchaikovsky and Sibelius, he prepared himself for a legal career. But his talent manifested itself so clearly that Rimsky-Korsakoff, whom he met when he was twenty-two, advised him to devote himself entirely to music, and it was under the Russian master that he received his first systematic training. The teacher's influence has always made itself felt in Stravinsky's brilliant orchestration and sensitivity to instrumental effects.

Stravinsky came to fame in the years before the outbreak of the first World War as one of the brilliant artists whom Serge Diaghileff grouped around him in the Ballet Russe. (For an interesting account of that eventful period, the reader is referred to Romola Nijinsky's biography of Nijinsky, the great dancer, and Haskell's book on Diaghileff.) THE FIREBIRD, performed by Diaghileff's Company in 1910, and PETROUCHKA, performed the following year, established Stravinsky as one of the most original spirits in the hectic pre-war scene. PETROUCHKA has remained the most popular of his works, and in brilliance of orchestration, dramatic power, verve, and melodic richness is generally considered his masterpiece. THE RITES OF SPRING, which appeared in 1913, created a furore in Paris by its brutal primitiveness, its strange rhythms and dissonances. For many years afterward, its performance in the musical centers of the world seldom failed to provoke violent demonstrations. Although the next twenty-five years saw a steady output of works—among them an opera, THE NIGHTINGALE, based on the fairy tale of Hans Christian Andersen; PULCINELLA, a ballet based on the music of the charming eighteenth-century master, Pergolese; a piano concerto in the style of Bach; as well as a number of compositions for chamber groups—the first three ballets still remain his most popular works and the ones most likely to be encountered at symphony concerts.

"Petrouchka"

PETROUCHKA was first performed during the famous season of the Diaghileff ballet at the Chatelet in 1911, with Nijinsky in the title role and Karsavina as the ballerina. A concert suite was arranged from the ballet by Serge Koussevitzky, conductor of the Boston Symphony Orchestra, in collaboration with the composer.

The action takes place at a carnival in a public square of St. Peters-

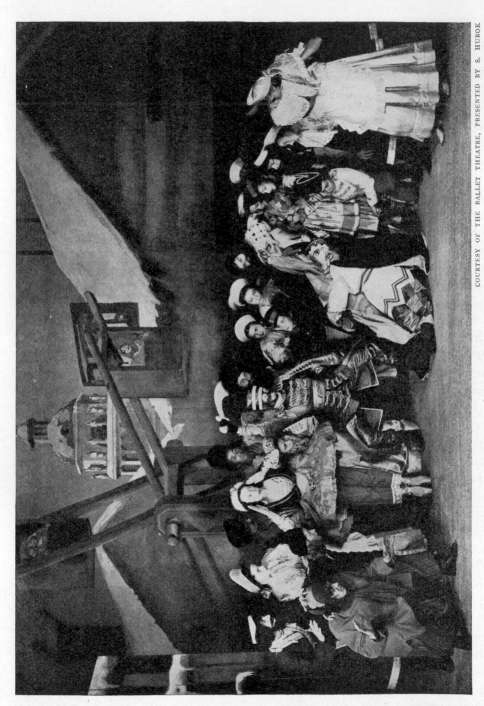

Stravinsky

A SCENE FROM THE BALLET "PETROUCHKA"

burg a century ago; the chief characters are a showman and the three puppets whom he exhibits, endowing them with human emotions in order to entertain his audience—the lovely Ballerina, the swashbuckling Moor, and the lovelorn clown, Petrouchka. The Showman blows his flute against the bustle of the carnival to attract customers to his puppet show. The puppets are brought to life; Petrouchka, ugly and the object of ridicule, falls hopelessly in love with the Ballerina, who prefers the Moor. After the puppet show is over the carnival continues; but behind the scene the sawdust tragedy plays itself out. At the height of the revelry Petrouchka is seen running across the stage of the puppet theater wildly pursued by the Moor who with a stroke of the sword crushes the unfortunate clown's head. He dies as the crowd gathers about, horrified. The Showman appears and explains to the crowd that his puppets are but stuffed dolls incapable of real emotion. He succeeds in convincing them; they depart. But at the end the ghost of Petrouchka appears above the booth, terrifying them with a grimace. There are obviously things in the lives of his puppets which the Showman does not understand. He has been wrong in assuming that his puppets have no souls. . . .

The Suite for concert opens with the boisterous *Russian Dance* from the opening scene of the ballet, music electric with the bustle and animation of the carnival mood. The music is taut and angular; this is the dance that the three stuffed puppets perform for the delectation of the unfeeling crowd. Notice the sharply contrasting timbres; the development of the theme by an interesting variety of instruments; the vivid ever-shifting rhythms; above all, the overpowering gusto and virility of the music.

The second part centers about the appearance of the Ballerina, accompanied by a dainty piano solo. Next the music depicts the sufferings of the love-smitten clown, his helpless rage at being rejected, his forlorn cries.

The third part is a brilliant carnival scene, one of the most colorful tone pictures from the composer's hand. A motley procession surges past our eyes—gay peasants, rollicking children, hawkers and fakirs and barkers, their cries intermingled with the tinny sounds of carousels and hurdy-gurdies. There is much dancing and gaiety that is rapidly dissipated as the crowd scatters at the arrival of a peasant leading a trained bear.

The peasant pipes a tune; the bear walks on his hind legs to a ponderous accompaniment on the double basses. The spotlight soon switches to a rich merchant who amuses himself by throwing money to the crowd. Gypsies dance, snatching at the wind-tossed bank notes. Then coachmen and hostlers perform a vigorous dance marked by great stamping of boots to typical Russian rhythms.

The final scene depicts the masquerade at nightfall. Clowning motives in the bass herald the approach of the masqueraders. Disguised as buffoons, devils, pigs, and goats, the merrymakers frolic together in a mad whirl. It is on this note that the concert ends, omitting the personal tragedy of the puppet who, from being put through the outer semblance of human emotions so unexpectedly, developed a soul—and a capacity for suffering—of his own.

Of course, the next step is to see the ballet as well as to hear it, if you can. Now for a more abstract and symbolic ballet by our own native composer, John Alden Carpenter.

John Alden Carpenter

The ballet has been assiduously cultivated in America; several of our contemporary composers have produced highly successful scores. One of the outstanding among these is SKYSCRAPERS by John Alden Carpenter (1876-   ), which not only is a fine example of modern tendencies in the art of ballet, but also presents to us in a racy, thoroughly alive idiom, the dynamic tempo, the vitality and surging rhythms of modern American life.

Carpenter, a descendant of John Alden, stands in the forefront of American composers. His music, delightful, intelligent, and witty, has attained wide popularity with the general public. SKYSCRAPERS is his best-known work; it was first performed at the Metropolitan Opera House in 1926 with scenery and costumes by the noted stage designer, Robert Edmond Jones. Arranged as a concert suite it has found a sure place for itself on symphonic programs.

"Skyscrapers"

The composer has built his music around the polarities of work and play, each, as he says, "with its own peculiar and distinctive rhythmic character." The fevered, restlessly pulsating rhythms of the work episodes alternate with the gay foxtrot and "Blues" rhythms of the play episodes. The ballet is divided into six scenes: 1. Symbols of Restlessness. 2. Abstraction of the Skyscraper; the Work that produces it; the Crowds passing it. 3. The transition from Work to Play. 4. An Amusement Park of the Coney Island type, and its varied, restless activities; a "flashback" to the idea of Work, and back again to Play. 5. The return from Play to Work. 6. Skyscrapers.

As in most ballet music, the rhythmic element predominates in this work; the rhythms of jazz, of foxtrot, of subways and motors and machines, of carousels and roller coasters—a brilliant and feverish conglomerate of the sounds and sights of the metropolis. The "symbols of restlessness" which permeate the first scenes; the blatant, hurdy-gurdy, "Coney Island" atmosphere of the fourth, with its hectic and synthetic gaiety; the *Dance of "Herself"* introduced by a muted trumpet; the *Dance of the Strutter*, the Negro scene which ushers in the *Blues; The Sandwich Man*, trudging along wearily between his gaudy placards; the factory whistle summoning the workers back to the shops, and the imposing chords at the end which drive relentlessly onward, symbolic of glittering skyscrapers thrusting against the sky —all these are interwoven in a score of compact brilliance that has humor and verve and a topical pointedness, capturing with rare felicity the drive and tension of American industrial life for which the skyscraper is so apt a symbol.

Note particularly the colorfulness of the orchestration: the use of the brass and complex piano parts in the "Symbols of Restlessness" scene; the woodwind and brass, in jagged rhythms, in the "Abstraction of the Skyscraper"; the happy-go-lucky dance tune on the banjo in the "Transition from Work to Play"; the muted trumpet and brass band effects in the "Amusement Park" episode; the crooning solo for English horn which introduces the "Negro Scene"; the imaginative use of trumpets and horns in the "Sandwich Man" scene; and the fierce power and glitter of the finale. Here is a wealth of melodic ideas, of striking harmonies that abound in pungent dissonances united with never-flagging rhythms in a composition of great excitement and forward drive.

For our last illustration, we have chosen Maurice Ravel's ever popular MA MÈRE L'OYE (Mother Goose) SUITE. (More of this composer and his impressionistic suite, DAPHNIS AND CHLOE, will be found in Chapter XXVIII, page 435.) These two ballets have been temporarily thrown out of proper perspective among the laymen by the abnormal popularity of Ravel's ballet BOLERO, a brilliant *tour de force* in the art of orchestration, an art and craft in which Ravel takes his rightful place beside the greatest in music history. One of the reasons we have chosen this particular work at this place is the value we can get in the way of appreciation of instrumental tone color, or timbre, if we will but listen carefully. (See also Chapter XI.)

Maurice Ravel: "Mother Goose Ballet Suite"

The MOTHER GOOSE SUITE music, originally composed for piano duet in 1908, was later orchestrated by Ravel and, like Debussy's AFTERNOON OF A FAUN, achieved popularity as a ballet. An interesting characteristic of Ravel is the fact that, although he transcribed for orchestra several compositions originally written for piano, his sense of style was so acute that the orchestral versions do not in the least have that "made-over" feeling that so often attends transcriptions, but seem to have a personality of their own quite distinct from the original form of the piece.

The *Suite*, arranged from the ballet music, consists of five children's pieces. The *Pavane of the Sleeping Beauty* has a slow somnolent grace. A *pavane* is an old stately dance of Spanish origin; Ravel's other pavane, *For a Dead Princess*, widely popular in this country, has achieved the distinction (?) of inspiring a foxtrot. Note the effect of two solo flutes, later English horn and flute.

To the second number, *Hop o' My Thumb*, Ravel appended a quotation from Perrault, the great French writer of fairy tales: "He believed that he would easily find his path by means of his bread crumbs which he had scattered wherever he had passed; but he was very much surprised when he could not find a single crumb: the birds had come and eaten everything up." Note the effect of the oboe solo over the muted first and second violins. Can you notice also the frequent change of time?

Third is *Laideronnette, Empress of the Pagodas*. *Pagoda* once indicated not only the fanciful little tower but also the idol or image lodged in it. When the Princess Laideronnette, who had been cursed at birth with supreme ugliness, entered her bath, the pagodas and their ladies—grotesque little figures with movable heads—"began to sing and play on instruments: some had theorbos made of walnut shells, some had viols made of almond shells; for they were obliged to proportion the instruments to their figure." Note that the quick theme played by the solo flute resembles the nursery tune "Chop Sticks," or "Peter, Peter, Pumpkin Eater," which all of us have played in our youth on the black keys of the piano. Such a scale is called a *pentatonic* scale. Many Chinese melodies are in such a scale, thus Ravel was making a proper musical pun.

Next comes the *Conversations of Beauty and the Beast.* In the meter of a slow waltz, with a double bassoon representing the Beast, this number is one of the most popular of the suite. Since Beauty was able to see through the ugly exterior of the Beast to the kind heart and fine soul underneath, she was able to release him from his enchantment. "The Beast disappeared, and she saw at her feet only a prince more beautiful than Love. . . ."

The first of the following musical illustrations, for harp with clarinet solo, is used to depict the "Beauty"; the second, which is played by the contrabassoon and which sounds an octave lower than written, is a delightful characterization of the "Beast."

The Fairy Garden, which closes the suite, reveals to us the composer in an unusually poetic mood. In slow three-four time, the movement sums up the spirit of fairy-tale magic. Here Ravel weaves a spell no less potent than that of the fairies and magicians who people the tales on which his music is based. How the strings, played very softly, contribute just the right "atmosphere" for the fairy waltzlike theme!

ADDITIONAL SUGGESTIONS FOR LISTENING

Among the popular ballet suites and excerpts that figure on symphonic programs and illustrate the nineteenth-century style in this genre are Tchaikovsky's SWAN LAKE, SLEEPING BEAUTY (also known as *Aurora's Wedding*); the charming excerpts from the ballets of the French composer, Léo Delibes (1836-1891), COPPELIA and SYLVIA; the ballet GAIETÉ PARISIENNE by the composer of *Tales of Hoffmann*, Jacques Offenbach (1819-1890); the *Bacchanale* from Glazounov's ballet THE SEASONS; and LES SYLPHIDES, the ballet arranged from the works of Chopin.

Other modern ballet suites that the reader will enjoy and that will give him an idea of some very delightful music of recent years are the popular ballets of Stravinsky, SACRÉ DU PRINTEMPS and THE FIREBIRD, to which we shall return when we discuss modern music; the gay music from THE INCREDIBLE FLUTIST, by the American composer, Walter Pison (1894-   ); Darius Milhaud's ballet LA CRÉATION DU MONDE (The Creation of the World), an interesting example of the use of the American jazz idiom by a European composer; Ravel's BOLERO, which attained wide popularity in America as a concert piece, although it was originally written as a ballet for the dancer Ida Rubinstein; *Yablochko*, or *Russian Sailors' Dance*, from Reinhold Glière's ballet THE RED POPPY, which is lustily satirized by his younger compatriot Dmitri Shostakovitch (1906-   ) in the *Russian Dance* from the ballet THE GOLDEN AGE; and Aaron Copland's BILLY THE KID.

Chapter XI

TONE COLOR IN MUSIC: THE ORCHESTRA

I. The Instruments of the Orchestra

NO DOUBT the listener's curiosity has been aroused from time to time up to this point as to what instrument was playing the theme at a particular moment. At least, it is hoped that such has been the case; in fact, during the analysis of Ravel's MOTHER GOOSE SUITE in the preceding chapter, we drew your attention to several instruments of the orchestra and we saw how the composer used the tone color of such instruments to depict, characterize, or incite a certain emotional effect. The time has now come to look into such matters more objectively and with more detail than was before possible.

We often speak of the character of tone produced by an instrument as *timbre*. Each instrument and each type of human voice has its own quality of tone, its distinctive color. The timbre of the violin differs from that of the bassoon; the soprano's tone quality is altogether different from that of the bass. Like the painter with his palette, the composer mixes his colors, blends or contrasts them as he sees fit. He must be as sensitive to timbre as the painter is to color, and he must have the same capacity for picturing the subtlest shadings of color in his imagination.

Timbre is a constituent element in every conceivable type of music. It is of prime importance in compositions for the various solo instruments—piano, violin, 'cello, organ, and the like. It is equally important in vocal music, whether solo as in the art song, or in ensemble and chorus as in opera and oratorio and in the blending of the various vocal timbres with the instrumental accompaniment. Above all, timbre enters as a predominant aesthetic consideration in the blending and contrasting of the different instrumental colors in the small ensemble, or chamber music groups (see Chapter XXV), and in that mighty instrumental aggregate, the modern symphony orchestra.[1]

If the reader were taking a course in music of the sixteenth century, most of the works that he would study would be choral. Since then, the instruments have forged ahead steadily, first to a position of equality with the vocal branch, and finally to a point where the symphony orchestra is the favorite instrument of our time—a many-tongued, wonderfully sensitive instrument on which the composer runs the gamut from a mysterious whisper to a tornado of sound, suitable beyond compare, as we saw in some of the modern ballets that we have just listened to, depicting the moods and rhythms, the furious activity and dynamism, of twentieth-century life.

In the history of music, this shifting of the spotlight from the vocal to the instrumental branch is one of the most significant changes of the past five hundred years. The instruments entered the domain of serious music timidly, at first mainly furnishing the accompaniment by doubling or duplicating the voice parts. The next step came when the madrigals of the Renaissance began to be performed occasionally by the instruments without the voices, probably when no singers happened to be available. Naturally, the composers of the period did not realize at once that instruments could manage an altogether different type of music from that which the voice could carry. They thought of the instruments as simply so many voices substituting for or duplicating the real things, and often inscribed their madrigals, "apt for voyces or viols."

The seventeenth century witnessed a steady development in the mechanical and tonal aspects of instruments, as well as in playing techniques. Throughout the century the instruments forged ahead in importance. Little *interludes* were introduced into the *madrigals* while the voices rested. Gradually these interludes took on a specifically instrumental character, independent of the vocal style. With the development of the opera, a new phase began: Monteverde, as we saw, began to exploit the dramatic possibilities of the instruments, their individual color and personality. Instrumental interludes began to play an increasingly important role in the opera. Most of all, it became fashionable to open the performance with a more or less ambitious overture, for instruments alone. These interludes and over-

---

[1] For pictures and more detailed descriptions of the instruments, see *Instruments of the Modern Symphony Orchestra and Band*, new and revised edition by Edwin John Stringham (New York: Carl Fischer, 1930), a useful and inexpensive book for the general music lover.

tures were loosely called *symphonias*, literally, a "sounding together" (from the Greek *syn*, "together," and *phonē*, "sound"). The path was thus opened for the emergence of what is, as far as many music lovers are concerned, the most important branch of the art—symphonic music.

The general composition of the orchestra as we know it was already fairly well established by the end of the eighteenth century. The Romantic movement in the nineteenth century, with its search for new effects, for picturesque tone colors and vivid description, naturally provided an enormous stimulus for expansion of orchestral resources, and for new developments in the art of instrumentation. Consequently, the past hundred years have witnessed a great growth in size of the orchestra, in the improvement of old instruments and the introduction of new, as well as in the artistic and technical standards of playing them. Whereas the orchestra of Mozart and Haydn usually contained about thirty-five players, our leading orchestras have well over a hundred expertly trained musicians, many of them artists on their instruments, who perform under the batons of gifted conductors the works of the masters of the past and the moderns alike with the greatest skill and artistic fidelity.[2]

The string choir

The modern symphony orchestra consists of four instrumental families or choirs: the string choir, the woodwind, the brass, and the percussion. The string group, considered the backbone of the orchestra, contains the four types of stringed instruments played with the bow: the violin, the viola, the 'cello, and the double bass. Each of these is based upon the acoustical law that by changing the length, thickness, and tension of the vibrating string we change the pitch of the tone. The player manipulates the bow with his right hand, setting the strings in vibration. With his left, he presses the strings at various points, producing different pitches. The strings have the great advantage, compared with a piano, for instance, of sustaining the tone as long as desired, modulating it the while (making it louder or softer).

It will be found helpful in studying the timbre of the various instruments to use the special records that illustrate the tone color of each instrument separately. The sound should be associated with the description in our text and with the appearance of the instrument.

[2] The author urges that at this point you listen to Serge Prokofieff's delightful *Peter and the Wolf*, wherein the instruments of the orchestra are pointed out in a most effective manner.

However, the real appreciation of instrumental tone color comes with repeated listening to the works of the masters, in the original orchestral environment.[3]

The violin is the "soprano" of the string choir. It is the foremost singer of lyrical melody; its legato possesses something of the warmth and expressiveness of the human voice. On the other hand, its agility in executing rapid notes makes it equally useful in intricate running passages. A number of special effects are possible on the violin: playing two notes at once, or "double stopping"; bouncing the bow on the strings (*saltando*); playing rapidly a number of staccato notes in one stroke of the bow (*spiccato*); plucking the strings (*pizzicato*); vibrating the left hand from the wrist as the finger presses against the string to produce that tremulous tone known as *vibrato;* playing with the wooden part of the bow to create a strange hollow tone (*col legno*); rapidly repeating the same note with brusque up-and-down strokes of the bow to achieve the *tremolo*, the favorite stand-by for producing effects of suspense, danger, fear and the like; sliding the left hand along the string while bowing with the right, which gives us the *glissando;* and pressing lightly at certain points of the string, which prevents the string from vibrating as a whole and brings into prominence the vibrations of its segments, thus producing those high-pitched, ethereal tones known as *harmonics*.

The four strings of the violin are tuned G-D-A-E, ranging from the full-throated expressiveness of the G string to the brilliance of the upper register of the E.

Its effective range is approximately three and a half octaves, beginning from G below middle C. The modern symphony orchestra has two groups of violins, known as the first and second violins, with about sixteen players in each.

The viola is held and played like the violin, but it is larger in size and produces a deeper, more veiled tone. It is the "alto" of the string choir. It is pitched five tones lower than the violin; that is, it cannot sing as high as the violin, but it compensates by being able to go lower. If it lacks the brilliance of the violin, the viola possesses a subdued

---

[3] Essential listening for this chapter includes: *Peter and the Wolf* by Prokofieff, "Instruments of the Symphony Orchestra" records for string, woodwind, brass choirs and percussion, "Introduction and Allegro" for strings or "Serenade" for strings by Elgar, Nutcracker Suite by Tchaikovsky, and selected solo and ensemble records.

charm and dignity of its own, which in the lower register takes on a
darkly brooding quality. The viola blends so well with the more
brilliant violin or the richer-toned 'cello that for many years its own
personality was subordinated to these two. But in the past century
composers grew more and more appreciative of its lyrical possibilities.
Its subtle coloring, now gently mournful, now coldly penetrating, has
come to assume an important part in the orchestral palette. Its four
strings are tuned C-G-D-A; and since most of its music lies between
the bass and treble clefs, for convenience it uses the alto (movable C)
clef (middle C is on the middle line):

It is capable of all the technical effects of the violin; its effective range
is slightly less—about three octaves, from the C below middle C. The
symphony orchestra usually contains from ten to twelve viola players.

The 'cello (shortened name for *violoncello*) is a still larger instrument and is propped between the player's knees. Tuned an octave
lower than the viola, it may be considered the "tenor" or "baritone"
of the string quartet. Its strings are thicker and over twice as long as
those of the violin; its tone is mellow and full-throated. Its capacity
for poignant emotion and sustained song have led composers to en-
trust to the 'cello some of their loveliest melodies. It is capable of the
special effects of the violin; is tuned C-G-D-A:

It has an effective range of over three and a half octaves, from C two
octaves below middle C. There are usually eight to ten 'cellos in the
modern symphony orchestra, which supply a warm, rich mass of tone
to the string section.

The double bass, known also as the contrabass or string bass, is
the lowest pitched and largest of the string family. It is about six feet
high; the player either stands, or sits on a high stool. It was originally
used mainly to duplicate the 'cello parts an octave lower—in other
words, to double the bass; hence its name. Its deep, heavy tone is
equally effective in portraying darkest gloom or gruff, heavy-handed
humor; but it seldom functions as a solo instrument. Its principal task
is to supply a firm base for the harmonic structure above it. Recently
it has acquired a new importance in jazz bands, where it is played in

"slapping" fashion to emphasize the beat, almost like a percussion instrument. The double bass is tuned E-A-D-G and sounds an octave lower than written:

Its sounding range is slightly over three octaves, from E three octaves below middle C. There are eight to ten double-bass players in the symphony orchestra.

Between the brilliant color of the violin, the soft "grays" of the viola, the rich glow of the 'cello and the powerful background of the double bass, the composer can look to the string section for an interesting assortment of tone colors and special tonal effects. When necessary, these instruments are muted by slipping a small contraption of metal, bone, or wood, called the mute (Italian, *sordino*), over the bridge. This lessens the sonority and produces a veiled, sensitive tone.

The harp, one of the oldest and most "romantic" of instruments, is a stringed instrument sounded by plucking. It was popular with the ancient Egyptians, Assyrians, Hebrews, and Greeks, and with the troubadours and minstrels of the Middle Ages. It was played by Alfred the Great; and, limned in gold on a field of green, it became the national emblem of Ireland.

The harp has a silvery, dreamlike tone that stands out among all the timbres of the orchestra. Beginners in composition are fascinated by its tone, and introduce it lavishly into their works; but masters of orchestral style know that its effectiveness depends upon sparing use. We will hear it used most effectively by Rimsky-Korsakoff to give the effect of Oriental languor in his SCHEHEREZADE. Debussy, Ravel, and other members of the Impressionist school (Chapter XXVIII) were very fond of the floating, silvery tones of the harp.

The range of the harp is five octaves. Its music is written like that for the piano. Chords on the harp are often "broken," that is to say, the tones are played in succession instead of simultaneously; whence is derived our name for a broken chord, *arpeggio* (from *arpa*, "harp"), an effect that appears frequently in piano music. The modern orchestra possesses one or two harps.

For our second listening project, hear the "String Choir" records from the available sets offered by the Columbia, Victor, or Decca companies, illustrating the various "Instruments of the Symphony Orchestra"; and for the third listening project, either hear the "Introduction and Allegro" for Strings, Opus 47, or the "Serenade" for Strings, Opus 28, by Edward Elgar.

The ranges of the instruments of the string choir and the harp are:

The woodwind choir

The woodwind section, with its haunting tone colors, is unquestionably one of the most fascinating and variegated parts of the orchestra. The members of this choir have sharply differentiated personalities that, whether in combination with one another or with the instruments of other choirs, contribute some of the most piquant colors of the modern orchestral palette. Since their timbre is so much more striking than that of most of the other instruments, the woodwinds have to be used with greater circumspection and sustained for shorter periods than the strings.

In the woodwinds, the tone is produced by a vibrating column of air within the tube: the shorter the air column, the more vibrations per second and the higher the pitch. The air is set in motion by a single or double reed (except in the flute); and it is the resultant reediness of tone that lends to these instruments their distinctive individuality. Each of the four principal members of this group—flute, oboe, clarinet, and bassoon—has a related family instrument so similar to it in construction that the player can change from one to the other without too great difficulty. The flute is related to the piccolo; the oboe, to the English horn; the clarinet, to the bass clarinet (and saxophone); and the bassoon, to the double bassoon. While all these are wind instruments—that is to say, blown with the breath—a number of them are no longer made of wood; but this does not affect their being classified as woodwinds. The saxophone is included in this group because, even though it is made of brass, it is a single reed instrument and possesses other characteristics of the woodwind choir; clarinets, flutes, and even oboes are sometimes made of metal.

The flute is one of the most ancient of instruments, having been extensively cultivated in its earliest form among the Egyptians and the Greeks. It is the most brilliant member of the woodwinds, as well as the most agile; it can execute rapid passages with greater dexterity than any of them. It is not a reed instrument at all; the tone is produced by blowing across a hole in the side called *embouchure*, instead of into a mouthpiece at one end. The modern instrument is held horizontally. The flute has a liquid tone that in the upper registers takes on a birdlike lightness and brilliance, while in the lower there is a veiled, expressive quality. The flute is the "coloratura

COURTESY OF THE METROPOLITAN MUSEUM OF ART

DOODLE-SACK PLAYER   *Dürer*

soprano" of the woodwinds, and is capable of legato melody as well as brilliant rapid passages.

The flute has a range of about three octaves, from middle C. The first octave has a veiled and fluid color; the second is smooth and clear; the upper register is sharp and penetrating. Romantic and Impressionist composers were very fond of the flute. Ravel makes effective use of it in *La Flute Enchantée* (The Enchanted Flute) from his

SCHEHEREZADE, as well as in the DAPHNIS AND CHLOE suite. Rimsky-Korsakoff uses it extensively in his SCHEHEREZADE (Chapter XV); Tchaikovsky in his *Dance of the Toy Flutes* from the NUTCRACKER SUITE (see next section); and Debussy assigns to it the celebrated opening theme of THE AFTERNOON OF A FAUN (Chapter XXVIII). There are generally two or three flutists in the orchestra; one or two may double on the piccolo.

The piccolo (from *flauto piccolo*, the Italian for "little flute") is half as long as the flute and sounds an octave higher. Its range is about three octaves, in the lower register very brilliant, in the upper, shrill and piercing. Its tone heightens the color of an orchestral climax, and it is much used for special effects, such as the whistling of the wind, the howling of a thunderstorm, and the like. The piccolo is used in military bands and in drum and fife bands. Its scintillating tone, suggesting the bizarre and even—as in Berlioz's DAMNATION OF FAUST—the infernal, has caused it to be nicknamed the "imp of the orchestra." It sounds an octave higher than written; therefore it is called a transposing instrument. One piccolo is used in the modern orchestra.

The oboe, a conical woodwind pipe terminating in a bell, is a double reed instrument and has a nasal, "pleading" tone that at times takes on a startlingly human quality. Possessing a certain lyrical, pastoral character, it is indispensable to the tone painters of pastoral scenes. In addition, its powers for expressing poignant emotion—whether grief, beseeching, or longing—made it one of the favorite instruments of the late Romantic and Impressionist composers. Saint-Saëns uses the oboe to represent the crowing of the cock in his DANSE MACABRE (Chapter XIII). Beethoven uses its mournful coloring in the *Funeral March* (second movement) of the "EROICA" SYMPHONY. Berlioz employs it to represent a shepherd in the "Pastoral Scene" of his SYMPHONIE FANTASTIQUE. The oboe may be considered the "lyric soprano" of the woodwinds. Its range extends two and a half octaves, from B flat below middle C. It is capable of brilliant and agile running passages, as well as of sustained melody. There are generally two or three oboe players in the full symphony orchestra, one of whom doubles on the alto oboe, the English horn. (For example, see MOTHER GOOSE SUITE, page 128.)

The English horn is not very well named, since it is neither English nor a horn. Some historians derive its name from a corruption of *cor angle* (bent horn) which gradually became *cor anglais* (English horn)—a plausible explanation. It is one and a half times as large as the oboe, transposing its sound a fifth lower than written. It may be considered the alto of the woodwind choir; it substitutes for the penetrating reediness of the oboe a plaintive quality all its own, vaguely nostalgic, sorrowful yet resigned. Dvořák entrusts to the English horn the famous melody of the *Largo* of his NEW WORLD SYMPHONY (see Chapter XIX).

The clarinet is a cylindrical pipe generally of wood, two feet in length, with a narrow bell at one end. It has a single reed mouthpiece. Its smooth, liquid tone is more colorful than that of the oboe; it has something of the agility and brilliance of the flute. The clarinet is the "dramatic soprano" of the woodwind choir. It has a great range of volume of tone, running the gamut from a mysterious whisper to the fullest sonority. Its lowest register has a specially haunting quality, while its capacity for pure, clear song in the upper register makes it most effective in lyrical passages. The clarinet, along with the violin, is one of the most useful instruments of the orchestra. Its range extends for about three and a half octaves, from the E below middle C. There are generally three clarinetists in the modern symphony orchestra, of whom one doubles on the bass clarinet. For examples of the instrument's versatile powers, listen to the lyric theme of the Princess in the third movement of Rimsky-Korsakoff's SCHE-HEREZADE (Chapter XV):

(note the smooth ascending and descending runs in the same movement); the wonderfully liquid tone of the clarinets in the first movement of Mozart's G-MINOR SYMPHONY (Chapter XXII); the imitation of the call of the yellowhammer in Beethoven's SIXTH SYMPHONY (*Pastoral*), and its use in combination with the horns in the same work, to give the shepherd's call after the storm. The clarinet has an extensive repertoire as a solo instrument. It is a transposing instrument (the written note and the tone that is produced from it are not the same); thus, the clarinet in B flat sounds down one step from the written note in the key of C, and the A clarinet sounds down a tone and a half.

The bass clarinet is, in structure, an enlarged clarinet that sounds an octave below the B-flat clarinet. Its tone is deep and full and encompasses a range of about three octaves. The lowest tones are extremely rich and powerful, resembling certain pedal stops on the organ. With its turned-up metal bell it might be mistaken for a saxophone, except that its body is made of wood. The richness and sonority of its tone, especially in the low register, lend themselves to solemnity and the ominous. In the second act of LOHENGRIN, Wagner allots the sinister motive of "warning" to the bass clarinet:

In DIE WALKÜRE, the bass clarinet carries the motive of Wotan's anger:

Wagner also gives it prominence in the tragic scene at the close of the second act of TRISTAN AND ISOLDE, where King Mark discovers the lovers and gives vent to his grief in tones of great dignity and pathos. The bass clarinet is a transposing instrument. If it is written in the treble clef, it sounds down a ninth; if in the bass clef, a second down. The orchestra includes one bass clarinet.

The clarinet reed was adapted to conical brass tubes by the French instrument maker Adolphe Sax, for whom the saxophone was named. These instruments, which come in several varieties—soprano, alto, tenor, baritone, and bass—combine the liquid quality of the clarinet with the soft reediness of the English horn and the lyricism of the 'cello. They have become closely associated with American jazz music—witness their effective use by Carpenter in his SKYSCRAPERS—and are effective both in sustained melody and in rapid, decorative passages. They did not enter the symphonic ensemble until modern times; although the reader may recall that Bizet assigned to the saxophone a passage of great beauty, the theme symbolizing "The Innocent," in the *Prelude* to L'ARLÉSIENNE. The French composers have always been partial to this liquid-voiced instrument. Debussy composed a RHAPSODY FOR SAXOPHONE AND ORCHESTRA; Saint-Saëns, Delibes, and Vincent D'Indy were fond of it. D'Indy has a quartet of saxophones in his opera FERVAAL. The American composer Werner Janssen (1899-   ) used the instrument memorably in his symphonic poem NEW YEAR'S EVE IN NEW YORK. Gershwin, Ferde Grofé, and Arthur Shepard have written effective passages for it.

The bassoon is the "bass" of the woodwinds. Its pipe is a conical tube about eight feet in length, folded or doubled upon itself and joined together in a block of solid wood. Since its primitive form bore some resemblance to a bundle of sticks—the tube was originally six to nine feet long, bent several times—the Italians named this instrument *fagotto*, a faggot. The instrument is capable of a dry, hollow tone that in staccato produces a somewhat grotesque effect, as a result of which it has come to be called the "clown of the orchestra." (Notice this effect, in the next section, at the opening of the *Chinese Dance* of Tchaikovsky's Nutcracker Suite, as well as the famous use of three bassoons to imitate the hopping of the broom in Dukas' Sorcerer's Apprentice, Chapter XIII.) At the same time, the bassoon is capable of lyric melody, of a sustained and expressive legato of solemn or passionate hue. It is nontransposing and sounds where written. The bassoon sings the serene, lyrical theme in the course of the second movement of Beethoven's Fifth Symphony (see Chapter XX).

The whimsical side of its versatile nature is expressed in the folk-song-like theme of the happy-go-lucky Kalendar Prince in Rimsky-Korsakoff's Scheherezade. (See Chapter XV.)

The bassoon has a range of about three and a half octaves. There are three bassoonists in the modern symphony orchestra, one of whom doubles on the contrabassoon.

The contrabassoon is the woodwind equivalent of the double bass. It is pitched an octave below the bassoon (sounds an octave lower than written) and can sound the deepest notes in the orchestral ensemble. It is a conical pipe of sixteen feet in length, doubled back upon itself four times and possessing a metal bell at its largest end. One is usually included in the modern orchestra. It is not often used as a solo instrument, its main function, like that of the double bass, being to furnish a foundation for the orchestral harmony. It figures also where a sepulchral or ominous color is needed, or for special effects—growling, rumbling, and the like. Ravel, in the *Beauty and the Beast* section of his Mother Goose Suite, used it to depict the Beast:

(Listen to the "Woodwind Choir" selections from the sets, "Instruments of the Symphony Orchestra," mentioned above.) The ranges and transpositions of the woodwind instruments are:

The brass choir

If the string choir provides the lyricism and the harmonic foundation for the symphonic web, and the woodwinds supply the subtle color effects, it is the brass choir that furnishes the patches of blazing color, the thunderous sonorities of conflict and triumph as also the sustained, organlike harmonies. In the instruments of this group—trumpet, French horn, trombone, and tuba—there is a cup-shaped mouthpiece against which the taut lips of the player act as a vibrating reed, and a series of valves to regulate the length of the column of air within the tube. For many years these instruments were able to produce only certain tones of the scale; the characteristic bugle calls, such as Taps and Reveille, are based upon these. As a result of a series of mechanical improvements throughout the nineteenth century, their limitations were overcome and they are now effective and useful members of the orchestral family. The brass instruments were very popular among the nations of antiquity, who made full use of their stirring, martial effects. Latin literature abounds in references to the *tibia* and *bucina;* and in the Old Testament story the walls of Jericho came tumbling down before them. In turn, the brasses may be stately, dignified, and organlike in sound, and they are often highly effective in melodic and lyrical passages.

The trumpet is the "brilliant soprano" of the brass choir. Its sharp, imperious tone is an indispensable element of all heroic climaxes, as we heard in the *Triumphal March* from AÏDA. It is equally useful in sustaining sonority or in executing complicated passages. By introducing a mute, a pear-shaped device, its tone takes on another character. When the muted tone is forced, we get a snarling, defiant effect. When played softly, the muted trumpet produces a sensitive flutelike tone. Jazz-band trumpet players are developing a large assortment of mutes, each with its special effect. Muted trumpets imitate the tiny trumpets of the Guild of the Tailors in the last act of DIE MEISTERSINGER:

Muted trumpets are also used effectively by Tchaikovsky in the middle part of the *Dance of the Flutes* from the NUTCRACKER SUITE. (See next section of this chapter.) The range of the trumpet is approximately two and a half octaves. There are three or four trumpets in the modern orchestra.

The horn, generally called the French horn because of its extensive use at the hunts of the French kings, is the most important of the brass instruments and one of the most beautiful voices in the orchestral family. It should not be confused with the English horn, which is an alto oboe and a woodwind. The French horn, which may be considered the "alto" of the brass choir, is easily identified through its flaring bell and complicated coils of tubing. It combines effectively with strings ·or woodwinds as well as with brass. It is the noblest of the brass instruments; its lovely tone is extraordinarily poetic and expressive. When played loudly, it takes on a character of majestic sonority. Descended from the hunting horn (*cor-de-chasse, waldhorn, jagdhorn*), it has retained its woodland associations: no other instrument conveys so well the sense of spacious outdoors, of magical remoteness. Weber made use of this quality in the opening of his "OBERON" OVERTURE. We heard a lovely passage for horns in the *Nocturne* from the MIDSUMMER NIGHT'S DREAM music:

The range of the horn is three and a half octaves. The fact that there are four to eight French horns in the modern orchestra enables the composer to write four-part harmony completely within this timbre. The horn in F sounds down a fifth. One of the most effective devices in symphonic writing is to give the horns sustained, noble harmonies while the strings and woodwinds weave an intricate tonal web about them. Wagner makes unforgettable use of the horns in his *Valhalla* motif in the majestic final scene of Das Rhinegold:

The tone of the horn may be "stopped" either with a mute or by inserting the hand in the bell of the instrument. The muted horn like the muted trumpet is capable of various effects. Forcing the tone gives a guttural, rasping quality. Played softly, the muted horn never fails to produce an effect of loveliness and remoteness. The snarling defiance produced by forcing the tone of the muted horn is well exemplified in the climax of the last movement of Tchaikovsky's Sixth Symphony, the *Pathétique*:

Among other outstanding horn passages may be mentioned the mischievous theme of Till in Richard Strauss' symphonic poem, The Merry Pranks of Till Eulenspiegel (see Chapter XVIII);

and the triumphant call of Siegfried in Götterdämmerung:

The trombone is a stately, nontransposing instrument that resembles the horn in its tone and the trumpet in brilliance and power. It is used for effects of solemn grandeur and great amplitude of tone. The trombone is the simplest of the brasses: instead of a complicated system of valves, it has a U-shaped sliding tube, because of which it is often called the slide trombone. This sliding tube lengthens or shortens the column of air in the tube, either lowering or raising the pitch. The trombone player must have a well-trained ear, for he himself determines the pitch of the tones by "sliding," and the slightest miscalculation brings dire results.

The pompous, rotund tone of the trombone is well exemplified in Wagner's "TANNHÄUSER" OVERTURE, when the trombones take over the solemn *Chorus of the Pilgrims:*

Similarly, the theme of the "Compact" between Wotan and the Giants, in the second scene of DAS RHINEGOLD, is given to the trombones, which play the phrase in brilliant unison:

There are three or four trombones in the modern orchestra. The range of this instrument, which may be considered the "tenor" (or ofttimes the "bass") of the brass choir, is two and a half octaves.

The tuba is an imposing-looking instrument (nontransposing), which fulfills the same function in the brass as the double bass in the strings and the contrabassoon in the woodwinds: it provides the harmonic foundation, combining with the other members of the choir more often than playing an independent part. It has a deep, heavy tone, and is a somewhat unwieldy instrument. Stravinsky makes it portray the Bear in his ballet PETROUCHKA; and Wagner appropriately uses it to depict the dragon in his SIEGFRIED:

The tuba has a range of two and a half or three octaves. The orchestra uses one tuba. (Listen to the "Brass Choir" selections from the sets, "Instruments of the Symphony Orchestra," mentioned above.) The ranges and transpositions of the instruments of the brass choir are:

(Consult a record catalog for examples of Brass instrument solos.)

The percussion group

This group, also known as the battery, includes the instruments that are sounded by being struck. These are the descendants of the drums and rattles of the jungle; most of them have no set pitch. Besides accentuating the rhythm, they heighten the sense of climax and add a number of very spicy color effects to the other instruments. Like all seasoning, they have to be used sparingly.

Most important of this group are the kettledrums or tympani, huge copper "kettles" across which sheepskin or calfskin has been stretched. They are sounded by striking with sticks that have large felt ends. The tympani have definite pitch, which can be changed by controlling screws or foot pedals. They are used to build up the orchestral volume of sound, for dramatic suspense, for thunderous climaxes. Nothing portends so fully the sense of death or doom as a roll on the muffled drum. On the other hand, this instrument can be stirring and lively.

The snare or side drum is the ordinary small military drum; its crisp, rattling tone is almost invariably associated with martial effects. The bass drum, familiar through its use in the dance orchestra, provides the regular beat for the military march as well as special effects, such as thunder or artillery.

The rest of this group includes a wide assortment of instruments, such as the tambourine, associated with Gypsy and Spanish music; the various primitive or Oriental drums, used to give the atmosphere of exotic music; and the castanets, whose clacking sound is an indispensable part of the Spanish dance.

The cymbals are large, slightly cupped disks of brass which, when struck together, produce an intensely dramatic effect. They add greatly to the excitement of orchestral climaxes.

The triangle, a metal bar bent into the shape of a triangle, when struck with a small metal rod, produces a light, tinkling sound.

The gong is a large disk of hammered metal, generally brass, of Chinese origin. When fairly struck with a large felt-headed stick it gives forth an ominous, metallic sound; but when softly struck it gives a mysterious effect.

The xylophone (pronounced zī′lȯ-fōn) consists of a series of tuned wooden bars or slabs of various lengths that are struck with two wooden mallets. It has a hollow, clanking sound, and is used with excellent effect in Saint-Saëns' DANSE MACABRE (Dance of Death) to imitate the rattling of the bones of the skeletons as they dance on the tombstones. (See Chapter XIII.)

Chimes are tubular bells suspended from a metal frame and struck with a hammer. They reproduce the tolling of bells.

Glockenspiel, or orchestra bells, consist of a set of steel or aluminum horizontal bars arranged ladderlike in two parallel rows, sometimes operated from a keyboard, more often played with two wooden hammers. They add a bright bell-like quality to the orchestral fabric.

The celesta, invented by August Mustel of Paris in the last quarter of the nineteenth century, is described in detail in the next section, in connection with Tchaikovsky's Nutcracker Suite, where it is used as a solo instrument for the first time in the *Dance of the Sugar Plum Fairy*. (See page 153.)

In addition to these percussion instruments, there is a varied assortment of whistles, rattles, wind machines, and similar noisemakers to create all the special effects that the intricate scores of a modern symphonic work may demand.

The piano is a stringed instrument in which the tone is produced by little hammers controlled by a keyboard. Technically, it is a percussion instrument. Pianists, however, vehemently disclaim any kinship with the family that includes the drum. We may sidestep the issue by listing the piano as a keyboard instrument, and let it go at that.

Since the piano can play both melody and accompaniment, it developed into a solo instrument (see Chapter XXVI), and as such has not been considered an integral part of the symphonic ensemble. Modern composers, however, are increasingly attracted by its percussive possibilities, which fit in with their prevailing moods, and are including it more and more often in their orchestral scores.

Arrangement of the orchestra

We may take the personnel of the Boston Symphony Orchestra as fairly representative of our great ensembles. There are 103 players: 63 strings, 16 woodwinds, 15 brass, 7 percussion, and 2 harps. Thus, the string choir amounts to about three-fifths of the total; the woodwinds and brass somewhat less than one-fifth each.

The strings contain 16 first and 16 second violins, 12 violas, 10 'cellos, and 9 double basses. The woodwinds contain 3 flutes, 1 doubling on piccolo; 2 oboes; 2 English horns; 3 clarinets, 1 doubling on bass clarinet; and 3 bassoons, 1 doubling on the contrabassoon. The brass has 6 French horns, 4 trumpets, 4 trombones and 1 tuba. The percussion has 2 kettledrums, or tympani; 3 in the battery, which includes the various small percussion instruments; and 1 celesta.

While each conductor varies the seating plan of his group to suit the acoustics of a hall or his personal taste, the general arrangement is more or less uniform. The orchestra is arranged in a huge semicircle about the conductor, who stands on a small platform or podium, directing with his baton. The various instruments are arranged in groups so as to blend properly.

SYMPHONY ORCHESTRA SEATING PLAN OF A NOVEL AND EXPERIMENTAL NATURE AS HAS BEEN USED BY LEOPOLD STOKOWSKI.

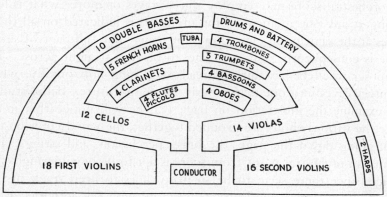

SYMPHONY ORCHESTRA SEATING PLAN OF A CONVENTIONAL TYPE GENERALLY USED BY ARTURO TOSCANINI AND MANY OTHER CONDUCTORS.

Orchestration

Writing for a full orchestra is no mean art. The composer must not only create his melodies; he must hear them in his imagination in the particular timbre, or tone color, of each single instrument or combination of instruments, selecting and blending his colors to achieve the exact shade he desires. He must know what theme will sound more effective on one group of instruments, and what on another.

He must be familiar with the personality, with the technical peculiarities, of each instrument, and assign to it only what it can do best. These are but a few of the problems in orchestration, the art of writing for orchestra. The popular notion that composers create their music at the piano and then arrange it for orchestra is altogether inaccurate. Although they may use a piano to assist them, composers generally hear their themes, to begin with, in a certain timbre. In this respect they differ from many writers of jazz music, who merely pick out their tunes on the piano and leave the orchestration to the arranger who specializes in that technique. Art composers, on the other hand, consider their orchestration as much an expression of their creative personalities as the melody itself. Indeed, great composers have so distinctive a method of orchestrating that often an experienced listener will be able to recognize Beethoven, Wagner, or Tchaikovsky merely from the way the orchestra is handled.

Orchestral score

The actual writing out of the parts for the instruments is known as scoring; the parts are arranged one below the other in the score. In piano music there are but two staves, the treble and the bass. A modern orchestral score may employ thirty staves or more: what is happening at any one moment in the orchestra is indicated on all thirty staves at the same point clear down the page. The full page of such a score is consequently only one line, to be read straight across. The composer in effect has thirty threads stretching horizontally, which he interweaves into one marvelously intricate texture. If the student will examine the illustration on page 151, he will notice that in the score the various choirs are grouped together, the woodwinds on top, then, going down the page, the brass, percussion, and strings. Following an orchestral work from score is apt to be bewildering to the novice, since there seem to be so many lines to keep track of; but with a little practice one learns to keep up with the activities of the various choirs quite easily. Following from score then becomes a most revealing way of listening to a symphonic work.

II. The Orchestra in Action

The "Nutcracker Suite"

For a glimpse of the orchestra in action, we have chosen the perennially popular NUTCRACKER SUITE that Tchaikovsky arranged from his NUTCRACKER ballet. The music, written in 1891, only two years before his death when he was at the summit of his powers, reveals to us a master of delicate orchestral colors and nuances.

The scenario for the ballet was taken from the elder Dumas' version of a fairy tale by E. T. A. Hoffmann, the writer of fantastic stories who exercised so powerful an influence upon the composers of the nineteenth century, particularly Schumann, Berlioz, and Wagner, although he is known today chiefly through Offenbach's TALES

FIRST PAGE OF SCORE OF "DER FREISCHÜTZ" OVERTURE   *Weber*

OF HOFFMANN. The ballet centers about a little girl, Marie, and the wonderful dream that comes to her on Christmas Eve after everybody else has gone to sleep. The toys and sweetmeats around the Christmas tree come to life; the plain old nutcracker she has received for her gift turns into a handsome young prince. Together they fly away to the court of the Sugar-Plum Fairy, where all the sweetmeats and the flowers come to dance for the happy young lovers.

1. *Miniature Overture.* Tchaikovsky omitted the bass instruments —'cellos, double bass and lower brass—from his little overture, thus achieving a light and graceful effect.

The second theme, by contrast, is a flowing melody of simple quarter notes played legato by the violins. The music works up to a scintillating climax for full orchestra, after which both themes are repeated from the beginning with an even longer climax at the end.

Notice that in order to achieve the effect of intensification upon which the climax is built, the music grows louder and faster, and mounts to the higher, more brilliant pitches. These are the three ways most frequently used to build an effective orchestral climax. It will be instructive to observe how the different composers use these ways.

The shrill pitches in high register evoke a sharper response from our nervous systems than do the low, mellow tones. For this reason, a climb to the upper register always produces an effect of intensification of emotion or brilliance of color. Conversely, a descent to the low register gives the impression of slackening, of fading color.

2. *March.* The march, with its brave opening flourish on trumpets, horns, and clarinets, is a gaily strutting affair. Here Tchaikovsky uses the rhythmic figure that occurs so frequently in trumpet and bugle calls, the triplet indicated by a small figure 3 over the eighth notes:

The dainty groups of notes that alternate with the flourish serve to remind us that this is a march for twirling ballerinas rather than for ordinary mortals.

The second theme is built on another of those pirouetting, staccato motives so dear to the heart of Tchaikovsky. Three flutes and a clarinet are echoed by violins and violas. Then the first theme returns in regular A-B-A form, with the strings and flutes providing new "sliding" effects in the accompaniment.

3. *Dance of the Sugar-Plum Fairy.* Nothing so well reveals Tchaikovsky's love of picturesque instrumental effects as his excitement at discovering the celesta, which he introduced into the orchestral family through this piece. He wrote enthusiastically to his publisher in June, 1891, after his return from America, that he planned to incorporate music for the new instrument—described as something between a piano and a glockenspiel, possessing a divinely beautiful tone—into his ballet. He instructed that it be ordered from Paris where he had discovered it and delivered in St. Petersburg in utmost secrecy, since he feared that Rimsky-Korsakoff and Glazounov might learn of it and, by using its effects before he himself should have a chance to do so, rob him of the glory of introducing it and detract from the sensation he expected to create.

The celesta, a member of the percussion group, consists of a series of small steel bars or plates set in vibration by hammers which are controlled by a keyboard like the piano. It has a range of four octaves above middle C. Its silvery, liquid tone captures perfectly the spirit of the Bountiful Fairy of Hoffmann's tale.

After a short pizzicato introduction on the strings, the transparent harmonics come floating gently downward:

This is interspersed with guttural comments by the bass clarinet that give a truly bizarre effect. The brief middle section ends with a brilliant cadenza on the celesta. (A *cadenza* is a flowery passage interpolated in a composition in order to show off the technical resources of the solo instrument or performer. Notice that the rest of the or-

chestra is silent during the cadenza, so as to focus attention more upon
the featured player.) The cadenza leads back to the opening phrase,
now played an octave higher than before. We therefore have here
another example of three-part, or A-B-A form. Strings sound in the
background; the silvery fairy floats aloft for a brief space—and fades
away.

4. *"Trepak" (Russian Dance).* The *Trepak* brings us the full
orchestra in an outburst of furious activity. One can see the figures
bobbing up and down, arms akimbo, heels flying, in a folk dance of
vigorous accents:

A contrasting theme appears, the first returns, in a clear-cut A-B-A
pattern. The orchestration is brilliant throughout. Tambourines add
gaiety to the proceedings. Ever faster and louder, the dance mounts
to the brilliant upper register, and ends on a note of wild abandon.

5. *Arab Dance.* This number summons up the languor and allure
of the East. Muted violas and 'cellos introduce a droning figure in
the bass that is reiterated with a kind of hypnotic insistence, alternating between piano and pianissimo. A tom-tom throbs dully in the
distance. Against this somber background two clarinets and an English horn intone the mysterious opening chords. The melody itself is
sung by muted violins; there is but one theme, which rises and falls in
a broad languid curve.

Presently an oboe lets out a long piercing wail in that nasal manner
associated with Oriental song. The violas and 'cellos drone on and
on; the tom-tom continues to weave its spell; the music fades away to
the merest whisper, *ppppp.*

6. *Chinese Dance.* Flutes and piccolos running shrilly up the
scale, forte, impart to the next dance its "Chinese" flavor. The strings
answer, pizzicato, with a droll seriousness that reminds one of a Pooh-
bah bobbing up and down. Throughout, the bassoons keep up a
steady staccato beat deep in the bass.

If we compare the second theme with the first, we notice that it does everything Theme I does, but in the opposite direction. Where Theme I runs up the scale to a trill and then jumps down along the tones of the chord, Theme II runs down the scale to a trill and then jumps up along the scales of the chord; in other words, it is an inversion of Theme I:

This device, rather difficult to handle effectively, attests again to Tchaikovsky's mastery of the technical resources of his art.

After the inversion, the theme is heard in its original form, giving us an A-B-A pattern. The music works up in a steady crescendo to the climax, fortissimo; and comes to an abrupt end.

7. *Dance of the Toy Flutes*. Next comes one of Tchaikovsky's happiest inspirations. A brief "vamp till ready" introduction leads to the airy tune of staccato sixteenth notes played by three flutes, piano. This sparkling music captures the very spirit of the dance. After a fragment of legato melody sung by the English horn, the theme is repeated:

The middle section, in contrast to the opening, lies in a lower register and is given to the brass choir. Here we have a famous passage for muted trumpet, the theme of sixteenth notes rising and falling in a gentle swell. After this, we return to the melody of the flutes in a clear three-part, or ternary, form.

8. *Waltz of the Flowers*. The *Waltz of the Flowers* has taken its place beside Johann Strauss' *Blue Danube* and *Tales From the Vienna Woods* as one of the world's beloved waltzes. Here we have Tchai-

kovsky's gifts as a ballet composer—a feeling for beautiful melody, for flowing line and the sheer excitement of movement—at their best. The gracious opening theme of the horns, the gay second theme with its suggestion of swirling figures, the middle section, which veers to a tender melancholy—all breathe a gentle nostalgia. True, these flowers grew amidst red plush and crystal chandeliers, and the world out of which they stemmed never really was as we have pictured it. No matter—they bring us the gentle aroma of their period preserved for us by a master of sentiment.

The introduction contains an elaborate cadenza for the harp, built of arpeggios, or broken chords. The reader should distinguish, incidentally, between an arpeggio and a scale. A *scale* is a series of neighboring tones. But an *arpeggio* is built of the tones of a chord, which do not necessarily lie next to each other. In a scale, therefore, we proceed stepwise, while in an arpeggio we jump along the tones of the chord.

After the final arpeggios of the cadenza fade in a gradual diminuendo, the French horns announce the suave waltz theme, softly, as from a distance:

French Horns (an octave lower)
Clarinet Solo

With the second theme, the swaying waltz movement gathers momentum. Notice how the string choir alternates with the woodwinds in a kind of dialogue—a favorite device in orchestration. Presently the first theme returns, A-B-A, embroidered with a charming countermelody.

The middle section opens with a graceful theme played by the flute and oboe, with the violins gliding downward in a countermelody. Now a lyrical melody emerges deep down in the violas and 'cellos. In returning to the preceding theme, Tchaikovsky cleverly reverses his orchestration: the violins carry the melody, while flutes and oboes glide downward in the countermelody. The middle section is therefore also an A-B-A pattern.

The first section is repeated substantially as before and worked up to a brilliant climax. The movement is accelerated, the volume increased; the orchestra rises steadily into the bright upper register, *fff*, overflowing with animation and brilliant color, bringing the ballet to a triumphant finale.

In form, the waltz presents us with an extended A-B-A structure in which each section is itself an A-B-A. This ingenious construction might be diagrammed as

$$
\begin{array}{ccc}
A & B & A \\
\cdot & \cdot & \cdot \\
\cdot & \cdot & \cdot \\
\cdot & \cdot & \cdot \\
aba & cdc & aba
\end{array}
$$

Notice how, throughout the suite, all the elements are combined—lilting melody, rich and vivid harmonies, compelling rhythms, simple, clear-cut structures, and imaginative orchestral coloring—into one unified effect.

For further introduction to the varied color palettes of the orchestra, listen to Saint-Saëns' clever suite, the CARNIVAL OF THE ANIMALS, which contains, among other numbers of interest, the popular and lovely 'cello and harp composition, *The Swan*. These may be supplemented by playing over the commercially prepared record series, "Instruments of the Symphony Orchestra," and similar sets that are generally available. (Consult your record catalog.) Get so you can "spot" any instrument of the orchestra as soon as it sounds. Perhaps you will become proficient enough to analyze several different instruments playing together—that is a real challenge to anyone, no matter how well educated musically he may be! Of course, the listener is urged to hear these instruments in the regular symphony concerts whenever possible—there is a wide difference in quality of sound between records, the radio, and the actual concert performance, even under the most favorable circumstances. (We have not included here an extended list of "Additional Suggestions for Listening," for most of the remainder of the text is an application of the ideas and principles enunciated in this chapter.)

Chapter XII

CLASSIC AND ROMANTIC ELEMENTS IN ART

OF THE several approaches an artist may choose to make toward his material, at least two or three seem more basic and elemental than the others. There is always the *Realistic*, or more or less exact imitation of nature, approach; but let us set that aside for a future chapter, leaving the two others for immediate discussion.

Thus, on the one hand, the artist may seek to give expression to the emotional experiences of mankind in their widest, most universal aspect. He will try to remain as objective as possible toward his material, fashioning it into the most polished, most enduring, shape. He will be concerned not only with what he says—the content—but also with the perfection of the manner of saying it—the form. If he is a composer, he will be deeply involved with developing tonal design and metamorphosis of germinal musical ideas as such to the utmost of their potentialities. Fundamentally, this creator is the artist-philosopher, whose duty it is to present rather than to question, to affirm rather than to rebel. He will exercise restraint, present emotion "recollected in tranquility"; he will aim for the conventional (in the best sense of the word) rather than for striking effects. He will work within established traditions, bringing them to a higher level, rather than striking out into new paths. Chastity of style, harmony, or outline, simplicity, balance, and self-control—these will be foremost among his ideals. In short, such a creator will be a *Classicist*.

Let us ponder a bit over that term, "classical"; but first let us try to define it somewhat broadly and, if possible, so as to include as many of the fine arts as we can. The dictionary tells us that *classical* means "resembling, modeled after, or in the spirit of, the highest forms of ancient Roman or Greek art." Thus, one might deduce that any art created since that time which embraces or is influenced by a style or temper similar to that which prompted, or characterizes, those ancient art works, may be said to be "classical." (Be careful to distinguish between the words "classic" and "classical"—consult an unabridged dictionary. Also bear in mind that each art medium will have its own peculiarities and that, in music especially, there will be many unique values.)

We refer you now to the picture of our "National Capitol Building" at Washington, D. C., page 48. You will see that there are unmistakable evidences of ancient Greek and Roman influences in this product of the Classical Revival during colonial times. Compare the Capitol building with the *Parthenon*, considered by many to be "the

COURTESY OF THE UNIVERSITY PRINTS, NEWTON, MASS.

THE PARTHENON FROM THE NORTHWEST   (*From a photograph*)

most complete example of the Doric style in temple architecture ever built." [1] This celebrated old temple was built by Iktinos and Kallikrates from the years 447 to 432 B.C.; it gives eloquent evidence to the highest degree of designing and building skill, and it is no wonder that it has been the marvel and inspiration of the entire western world for the past 2400 years—so much so that the building, though a mere ruin, may be considered the very symbol of perfection. Here, in a

---

[1] Read Chapters III and IV of *Art in the Western World* by David M. Robb and J. J. Garrison (New York: Harper and Brothers, 1942).

single edifice, are exemplified: the perfect consonance of purpose and design, the attractive severity of line and surface, the epitome and triumph of mathematical and formal perfection, a monument to impersonal and epochal expression, a model of quiet serenity and nobility without pomp and overindulgence of fancy; and there are also exemplified minutely calculated effects that never become ostentatious or conspicuous in themselves. Finally, one can see in the *Parthenon* the ideal achievement in the relationship between the separate parts and the whole. Such richness of virtues was destined to fire the ideals of beauty in man in all the fine arts through twenty-five centuries, and to serve him as a perpetual model for those attributes he has chosen to call the spirit or temper of "classicism." [2]

Now let us look at the reproduction of the classical painting, "Orpheus and Eurydice" (page 161), by the French artist, Nicolas Poussin (1594-1665). The subject matter, or literary content, of this story has served as the basis for more operas than has any other. It is a classical tale, in the exact sense, and it is "told" in such a way that moral, intellectual, and emotional elements are set forth with utmost clarity of means. There is in this picture the positive spirit of the ideal perfection, and the absence of excessive sensuality and flamboyance. Although the artist was not without influence from the early spirit of the *Baroque* (see page 399), he steadfastly held to the ideals of beauty as passed on by ancient cultures. He strove to create paintings that evidenced harmony, concord, and masterly control rather than turbulence, discord, and ecstatic emotional expression. His figures seem to be enlivened Greek statues—note the postures, as though they were arrested gestures during a dignified and graceful Greek dance. Poussin seeks to charm the appreciator, to mollify rather than to startle by novelty or shock by boldness of expression; all is polished perfection, as near as he could achieve the ideal.

In striving for such ideals, Poussin was not unlike Corneille and Racine in the theater, wherein man asserted his mastery over himself and his mundane fate through the control of his emotions and actions by the intellect—really an ancient "classical" idea. So the paintings of Poussin reflect that same kind of control and mastery of one's emotional expressions by means of a well-ordered and meticulously executed plan or design. Nothing was left to chance or to momentary

---

[2] By the word "temper" we mean "The quality of mind with reference to the passions, emotion, or affections; nature or disposition of; medium; organization; form." See the *Standard Dictionary*. We also use the words "spirit," "tendency," "element," "character," throughout the text as closely akin in meaning.

ORPHEUS AND EURYDICE *Poussin.*

extemporization. He was consciously concerned with making everything he painted exemplary of the characteristic rather than of the transient incident, or exception, or personalized interpretation—a trait also marked in the aspects of conventionality that exist in "classical" music. We must observe, however, that though the emphasis is on the formal manner rather than free fancy, the latter is by no means absent; it remains a matter of control and degree of emphasis. One is reminded of some of the artistic ideals of the Renaissance. Internal units of design, as in the *Parthenon*, are subordinate but organically contributory to the whole. Here, in "Orpheus and Eurydice," are those qualities which have provoked the term "heroic landscape." It is unlike any scene one may have witnessed; rather, it is the ideal and perfect landscape for the setting of the picture.

On the other hand, the artist may seek to project his own personality into his art, to view the world about him through the lens of intense personal feeling. He will be proudly subjective and proclaim his very differentness from other men. He will revolt against the established order of things, a passionate rebel against all traditions and forms. He will stress feeling rather than reflection; content rather than form (though he will not abandon the latter, by any means); and he will hanker after what is strange and picturesque. Giving free rein to his imagination, he will prefer the bizarre and the particular to the serene and the universal. He will seem to lean toward mysticism and fervor rather than toward lucidity and discipline of the intellect; yet he will not be devoid of the latter. Technic and design will not be ends in themselves; instead, they will be the means for the projection of his individual, intensely emotional utterance. He will be novel, bold, and individual rather than characteristic and conventional. In short, such a creative artist would represent the *Romantic temper* in art; he would be a *Romanticist*.

Here again, it is best that we seek to define our terms as much as possible. The dictionary tells us that the romantic is: "founded upon or influenced by what is extravagantly ideal; sentimental rather than rational; visionary; pertaining to or suggestive of the strange and fantastic; picturesque, imaginative, wild (*sic!*), fictitious, dreamy, . . ." Compare these attributes with those we have just discussed in "classicism." No doubt extended and varied experience in the appreciation of actual art works of both schools will prove to be better definers than our old and constant friend, the Dictionary.

At any rate, let us first consider the reproduction of the picture, "The Abduction of Rebecca" (see page 163), by another French

COURTESY OF THE METROPOLITAN MUSEUM OF ART, NEW YORK

ABDUCTION OF REBECCA   *Delacroix*

painter, Ferdinand V. Eugene Delacroix (1798-1863). Here is action, drama, force, conflict, novelty, and what might well be called ordered disorder. The picture is a highly personalized expression in which a certain deliberate indefiniteness of line and form contrast strongly with the type of drawing we ordinarily see in classic realism. Delacroix has put into the picture novel and highly imaginative contents (plastic as well as literary); he has provided striking contrasts in design and composition, and he has used color in a vivid and dynamically moving manner. Rather than trying to conform to an ideal or a convention (which is another way of saying general acceptance of an ideal), the painter has projected a very individualized picture, and he has expressed it in a manner and with the means that best suited his fancy at the moment. He is not moralizing; yet he is telling a story, and with it he is giving one a psychological insight into the characters of the drama in a most uncanny manner. Over all, the picture involves an extra-plastic art—literature. The exciting moment of the tale that he desires to depict is evidently of greater importance to him than the traditional classical perfection of details of line and form, or faithfulness to reality and regularity. Yet all these elements may be found in the picture, to a degree and well subordinated. Finally, the onlooker is a much more active "participant" in the picture than is the case with the Poussin work.

One is quite right in considering Delacroix the leader of the French Romantic "school"; by means of the high flights of his poetic imagination, one has a fleeting glimpse into the future, yes, even into our own day—and one might just as truthfully say the same of Poussin!

There are a number of common attributes in the two schools we have discussed, and a number that are opposite ends of the same pole; there are also a few that are unique in each instance, though these are very few indeed. The reader will do well to emulate the mystery-story teller by "enumerating at this point" the stylistic attributes that are peculiar to each type, those that are conflicting and, most important, those that differ largely through combinations and accents. Let us develop some of these ideas still further.

Nineteenth-century critics, sharing the love of their age for neat, water-tight classifications, used the labels *classic* and *romantic* with much assiduity; with the result that there emerged two concepts or styles that were then considered diametrically opposed to each other —the first rigidly excluding the second. Yet it takes little reflection to understand that each might be a complement of the other; that neither exists often in pure form; that, on the contrary, the classic and the romantic often co-exist; and that the differences between them are often due to the degree of emphasis of values rather than complete opposition of kind. Indeed, one is frequently impressed by the fact that both tempers are present in the same artist. There are strong Romantic elements in the works of such Classicists as Virgil, Corneille, David, and Haydn. Conversely, there are powerful Classical tendencies at work in the art of such Romanticists as Millet, Swinburne, or

Brahms. The composer who is most often held up as the epitome of the Classical spirit, Mozart, wrote measures that, for sheer emotional expressiveness and imagination, have not their superior in all music; while such figures as Shelley or Chopin, who are with equal consistency represented as types of the Romantic artist, display in their finest work a purity of form, a mastery of technique and design, that bear comparison with the great figures of the Classical school.

Equally misleading is the practice of labeling a period either *Classic* or *Romantic,* and then forcing everything created within the period to fit the label. So often has the eighteenth century been marked off as the special province of the Classical spirit in art, and the nineteenth relegated to the Romantic, that the student is likely to get the impression that between 1799 and 1801 Classicism died and Romanticism came into being. The error will be avoided if we consider the two tendencies as signposts revealing general trends, with generous overlappings on both sides, rather than as rigid categories. Actually, the eighteenth century—the age that saw the culmination of Classical form in music in the symphony—produced such utterly unclassical works as Rousseau's *Autobiography,* Hogarth's "Shrimp Girl," Mozart's *Abduction from the Seraglio,* the lyrics of Robert Burns, the poetry and drawings of William Blake. On the other hand, the qualities that we lump together under the general concept of Romanticism —the intensely subjective approach to life, the emphasis upon deep feeling, the revolt against arbitrarily imposed restraints, the preoccupation with the supernatural and the picturesque—being of the very essence of man's personality, have flourished in one form or another throughout all periods, and may be found, now stronger, now weaker, from the Psalms, Homer, and Sophocles, to Virgil and Catullus; from Dante and Petrarch to Michelangelo and Dürer; from Shakespeare and Rembrandt, Bach and Haydn, to Goethe, Schubert, Beethoven, and the moderns.

The point that emerges from all this analysis is that classifications in music, poetry, or painting cannot and should not be applied as rigidly as in botany, zoology, or chemistry. If used with circumspection, such labels as *Classic* and *Romantic* are most helpful in giving us insight into the nature of art and a better appreciation of the style of the artist and his relation to his epoch. But the concepts must always remain flexible, fluid, and dynamic; otherwise they will lead us to a static attitude that is alien to the nature of art. Such connotations should be aids rather than stumbling blocks, or they would be better left unused.

The distinction between Classical and Romantic has been connected with an exaggerated distinction between form and content. It has been pointed out again and again that the Classical artist subordinated content to form, while the Romantic artist subordinated form to content. Since, in discussing so abstract a matter as style in art, there is an habitual temptation to drive the point home by exaggerating the distinctions behind it, the stress on these combinations of form and content inevitably led to the notion that the Classical artist was all form and no emotion, while the Romantic artist was all emotion and no form. No art work can exist if it possesses only one of the elements. A work given form without feeling and inspiration is no more than a technical stunt and has neither life nor meaning. Witness the thousands of perfectly formed fugues, sonatas, and symphonies composed by well-meaning musicians who followed all the rules but had nothing vital to say, that have been relegated to the oblivion they so richly deserved. Conversely, unless the artist can channel his emotion and direct it into a communicable art form, his work will be an incoherent jumble of rapture and exclamation points.

As applied to Western European art, the terms *Classical* and *Romantic* generally refer to the two great art styles that prevailed in the second half of the eighteenth and the whole of the nineteenth century and that were separated by the gigantic social upheaval brought about by the French Revolution. It can readily be seen why the eighteenth century, dominated by an ultraconservative aristocracy, has come to be known in the history of human thought as the *Age of Reason,* and in the history of art, as the *Age of Classicism.* The nobility of the old regime, that semifeudal agricultural aristocracy whose power was soon to be overthrown by the rising industrial and mercantile *bourgeoisie,* had brought the business of living to the level of a fine art. The accent was definitely on correct form rather than on deep feeling, on the manner rather than on the matter. Emotion was channeled within the confines of an exquisite art just as brooks were channeled within the balanced landscape of a formal garden. The artist working under the system of patronage had to satisfy the fastidious tastes of his noble benefactor. He did not lack either deep feeling or imaginative power. But within the prevailing social framework it was inevitable that he placed enormous emphasis on the chiseled line, the exquisite finish, the restrained manner, the serene and objective vision that have come to be associated with Classical art.

The nineteenth century, on the other hand, presented a completely different picture. The aristocracy had been supplanted in power by the *bourgeoisie;* the cult of personal freedom, of aggressive individualism, had taken hold of the new industrial society. The world-shaking slogan of the Revolution—Liberty, Equality, Fraternity—released forces that had been pent up for centuries; the artificialities and restraints of the old order were swept aside. Emancipated from his subservience to kings and courts, the artist now addressed an audience of his social equals. He could dare to be himself, to express his innermost feelings, to defy the stifling conventions. Intensity of feeling and picturesque effect were his natural idiom, as the classic style had been the natural idiom of his predecessor. The difference of expression did not mean that he was not as careful a craftsman, as great a master of technique, as the eighteenth-century artist. It meant simply that his interest in technique was subordinated, owing to the prevailing social pattern of the age, to the emotional and subjective, to the Romantic elements of artistic expression.

We may get a good insight into the relative values of the two idioms if we compare the didacticism, the impersonality, the objective "sweet reasonableness" of a passage such as the closing lines of Pope's *Essay on Man,* written in the 1730's and characteristic of the Age of Reason:

> Submit: in this or any other sphere,
> Secure to be as blessed as thou canst bear;
> Safe in the hand of one disposing Power,
> Or in the natal or the mortal hour.
> All Nature is but Art unknown to thee;
> All chance, direction, which thou canst not see;
> All discord, harmony not understood;
> All partial evil, universal good;
> And spite of Pride, in erring Reason's spite,
> One truth is clear, *Whatever is, is right.*

with the passionate lyricism, the subjectivity and intense feeling of a poem such as Shelley's "Ode to the West Wind," which has so often been cited as the quintessence of the romantic attitude:

> Oh! lift me as a wave, a leaf, a cloud!
> I fall upon the thorns of life! I bleed!
> A heavy weight of hours has chained and bowed
> One too like thee—tameless, and swift, and proud. . . .

Or Heine's poignant:

> Out of my great, great sorrow
> I make my little songs. . . .

Or Byron's bitter:

> I have thought
> Too long and darkly, till my brain became,
> In its own eddy boiling and o'erwrought,
> A whirling gulf of phantasy and flame:
> And thus, untaught in youth my heart to tame,
> My springs of life were poisoned.

Or the no less significant hymn to the night in the love scene of Wagner's TRISTAN AND ISOLDE with its longing for oblivion:

> O sink down upon us, night of love,
> Let us now forget that we live,
> Take us up within your arms,
> Free us forever from the world!

Or Rousseau's defiant: "I am different from all the men I have ever seen; if I am not better, at least I am different!" Here we have the prevailing attitudes of the romantic artist. So, too, we might compare the delicate landscapes with their nymphs and shepherdesses of Watteau and Fragonard with the grand sweep and melodrama of the canvases of Delacroix and Géricault; or the exquisite finish of an early minuet by Haydn or Mozart with the surge and thunder of a composition by Wagner or Tchaikovsky.

The Romantic Movement in Music[3]

We have drawn a distinction between the spirit, or temper, of Classicism, and a contrasting spirit, or temper, of Romanticism as concepts in art that are limited to no one century; and the Age of Classicism and the Romantic Period as the epochs when the qualities associated with either one or the other tendency appeared to predominate. For the music lover, the Romantic Movement is of particular interest, since practically nine-tenths of the music we hear today was either inspired by it or came under its influence. To begin with, the two masters who are most often held out as perfect examples of the Classical style, Mozart and Haydn, showed strong Romantic characteristics, especially in the works written in the latter part of their careers. Mozart died in 1791, two years after the beginning of the

---

[3] Essential listening for this chapter includes: *Minuet* from SYMPHONY IN E FLAT by Mozart; *Liebestod* music from TRISTAN AND ISOLDE by Wagner; and the Overture-Fantasy, ROMEO AND JULIET, by Tchaikovsky.

French Revolution; Haydn did some of his most important work in the following decade.

Beethoven, Weber, and Schubert encompassed the transition from the Classical style to the spirit of the new century. Mendelssohn, Chopin, and Schumann saw the full unfolding of the Romantic Movement. Wagner, Liszt, Berlioz became the prophets of mid-nineteenth-century Romanticism. Brahms, Tchaikovsky, Grieg, Dvořák, Smetana, César Franck, Moussorgsky, Rimsky-Korsakoff, Saint-Saëns, Massenet, Gounod, Bizet, Verdi, Puccini, Elgar, Mac-Dowell—these composers are of the Romantic Movement. One need not extend the list to make it apparent that for all practical purposes the general public of today still lives, musically speaking, in the Romanticism of the nineteenth century. And even after the twilight of Romanticism, when the interlude known as post-Romanticism bridged the gap between the nineteenth and twentieth century, the outstanding men—Sibelius, Richard Strauss, Debussy, Ravel, Falla, and their compeers—still preserved in new guise many of the influences of nineteenth-century Romanticism.

In the following chapters, we shall study in detail a number of compositions that exemplify various characteristics of musical Romanticism. As an introduction, let us now listen to and compare an example of the Classical style such as the *Minuet* from Mozart's SYMPHONY IN E-FLAT MAJOR, with a piece of Romantic music such as the *Liebestod* from Wagner's TRISTAN AND ISOLDE. The choice of such extreme examples of the two styles will the more clearly demonstrate the differences between them.

Perhaps the first thing that strikes us, as we listen to the two compositions, is the fact that Wagner's orchestra is so much larger than Mozart's—a fact due to the tremendous increase in symphonic resources during the Romantic Period. From this increased size of orchestra there spring several other differences. Wagner's orchestral writing is much more involved than is Mozart's. Where Mozart's is a wonderful example of economy of means, Wagner piles on his effects with a lavish hand. Mozart relies in the main on his string section with an occasional touch of color from the woodwinds and brasses. Wagner revels in the timbres of clarinet, oboe, flute, bassoon, and in the sonorities of the brass, and the sweep and power of the strings. The dynamic range in Wagner's music, the contrast between soft and loud, and the intensity of the climax, are naturally much greater in the Romantic master than in the Classical. The *Minuet* represents a simple and limpid texture; the *Liebestod*, on the other hand, is an elaborate tonal tapestry of great opulence and splendor. It should not be assumed that the characters of these two works mark all the works of Wagner and Mozart as being similarly differentiated.

In regard to form, the *Minuet* consists of regular phrases and periods and sections all stemming out of a clear-cut, four-measure structure. In contrast, Wagner's music sweeps forward with either no segmentation at all, or with sections that run together in a continuous movement. In Mozart, the qualities of symmetry, balance, and contrast are presented in a graceful, easily perceived architecture. In Wagner, there is a mighty flow of sound, as of a current that threatens to surge over its banks. Mozart's writing stays securely within the key; that is to say, it is predominantly diatonic. Whatever modulations there may be are carefully prepared and negotiated. Wagner modulates continually in a restless chromaticism charged with emotion. Mozart's harmony is in the main consonant; the discords are placed at strategic points and resolved almost immediately; the prevailing mood is one of well-being and satisfaction. Wagner's harmony, on the other hand, abounds in dissonance, in active tones left palpitating in suspension, in all the accents of despair and longing. Mozart is suave and urbane, restrained and rationally objective; his melody is crystal clear, his harmony transparent. Wagner is tragic, sensuous, and passionate. Mozart's is a music of pure beauty and delicate emotion, a song of sunlight and sensibility; Wagner's is a music of night, of ecstasy, of strange and hidden things.

Between these two extremes are innumerable shadings where one may find the characteristics of one style imperceptibly blending with those of the other. It is the combination of the many factors involved that produces the total stylistic effect. Through the detailed analysis of the compositions we shall examine in the next chapters, as well as of others that the reader might hear, it is hoped that he will gain an insight into the manner in which the composer manipulates and combines the various elements and concomitants of style, and will thus become sensitive to the subtle and distinctive quality of the great art styles in music—Classical and Romantic, Baroque, Impressionistic, post-Romantic and Contemporary, and the three basic and universal tempers of Classicism, Romanticism, and Realism.

Program music

One of the most important developments in the Romantic Movement was that, under its influence, music moved closer to its sister arts, poetry and painting. Composers chose to tell stories, to paint scenes, and to convey general poetic ideas and moods. Such literary and pictorial influences provided an enormous stimulus to the writing of program music—music, that is, with a story or synopsis attached to it.

From the beginnings of the art, composers had often turned out musical imitations of birds, brooks, battles, and hunting scenes. It was in the nineteenth century, however, that the descriptive and narrative tendencies emerged to a position of general dominance in European music. For this reason, even though program music in no sense originated in the nineteenth century, it has come to be considered one of the most characteristic developments of the Romantic Movement in music.

Program music is to be distinguished from *absolute*, or *pure*, music in which the composer attached no specific literary or pictorial connotations to his themes, but worked them out in purely musical terms.[4] Thus, Beethoven's FIRST SYMPHONY or Mozart's SONATA IN A MAJOR are examples of absolute music; Liszt's *Faust* SYMPHONY, Tchaikovsky's *Overture-Fantasy* ROMEO AND JULIET are examples of program music. The distinction between the two types is often a subtle one. Naturally, all music tells something to the listener. However, if the composer has given the listener no extramusical clue as to what he had in mind when he composed the music, no literary or pictorial association, actual or divined, we may consider it absolute or "pure" music. If, on the other hand, the composer indicates either through his title or through his remarks about the composition that he was influenced by or had in mind a definite literary, pictorial, or general poetic idea, we consider it program music.

For many years a fierce controversy raged among musical estheticians as to the respective merits of the two genres. The problem no longer seems as important as it once did. There is great absolute music as well as mediocre; there is great program music as well as mediocre. The chances are that if a composer has something worth while to say, he will say it no matter which style he is writing in. It is fairly apparent that, program or not, the music should be able to stand on its own feet as good music and to be appreciated as such. No program, however fanciful or picturesque, can supply imagination or power if the music itself is weak or dull. Certain composers,

---

[4] See article "Absolute Music" in Grove's *Dictionary*. Our use here is largely based on that definition. This term, though general, is unsatisfactory and leaves much to be desired. The best discussion is "On the Elements of Expression in Music" by Donald N. Ferguson, University of Minnesota, 1944.

as Beethoven and Brahms, seemed to gravitate more naturally toward the absolute type; their musical imagination seemed to function best when unhampered by extramusical associations. On the other hand, some like Wagner, Liszt, and their disciple, Richard Strauss, appeared to need the stimulus of a literary or pictorial program to spur them on to creation. Still others, like Tchaikovsky and Sibelius, have written copiously in both genres.

For our immediate and particular purpose, the program has a definite value. The person who has thought all his life in terms of verbal language in which each word has a concrete meaning inevitably feels bewildered when confronted with a language that consistently avoids all specific connotations. "But what does it mean?" is his first reaction. By tackling program music first, instead of absolute, we can reduce this bewilderment to a minimum. The pictorial and literary associations will assist the student through the initial period while he is still learning the vocabulary and the meaning of absolute musical expression. After that he will be free either to lean on the composer's story, or supply his own, or do without any at all.

If the enormously increased "programming" of music was the most striking characteristic of the art during the Romantic Movement, it will be found that the program was generally of the kind that fitted in with the prevailing literary mood of the period. We shall discuss this problem at greater length in the chapter on Franz Liszt (see Chapter XVI). At this point we may observe that the Romantic composers were influenced by the same poets from whom the literary Romanticists drew their inspiration, chief among them such figures as Shakespeare and Goethe, Dante and Schiller.

In the chapter on the orchestra we pointed out the enormous strides made in the art of orchestration during the nineteenth century. We can now see why these strides were made. In their search for new emotional effects, for picturesqueness and atmosphere, for brilliant and exotic coloring, the Romantic composers turned in far greater degree than did their Classical predecessors to the element of tone color as such. Certain general factors unquestionably helped: the mechanical improvements in instruments; the marked development of the orchestra in size and in the playing ability of its members; the general rise in the level of instrumental proficiency. In addition, there were important changes in the social conditions surrounding the making of music, such as the rise of a widespread middle class with an interest in the art, replacing the former patronage that had been limited to the nobility. With the rise of a music-hungry public, there came also the public concert as an important social institution, instead of the private musicales at the homes of the aristocracy that had characterized music-making in the eighteenth century. This public encouraged and was able to support orchestras much greater in size than those of the nobility; and the orchestra consequently forged ahead steadily in importance.

Yet, despite all these external encouragements, the central stimulus to the growth of the orchestral art lay in the very nature of the Romantic composer's attitude toward his art: in the exuberant emotionalism that demanded rich color effects and new expressive devices; in the unprecedented interest in the feelings evoked by the distinctive timbres of the different instruments and by strange combinations untried until then. We may therefore consider tone color—the reliance upon novel or picturesque orchestral effects—as the second outstanding characteristic of musical Romanticism; and we shall have frequent occasion to point out examples of it in the compositions we study.

Peter Ilyitch Tchaikovsky (1840-1893)

We begin our study of the Romantic style with a work by the composer who represents perhaps as fully as any other the spirit of late nineteenth-century Romanticism. Both in choice of subject and in spirit, the ROMEO AND JULIET OVERTURE fantasy exemplifies several important features of the program music of its time.

Biography

Peter Ilyitch Tchaikovsky was born at Kamsko-Votinsk in 1840, the son of a government official. He gave no early signs of his future eminence in music and did not, in fact, undertake serious musical study until after he had graduated from the School of Jurisprudence in St. Petersburg. For two years longer, while working in the Ministry of Justice, he vacillated between an official and musical career. At twenty-three, however, he made his decision, relinquished his post, and devoted himself rigorously to his studies in composition. In a letter to his sister he justified his choice, declaring that he must do the work for which he felt fitted. Whether he was to become a celebrated composer or merely a struggling teacher, his conscience would be clear and he would not grumble at his lot. In two years' time he completed his course at the Conservatoire of St. Petersburg and was awarded a silver medal for his setting of Schiller's "Ode to Joy."

For the next twelve years he occupied the post of professor of harmony at the newly founded Conservatoire at Moscow. The great pianist, conductor, and director of the Conservatoire, Nicholas Rubinstein, speedily recognized his pupil's gifts; he performed Tchaikovsky's works almost as soon as they were written. Slowly, doggedly, the young composer forged ahead. To this period of his life belongs the ROMEO AND JULIET OVERTURE, now one of the best beloved of his compositions, although it was hissed at Paris and Vienna when first performed; and the PIANO CONCERTO IN B-FLAT MINOR, which Rubinstein pronounced absolutely worthless and unplayable when he first saw it but which he later performed throughout Europe with the most brilliant success.

The Moscow period in Tchaikovsky's career came to an end in 1877 with his brief and unhappy marriage, followed by complete nervous collapse. The same year brought into his life Mme. Nadejda von Meck, the benefactress who for the next thirteen years supported him with a generous annuity, making it possible for him to give up his onerous duties at the Conservatoire and devote himself completely to composition. Their relationship forms one of the strangest chapters in musical biography. Although both lived in Moscow, they never met, carrying on their friendship through a series of intensely revealing letters. These, published in English by Mme. von Meck's grandniece and Catherine Drinker Bowen under the title of *Beloved Friend*, furnish an interesting sidelight on the composer's character and music.

From 1877 until his death in 1893 Tchaikovsky produced, in a steady stream, the works upon which his fame rests. Success did not come easily; but he was sustained by the devotion and encouragement of a little band of trusted friends and by the inner conviction that his music would ultimately come into its own. In the last years of his life he overcame his almost morbid fear of strangers sufficiently to undertake concert tours and popularize his works; and he had the satisfaction of seeing himself become a European figure. In 1891 he was invited to come to America to conduct the opening concert at Carnegie Hall. Two years later, at the Jubilee celebration at Cambridge University, he was honored with the degree of Doctor of Music. He returned to Russia to finish his SIXTH SYMPHONY, the *Pathétique*, considered by many his greatest work; went to St. Petersburg to conduct it; fell ill with cholera a few days after the first performance; and died on November 6, 1893, at the age of 53.

If in his personal life Tchaikovsky was emotionally unstable, vacillating, hypersensitive and subject to severe spells of depression; if he could write: "To regret the past, to hope in the future, and never to be satisfied with the present—this is my life," in everything pertaining to his art he was the careful craftsman, the tireless and completely devoted worker for whom musical creation was the supreme function of living. A child of his age, only through music did he find the strength, the meaning, the sense of pattern that life itself denied to his overwrought temperament. The music written out of such compulsion is of necessity intensely subjective, sometimes to the point of morbidity; but it possesses a sincerity, an emotional exuberance, a richness of melody, and a brilliance of orchestral coloring that have endeared it to the broad masses of music lovers and made Tchaikovsky a century after his birth one of the most universally loved of composers. Nothing, surely, gives us so complete an insight into the intensely personal attitude of the man toward his art than the moving letter to Mme. von Meck in which he pays tribute to music:

You see, my dear friend, I am made up of contradictions, and I have reached a very mature age without resting upon anything positive, without having calmed my restless spirit either by religion or philosophy. Undoubtedly I should have gone mad but for music. Music is indeed the most beautiful of all Heaven's gifts to humanity wandering in the darkness. Alone it calms, enlightens, and stills our souls. It is not the straw to which the drowning man clings; but a true friend, refuge, and comforter, for whose sake life is worth living. Perhaps there will be no music in heaven. Well then, let us give our mortal life to it as long as it lasts.[5]

Overture fantasy "Romeo and Juliet" (1869)

Tchaikovsky was twenty-nine years old when he wrote the ROMEO AND JULIET OVERTURE. This was, indeed, the first work in which his creative personality fully revealed itself. After three-quarters of a century, it still remains as one of the peaks of Romantic program music—definitely conceived and built upon a literary story.

The Overture was dedicated to the composer Balakirev, the leader of the Russian nationalist school, who suggested the literary basis of the subject. Tchaikovsky seems to have had some trouble in getting started. Balakirev wrote him to keep trying:

First get enthusiastic over the scheme. Then arm yourself with galoshes and a walking-stick and go for a walk along the boulevards. Begin with the Nikitsky, let yourself be thoroughly saturated with your sub-

---

[5] Catherine Drinker Bowen and B. von Meck, *Beloved Friend*. (New York: Random House, 1937.)

ject; and I am convinced that by the time you reach the Stretensky
Boulevard some theme or episode will have come to you.[6]

The advice seems to have worked, for shortly afterward we find
Balakirev writing:

I am delighted that the child of your fancy has quickened. God grant
that it come to a happy birth. . . . Do send me what you have done so
far, and I promise not to make any remarks—good or bad—until the
thing is finished.[7]

When Tchaikovsky complied with this request, Balakirev wrote
back:

As your overture is all but finished, and will soon be played, I will tell
you what I think of it quite frankly. . . . The first subject does not
please me at all . . . it has neither strength nor beauty, and does not
sufficiently suggest the character of Friar Laurence. Here something
like one of Liszt's chorales, in the old Catholic Church style, would be
very appropriate. Your motive is of quite a different order, in the style
of a quartet by Haydn, that genius of "burgher" music that induces a
fierce thirst for beer.[8]

The famous Romeo theme—its lyric loveliness has survived even
a popular fox-trot version—Balakirev considered "very pretty, although rather colorless." The Juliet theme he called "simply fascinating."

I often play it, and could hug you for it. It has the sweetness of love,
its tenderness, its longing. . . . I have only one thing to say against this
theme: it does not sufficiently express a mystic, inward spiritual love, but
rather a fantastic passionate glow which has hardly any nuance of Italian
sentiment. Romeo and Juliet were not Persian lovers, they were Euro-
peans.

The first performance took place in 1870 at a concert of the
Moscow Musical Society. Unfortunately, Nicholas Rubinstein, who
conducted, had just been involved in a lawsuit concerning his right
to dismiss a student from the Conservatoire, and the entire musical
world of Moscow was on hand to demonstrate its solidarity with him.
A friend of Tchaikovsky's wrote:

---

[6] M. I. Tchaikovsky, *Life and Letters of Peter Ilyitch Tchaikovsky*. (New York:
Dodd, Mead and Company, 1924.)
[7] *Ibid.*
[8] *Ibid.* The three excerpts that follow are also from this work.

From the moment Rubinstein came on the platform until the end of the concert he received an extraordinary ovation. No one thought of the music; and I felt indignant that the first performance of "Romeo and Juliet" should have taken place under such conditions.

Tchaikovsky too was dispirited over the reception of his work:

My overture "Romeo and Juliet" had hardly any success here, and has remained quite unnoticed. . . . After the concert a group of us went to a restaurant. During the whole evening no one said a word to me about the overture. And yet I longed so for appreciation and kindness.

Considering that it is now one of the works upon which his fame most securely rests, the overture made its way into the European repertory with unbelievable slowness. In 1878 Tchaikovsky wrote to Mme. von Meck: "My overture . . . has been played in every capital, but always without success. In Vienna and Paris it was hissed; a short time ago it met with no better reception in Dresden!" At the end of the letter he eloquently affirmed his deep inner faith in the ultimate victory of his work:

If fame is destined for me, it will come with slow but sure steps. History convinces us that the success which is long delayed is often more lasting than when it comes easily and at a bound. . . . An artist should not be troubled by the indifference of his contemporaries. He should go on working and say all that he has been predestined to say. He should know that posterity alone can deliver a true and just verdict. . . . Perhaps I can accept my modest share of success with so little complaint because my faith in the judgment of the future is unshakable. I have a foretaste during my lifetime of the fame which will be meted out to me when the history of Russian music comes to be written. For the present I am satisfied with what I have already acquired. I have no right to complain. I have met some people on my way through life whose warm sympathy for my music more than compensates me for the indifference, misunderstanding and ill-will of the others.[9]

The word *overture* (from the French *ouvrir*, "to open") originally referred to an orchestral composition played as an introduction to an opera, oratorio, ballet, or play, which generally prepared the audience for what was to follow by presenting the principal themes of the work. Being essentially a "curtain raiser," the conventional overture was spirited, swift-moving, and closed with a rousing finale. Many overtures became so popular that they began to be performed at concerts independently of the opera or play for which they had been written. Some of them survived long after the work itself had been forgotten. From this custom was derived the second meaning of the word: a concert piece for symphony orchestra built around a strongly dramatic or pictorial theme and lending itself to brilliant and theatrical treatment. Whether the overture is an introduction to an opera or an independent concert piece can generally be determined from the title. Thus, *Overture* to TANNHÄUSER indicates the existence of an opera by that name; while 1812 OVERTURE or ROMEO AND JULIET OVERTURE refers to an independent concert piece built around a respective theme.

ANALYSIS. The Overture opens in the pale twilight of a medieval chorale symbolizing the good Friar Laurence. (A *chorale* is a simple, hymnlike tune.) The churchly chords are played in simple four-part harmony by two clarinets and two bassoons *andante quasi moderato*, (fairly slow, almost in moderate tempo), in quadruple meter:

The mysterious effect is enhanced by ethereal arpeggios on the harp. The chorale returns on the woodwinds with a running accompaniment in the strings. Gradually, with a *poco a poco accelerando* (faster little by little) and a steadily mounting crescendo, we are thrown into the fury and strife of the Feud theme, whose brusque, irregular accents aptly describe the ancient grudge and new mutiny of the Capulets and Montagues. The tempo is allegro; the theme is announced with the full orchestra in action, forte, and with those upward and downward sweeps on the violin that are so characteristic of Tchaikovsky's style:

A passage of mounting excitement through the running passages on the strings brings us the repetition of the Feud theme, this time fortissimo. Then the tumult dies; out of a tremulous background there emerges the love song of Romeo, with its broad lyric curve and poignant harmonies, sung by a solo English horn and muted violas. *mf, dolce* (sweetly) and *espressivo:*

This song is answered immediately by the Juliet theme on muted violins playing in four-part harmony. The strings are therefore divided—that is, they are not playing in unison. Lawrence Gilman remarks, "There are not many things in modern music more justly and beautifully expressive, more richly poetic, than the mood of the enraptured pair as they watch the coming of the dawn in Juliet's chamber."

The two themes are now repeated in a somewhat more developed form that closes the first section of the work.

In the middle section, the violins again take up their broad sweeps. The Feud theme is presented in an exciting development, with echoes of the Friar Laurence motive in the horns, as though warning of impending disaster. The mood of strife is built up through a gradual intensification until the entire orchestra is alive and seething. A broadly sweeping passage on the strings leads us into the third section, which recapitulates the thematic material of the first with important changes. The Feud theme is heard fortissimo, substantially as before. Then comes the Juliet music, *dolce espressivo* (sweetly expressive). And after that the Romeo theme is developed in one of those eloquent crescendos so dear to the heart of Tchaikovsky—wave upon wave of ingratiating sound, striving upward, accumulating, until the entire orchestra is surging forward in a mighty outpouring. The glow fades; stern outcroppings of the Feud theme carry us from the music of love to that which portends death. The epilogue is in a moderate pace, marked by the somber chorale of the prologue, while celestial arpeggios on the harp are heard above the muffled drum that beats a dirge for the dead and eternally faithful lovers. The spirit and mood of the Shakespearean play is thus told in the art of music by a master, in the spirit of Romanticism.

Chapter XIII

THE SYMPHONIC POEM:
TONE PAINTING, NARRATIVE, AND MOOD

W E HAVE just listened to an extended orchestral composition one purpose of which was to project through music the moods, emotions, and story suggested by a literary theme—the ROMEO AND JULIET OVERTURE by Tchaikovsky based on the play by Shakespeare. In spite of the fact that this story served as the basis for the overture and prescribed the sequence of events to a great extent, the composer was careful to see that the musical work had a structure and organization of its own, aside from the dictates of the underlying drama; and, in several instances where the sequence of events in the story were in conflict with what the composer considered desirable musical structure, the musical significance determined the issue. Thus, certain musical themes appeared, were contrasted and developed, and reappeared within a broadly traditional musical framework; and the composer gave these themes and the process of musical development an interest and importance in themselves. One can see here the workings of the classical as well as the romantic tempers.

The point becomes clear when we realize that in Shakespeare's play Friar Laurence appears in the middle of the play, while in the musical narrative the chorale symbolizing the Friar serves as prologue and epilogue. In short, the composer was guided by purely musical as well as literary considerations in the composition of his material—even if his themes possessed more or less precise symbolic literary connotations.

We now come to the most highly developed type of program music—the symphonic poem or tone poem—in which the form is completely free and determined to a great extent by the literary or pictorial program. Just as the symphony represents the highest level of organization in absolute music, the symphonic poem or tone poem is the most ambitious type of composition in program music. The symphony was perfected by the masters of late eighteenth-century

Classicism. Similarly, nineteenth-century Romanticism, with its strong admixture of literary and pictorial influences, turned enthusiastically to the symphonic poem.

A symphonic poem does through music what a poem does through words: it tells a story, paints a scene, describes or projects a mood, or presents a general poetic idea in musical symbols. The time was when the designation *symphonic poem* implied that the composition projected a story, and *tone poem* that it concerned itself principally with scene or mood; but now the two terms have become practically interchangeable. The symphonic poem has no fixed form, this being shaped in each case by the necessities of a particular program, with the transformation in the musical themes paralleling and reflecting changes in the poetic or literary idea. Naturally, the program in many cases clearly reveals the prevalent literary influences of the period. Thus, in the three tone poems that have been selected as an introduction to the form—Saint-Saëns' *Danse Macabre*, Moussorgsky's *Night on Bald Mountain*, and Paul Dukas's *Sorcerer's Apprentice*—we find in the music the same embodiment of the fantastic and the bizarre that played so prominent a part in the Romantic literature of the time.[1]

While we shall confine our immediate study to the three typical symphonic poems just mentioned, and though future pages of this book will present additional examples of this form, it might be well to mention here a comparatively rare occurrence in music—a symphonic poem inspired by a painting.[2] This is Sergei Rachmaninoff's *The Isle of the Dead*, after the painting of the same name (see page 183) by Arnold Böcklin (1827-1901). The poem was written in Paris, in 1909, where the composer first saw the painting. It is scored for a large orchestra and the work begins with a figure in the 'cellos suggestive of the quiet lapping of the water, then a softly intoned French horn theme is heard which serves well throughout the poem. A climax is reached and the "Chant of the Dead," *Dies Irae*, comes forth from the brasses. Gradually the work calms down and a theme appears in the strings which is somewhat reminiscent, and a development, of the horn theme heard at the beginning. This theme is worked

---

[1] Essential listening for this chapter includes: *Danse Macabre* by Saint-Saëns, *Night on Bald Mountain* by Moussorgsky, and the *Sorcerer's Apprentice* by Dukas—in that order. Rachmaninoff's symphonic poem, "The Isle of the Dead," may be considered as suggested supplementary listening.

[2] A more recent example of such an inspiration is Paul Hindemith's *Mathis der Maler,* originally an opera inspired by the Isenheim alterpiece by Matthias Grünewald. The music is usually heard as a symphonic suite.

ISLE OF THE DEAD

This striking romantic picture sets forth moods of eternal peace, tranquility, sorrow, and tragedy. The literary content is obvious; but equally forceful and not observable in the half-tone cut is the intensification of the forms conveyed through the contrasting colors of the black cypress trees, the towering red cliffs, the white mausoleums, and the stark figure standing in the boat. It is interesting to observe how the composer Rachmaninoff expressed the feelings aroused by the painter Böcklin.

COURTESY OF THE METROPOLITAN MUSEUM OF ART, NEW YORK

Böcklin

up to the real climax of the composition when the horn theme played in the beginning is loudly intoned by the brasses. Little by little the mood subsides; finally the symphonic poem closes with the material of the opening section being heard once more, and quiet reigns. (Rachmaninoff was born in Russia in 1873 and died in the United States in 1943. He is more generally known for his short piano pieces, songs, his four concerti for piano, and his three symphonies.)

Camille Saint-Saëns (1835-1921)

We pointed out earlier in this chapter that Romanticism was a middle-class art, as opposed to eighteenth-century Classicism, which was essentially aristocratic in nature. The middle class, however, was too firmly rooted in practical affairs to float indefinitely in the mists of the supernatural and the bizarre. Thus there developed within the framework of literary Romanticism, and side by side with the emotional excesses of a Hugo, a Byron, or a Poe, a tradition of Realism which ran down the century, from Balzac and Flaubert to Dickens, George Eliot, and Thackeray, culminating at the end of the century in the Naturalism of Zola, de Maupassant, Thomas Hardy, Ibsen, Chekhov, and the American school.

It need hardly be said that this tendency to capture all aspects of reality in literature made itself felt also in music. Liszt, Berlioz, and their contemporaries of the middle of the century based their program music on highly symbolic and quite general literary or pictorial elements presented with a maximum of poetic suggestion. Throughout the last quarter of the century there was a steady movement in program music toward Realism, culminating in the 1890's in the tone poems of Richard Strauss (Chapter XVIII) which, substituting literalness for suggestion, may be considered the musical counterpart of the tendency represented by Zola. The beginnings of this tendency may already be traced in a work such as Saint-Saëns' (pronounced săn'säns') *Danse Macabre* (Dance of Death), written in 1874, that combines the love of the macabre we have noticed in Romanticism with certain elements of satire and literalness that were to dominate the program music of the end of the century. The symphonic poem of the Frenchman, Saint-Saëns, may therefore be considered as a kind of middle point between the tone-poem style of Liszt and that of Richard Strauss.

Biography

Camille Saint-Saëns, known to the American public mainly through the ever-popular *Danse Macabre*, the *Swan*, which the great

Pavlowa transformed into a famous dance, and the aria *My Heart at Thy Sweet Voice* from the Opera SAMSON AND DELILAH, began his long and supremely successful career as a wonder child. He composed at seven, gave his first piano recital at eleven, and won a prize in organ playing at the Paris Conservatoire at fourteen. His first symphony was performed when he was eighteen; at twenty-two he was appointed organist of the Madeleine, one of the most famous churches in Paris. He was thus spared much of the disappointment and bitterness that beset so many great musicians. Indeed, after the seventies his career was an almost uninterrupted succession of triumphs. He composed steadily in almost every branch of music and made brilliant concert tours as organist and pianist; his piano and violin concertos, his operas, symphonies, and tone poems were performed throughout Europe. He received the order of the Legion of Honor in 1868, was elected a member of the French Institute in 1881, and was given the honorary degree of Doctor of Music by Cambridge University in 1892. Witty, facile, and a tireless worker, he found time from his musical activity to dabble in literature, producing a volume of poetry, several farces, a number of essays on music and the theater, and, curiously enough, some papers on scientific subjects.

Saint-Saëns' music is brilliant rather than moving, pleasant rather than profound. For this reason, a good part of his output is not bearing up too well under the test of time. A thorough craftsman and a master of orchestration, his melodies are facile, his ideas interestingly worked out. But he is definitely a product of his period, rather than one of the chosen few who stand above all limitations of time and place. He appeared at a time when the French nation was completely apathetic to its own living composers. He devoted himself tirelessly to the cause of French music and, through the *Société Nationale de Musique*, which he helped found, fought for recognition for the young composers of the new French school. The wave of nationalism that swept France as an aftermath of the Franco-Prussian War helped bring the movement to its ultimate success. When the influence of Wagner came to dominate the musical life of the Continent, Saint-Saëns stood up for the particular qualities—clarity, measure, poise—that his great contemporary, Anatole France, considered the essence of the Gallic spirit in art. He was in effect one of the most important influences in initiating and molding the modern French symphonic school. His was, however, the peculiar fate of all reformers who outlive their period: he began as a flaming radical in music, became more and more conservative as he went along, and ended completely out of sympathy with the very developments that he himself had been instrumental in getting under way. The last of the great nineteenth-century composers, he survived in a world completely alien to that which he had so ably represented; his death in 1921 at the age of eighty-six marked the end of an era.

"Danse Macabre" (Dance of Death)

Death had been a popular theme in art during the Middle Ages and the Renaissance. Holbein's famous "Dance of Death" shows the grim figure playing a *strohfiedel*, the medieval ancestor of the xylophone, which Saint-Saëns used so effectively in this work to imitate the rattling of skeleton bones. The Age of Classicism, of the Enlightenment, naturally discouraged the use of such obviously melodramatic themes. But when Romanticism turned for inspiration to the Middle Ages—just as Classicism had turned to antiquity—death became again a motif in art. In their reaction from the reason and light of the eighteenth century, the early Romantics swung so far toward the Gothic that an almost morbid preoccupation with horror and strangeness soon became one of the mannerisms of the movement.

Danse Macabre was written in 1874 and first performed the following year. Saint-Saëns originally wrote it as a song, but since the melody turned out to be somewhat hard to sing, he used it as the basis for his orchestral piece. The poem that served as his inspiration seems rather crude and dated now, but it must be remembered that half a century is a long time for second-rate literature. Cazlis' poem has been translated as follows:

> Ziz, zag, zig, Death in cadence
> Striking a tomb with his heel,
> Death at midnight plays a dance-tune
> On his violin.
>
> The winter wind blows, the night is sombre,
> Moans are heard in the linden trees;
> The white skeletons flit through the shadows,
> Shrouded shapes moving strangely.
>
> Zig, zag, zig, each one is frisking;
> The bones of the dancers rattle . . .
> But pst! suddenly the cock crows!
> They quit the dance, they run, they fly,

Around this rather obvious program the brilliantly ironic Saint-Saëns, with a kind of grim relish, constructed a composition that shocked and startled his contemporaries, although its devices have become familiar through incessant repetition. The twelve strokes of the clock sounded on the harp and the mysterious plucked strings of 'cellos and bass violins set the scene. Death tunes his fiddle, with the E string lowered out of tune; the dance opens with an appropriately cheerless theme on the flutes leading to the waltz tune proper. The xylophone imitates the clanking of skeleton bones, while chill chromatic scales suggest the howling of the night wind. (*Chromatic scales* are scales that ascend or descend in half steps—that is, they include the sharps and flats. They belong to no particular key, and present twelve semitones, or half steps, within the octave. They are much used in "picture music" for storms, howling of the wind, and so forth.)

chromatic scales.

After a brief lyrical interlude in the violins, as though two specters had met who remembered each other from happier days, the chromatic scales return, the dance grows ever faster, louder, more abandoned. Suddenly the horns announce the glimmer of dawn; the oboe imitates the crowing of the cock. Death packs his fiddle; the specters unwillingly trudge back to their graves; the ghostly revel is over.

When *Danse Macabre* was first performed in London in 1879, the critic of the *Daily News* threw up his hands, calling it "horrible, hideous, and disgusting," and an example of the "intense and coarse realism that is entering into much of the musical composition (so-called) of the day." Saint-Saëns enjoyed the outcry; but his music aged more rapidly than either he or his critics suspected. What was so shocking to the 1870's has become fairly tame to the audiences of the twentieth century.[3]

---

[3] The work is one of a series—Berlioz' SYMPHONIE FANTASTIQUE, Liszt's DANCE OF DEATH and MEPHISTO WALTZ, Gounod's FAUST and Boito's MEPHISTOPHELES—in which the "diabolism" so dear to the Romantic poets and novelists found musical expression. From the horror stories of Mrs. Radcliffe to the fantastic tales of E. T. A. Hoffmann, from the "Ancient Mariner" and "Christabel" and "Kubla Khan" to the tales of Poe, the visions of De Quincey, and the novels of Victor Hugo, the love of the supernatural, the strange, and the picturesquely macabre constituted one of the strongest motifs in literary Romanticism.

ANALYSIS. The two main themes out of which the composition is built offer an excellent contrast to each other. The first consists of rapid eighth notes, staccato, in brusque rhythmic patterns:

The second is a flowing, legato, waltz theme, consisting of half and quarter notes, all held together by a *slur*. (This word indicates the curved line covering the notes as a sign that they are to "melt" into each other in legato fashion.) The melody is presented with a kind of ironic warmth by all the strings in unison:

Besides the numerous variations in which the two principal themes are presented, we hear also, well on in the composition, a travesty of the *Dies Irae*, the medieval, impressive *Hymn to the Dead*:[4]

The orchestration is expertly done, making use of all the colors and contrasts of the various choirs and instrumental combinations. Notice how, when Saint-Saëns begins to build toward his climax, we hear the opening notes of Theme I bandied about in quick succession by trombones, horns, oboes, clarinets, and flutes, each imi-

---

[4] The traditional chant is as follows:

tating the other. As the music mounts in intensity in the final section, the brilliant voices of flute and piccolo are added to the ensemble. Noteworthy, too, is the effect of rattling bones on the xylophone; the mysterious horns, as though from a distance, signaling the coming of dawn; and the oboe announcing cockcrow. A violin shudders as the wraiths flit away. We hear a last fleet echo of the opening theme, and two chords plucked furtively on the strings (pizzicato) brings the piece to a close.

The form of *Danse Macabre*, like its orchestration, bespeaks the master craftsman. There are three sections: the first, in the nature of an introduction, includes the striking of the clock and Death tuning his violin; the second consists of the dance proper, in which the two main themes of the waltz are worked out; the third is a sort of *postlude*, which recalls some ideas of the first section. We shall meet this device again and again in symphonic literature; the final measures, reminding the listener of the opening, help unify the entire musical structure. (This restatement-after-contrast is a basic form in all the fine arts, and the minor arts as well.)

Rhythmically the music is compelling, particularly in the swaying triple meter of the waltz theme. The tempo is clear-cut. The piece begins in moderate waltz time—*mouvement modère de valse.* (As a nationalist, Saint-Saëns used French indications instead of the conventional Italian.) As the dance gets under way and approaches the climax there is a steady speeding up (accelerando). With the coming of dawn we return to Tempo I, known as *Tempo Primo*, or the first tempo. Thus, sections one and three, the prelude-postlude frame, are in identical tempo.

Equally simple is the dynamic design in *Danse Macabre*. The music opens *ppp* (pianississimo) the merest whisper; proceeds gradually to pianissimo and piano. The second theme enters forte, works up to fortissimo, and finally, at the climax, *fff* (fortississimo). With the return to Tempo I, the gradation of the opening is reversed: *p* leads to *pp*, and the music dies away *ppp*. We see here how both tempo and dynamics help to bring out the structural element of the prelude-postlude form—another instance of how the diverse elements of music supplement one another in producing the total effect.

Modest Moussorgsky (1839-1881)

Biography

Modest Moussorgsky was born in Russia (Pskov) in 1839, of a family of landowners. Like many sons of the gentry he was prepared for a military career and became an officer in one of the fashionable Guards regiments. Like Tchaikovsky and Rimsky-Korsakoff, he began as a musical dilletante. Like them, too, he came under the influence of Mily Balakirev, the leader of the Russian national school. It was only then that he decided to devote himself to a musical career. He resigned his commission when he was nineteen and embarked upon a musical career rich in achievement yet darkened by the shadow of great hopes left unfulfilled. Moussorgsky aimed at naturalism in music, at uncompromising honesty as he himself felt it, and at simplicity. He was profoundly interested in the nationalistic folk arts, especially folk songs. Technique as such was, for him, a species of artifice. Consequently, he never became as dexterous or as polished in musical composition as either Tchaikovsky or Rimsky-Korsakoff. On the other hand, he submitted much less than they to the traditional influences, Italian, German, and French; he stands today as one of the most indigenous of the Russian nationalist composers, his nationalism reaching its peak in his historical music drama, BORIS GODUNOFF.

Moussorgsky's life became a continual struggle against poverty and lack of appreciation on the part of the musical public of his time. He held an ill-paid government post; his personality, although most attractive and endowed with charm, was not strong enough to withstand the continual disappointments and strain to which he was subject. He sought refuge in drink and drugs, which ended by sapping his powers for sustained creative effort. He was able to finish small pieces—the wonderful songs, and the piano compositions of which the best known is the suite of sketches, PICTURES AT AN EXHIBITION. But most of his large works, operatic and orchestral, were either abandoned midway or left unfinished at his death. The manuscripts that he left were completed by his musical friends, chief among them Rimsky-Korsakoff. These include the comic opera THE FAIR AT SOROTCHINSK, the opera KHOVANTCHINA, the orchestral fantasy NIGHT ON BALD MOUNTAIN, and BORIS GODUNOFF, the historical opera.

"Night on Bald Mountain"

In 1860, when he was twenty-one, Moussorgsky wrote to Balakirev of "a most interesting work" he had been commissioned to do:

music for the first act of THE BALD MOUNTAIN, to be based on Megden's drama, *The Witch*. It was to describe a gathering of the witches as they practiced some of the mysterious rites of their craft, a pageant of sorcerers, and in the finale a dance in tribute to Satan. Moussorgsky was hopeful about the composition: he considered the libretto unusually good and announced that he had already conceived some of its themes.

As in the case of Tchaikovsky's ROMEO AND JULIET, Balakirev does not seem to have shared his protege's enthusiasm. Two years later Moussorgsky wrote to his mentor concerning the work that he was not to be shaken in his belief that his music was entirely satisfactory. He felt that the music was a genuine expression of the story it conveyed, "without tricks or pretensions," and that he had discharged the task set him to the best of his ability. He remained adamant in his determination not to alter the plan or its development, but consented to change the percussion, which he admitted he had misused. He rewrote the fantasy in 1867, and intended on two occasions to introduce it into a dramatic work: once into a fairy opera MLADA, of which he, Rimsky-Korsakoff, Alexander Borodin, and César Cui were each to write portions, and in which the symphonic poem was to serve as background for a fantastic scene, "The Sacrifice to the Black Goat on Bald Mountain." The scheme fell through because of financial reasons, and again in 1877, when he intended to introduce it as an interlude in his unfinished opera THE FAIR AT SOROTCHINSK.

The score was revised by Rimsky-Korsakoff, after Moussorgsky's death, and received its first performance in 1886 when Rimsky-Korsakoff conducted it with great success. It was the first work that earned for the composer the popular acclaim that had been denied him during his lifetime.

Rimsky-Korsakoff appended Moussorgsky's program note to the score:

Subterranean sounds of supernatural voices. Appearance of the spirits of darkness, followed by that of Satan himself. Glorification of Satan and celebration of the Black Mass. The Sabbath Revels. At the height of the orgies the bell of the village church, sounding in the distance, disperses the spirits of darkness. Daybreak.

ANALYSIS. The tone poem opens *allegro feroce* (fast and fierce), with a turbulent figure in the strings against which trombones, tuba, and bassoons thunder the Satanic theme:

The dance that ushers in the "glorification of Satan" is saturated
with the Russian folk idiom and appears in strongly marked rhythms
in the oboes and clarinets, presenting an effective contrast to the
opening theme:

After the movement has somewhat slackened, the allegro feroce
of the opening returns, the brass weaving its theme against rapid
chromatic passages in woodwinds and strings. A new dance theme
appears, at first in fairly slow tempo, but gradually working up to a
frenzied climax.

At the height of the festivities the bell tolls mournfully six times.
Strings and harp tranquilly announce the coming of dawn in a coda
suffused with poetic feeling.

The music has verve and gusto, permeated by a supernatural aspect. Like the ROMEO AND JULIET OVERTURE, it is the work of a
young and ardent imagination, projected with such sincerity of feeling and richness of fantasy that it needs no further intermediary between the composer and his listener.

Paul Dukas (1865-1935)

THE SORCERER'S APPRENTICE was written in 1897, almost a quarter
century after *Danse Macabre*, in what has come to be known as the
post-Romantic era. This was the transitional period from the nineteenth century to our own, when the great Romantic tradition had
given way to a *fin de siècle* spirit—the Mauve Decade, as Beer aptly
called it, the period of Oscar Wilde and the *Yellow Book*, of Whistler
and Aubrey Beardsley. The rich emotionalism of the ROMEO AND
JULIET OVERTURE, the demonic imaginativeness of NIGHT ON BALD
MOUNTAIN or *Danse Macabre* were retreating before the sophistication and the objectivity that characterize the modern temper; we are
already in the atmosphere of the Straussian tone poem. From a purely

technical standpoint, the experiments of Berlioz, Liszt, and Wagner in orchestral writing had opened to their followers a new world of dazzling color effects. It was out of this combination of influences that a number of exciting orchestral works, of which Dukas' joyous orchestral scherzo is typical, came into being.

Biography

Paul Dukas (pronounced dü-kăhs′) was one of the most distinguished French composers of his time. Born in Paris in 1865, he entered the Conservatoire at the age of seventeen and soon displayed a talent for composition. His first symphony was performed in 1896. The following year, when he was thirty-two, he wrote L'APPRENTI SORCIER (The Sorcerer's Apprentice), which has remained his most popular work. His operatic setting of Maeterlinck's ARIANE AND BLUEBEARD also won much acclaim. He was not only a versatile musician but also won distinction as teacher, editor, musical critic, and essayist. He was a member of the Legion of Honor, professor of orchestration at the Conservatoire, and holder of an official post in the ministry of fine arts.

"The Sorcerer's Apprentice"

The program upon which Dukas based his composition concerns the sorcerer's apprentice who could start a magic spell but could not stop it. The theme had been popular for centuries—*The Golem* and *Frankenstein* are two famous variants—and may be traced back to the Roman poet Lucian. In Goethe's version the young apprentice has repeatedly watched his master utter a charm over a broomstick, whereupon the stick sprouted hands and feet and carried out the magician's bidding. One day, after his master goes out, the apprentice utters the charm and orders the broomstick to fetch water for his bath. When he tries to stop the stick he realizes to his horror that he has forgotten the formula for removing the spell. The stick continues to haul the water; the apprentice falls into panic. He seizes an axe and splits the stick in half, whereupon two sticks proceed to fetch water. Just as the mounting flood threatens to engulf the luckless boy, the sorcerer returns, pronounces the formula, and with a brusque command sends the broom back to its corner. The apprentice has learned his lesson.

ANALYSIS. The introduction is in a lento movement (*lento* means slow, like *adagio*). The atmosphere of enchantment is established at the outset by the violas and 'cellos playing *harmonics*. These, the

MICKEY MOUSE AS THE SORCERER'S APPRENTICE   *From "Fantasia"*

reader will recall, are the flutelike tones in the very highest register
produced by touching the finger lightly to the string at certain points,
causing it to vibrate in small segments, to produce an effect of delicacy
and charm.

The theme of the magic spell is chanted piano by the muted violins,
a plaintive melody in high register descending gradually in a series of
little leaps:

The woodwinds and brass answer brilliantly with the choppy,
staccato theme of the broom. (See ensuing example.)

Notice the interesting contrast between the two themes out of
which the composition is woven: the first in high register, languidly
legato, played by the strings; the second in low register, brusque and
staccato, given to woodwinds and brass.

Presently the apprentice utters the fatal formula. There is an ominous silence. Then the uncanny business begins, allegro and piano, with three bassoons and a contrabassoon keeping up a curiously hopping rhythm in the deepest register.

The music works steadily into a mood of feverish activity. The theme of the magic formula returns fleetingly, now plaintive, now with gleeful malice; the broom theme is tossed about among clarinets, bassoons, horns, and trumpets, while the rest of the orchestra weaves a shimmering background of chromatic scales. The mounting consternation of the would-be wizard is portrayed with brilliant drollery; horns and trumpets fortissimo blare out his frantic cries for help. The movement climbs steadily to the point where he splits the broom in two. There is a breathless pause—and then the cursed activity begins anew, with bassoons and contrabassoon as at the beginning. The movement mounts in a steady crescendo to the final climax: the Sorcerer, announced by thunderous blasts in the brass, returns and puts an end to the spell. We hear again the magical chords of the introduction as the apprentice comes to, a sadder and wiser man. A final blast of the orchestra sends the broom back to its corner.

The work reveals Dukas as a composer of brilliant imagination and wit, a master of orchestration and color. From the moment when the broomstick begins its activity there is a rhythmic pulsation that sweeps the listener along with a kind of relentless energy. The meter, as the signature indicates, is $\frac{9}{8}$, a compound of triple meter; the student will have no difficulty in feeling the triple beat as soon as the movement gets under way. In general, the composition is more sophisticated and modern than *Danse Macabre*. The melodic line is jagged and brusque; the harmonies rich and complicated; the orchestration remarkably varied.

Dukas called his piece an "Orchestral Scherzo." Like Mendelssohn's "Scherzo" from the *Midsummer Night's Dream* music, Dukas' piece is strongly rhythmic and movemented; but where Mendelssohn's "Scherzo" is delicate and elfin, Dukas' is gaily boisterous. The structure is simple. There is the unifying prelude-postlude formation that we noticed in *Danse Macabre* in the Magic Spell theme. The movement itself falls into two parts: from the point where the broom begins until the moment when the apprentice splits it in two, and from then on until the return of the sorcerer. The dynamic scheme fits this structure: prelude and postlude generally pianissimo (interspersed with outbursts of furious energy when the broom theme is introduced); while in the two halves of the work itself there is a steady crescendo from the pianissimo of the three bassoons to the full orchestral outburst at each climax. The tempo outline fits this scheme. The introduction is lento, the action proper allegro with a steady accelerando to the climax, and the postlude is marked *Tempo I*, the same as the introduction.

The composition is largely built on the broom theme. The contrasting material includes the enchantment theme and a playful subsidiary theme that flits through the body of the work. But Dukas has relied for the necessary variety not so much on diverse thematic material as on the richness of his orchestral palette. Thematically, this piece is much less diversified than some of the others we have listened to; yet because of the brilliant handling of the orchestra, it sustains the interest of the listener throughout. Notice that Dukas, like Moussorgsky and Saint-Saëns, has used chromatic scales throughout the work to create a feeling of agitation and climax. It is evident that the chromatic-scale passage was a staple device in nineteenth-century program music. We shall encounter it again and again in symphonic climaxes.

Chapter XIV

NATIONALISM IN MUSIC

O F THE utmost significance to musical Romanticism was the up-
surge of nationalism that manifested itself throughout Europe during
the nineteenth century. Napoleon's dream of a subjugated continent
crumbled before the outburst of patriotism that demanded Spain for
the Spaniards, Holland for the Dutch, Italy for the Italians. Both
among the small nations struggling for their liberty and the large
states bent on fulfilling their expansionist ambitions, nationalism became an ideal worth fighting and dying for. This sentiment fitted in
excellently with the prevailing mood of the Romantic movement.
Romanticism had taken over the abstract Rousseauesque notion of a
"return to nature"; nationalism transformed this into a return to the
natural beauties of one's own homeland. Romanticism had encouraged
an interest in the humble joys and sorrows of the common folk;
nationalism shifted this interest toward an enthusiasm for the folklore and folkways of one's own people. Thus the Romantic artist
became a nationalist artist.

Nationalism and the Arts

In literature, painting, and music we have the rise of strongly
nationalist schools out of which emerged some of the most memorable
work of the period. The legends of the national hero furnished inspiration to such dissimilar works as the Arthurian poems of Tenny-
son, the historical novels of Walter Scott and Dumas, the SIEGFRIED
cycle of Wagner, the poetry of Pushkin in Russia, of Robert Burns in
Scotland, of Mieczkewitz in Poland. David, in his epic canvases, aimed
to perpetuate the glory of Napoleon; Constable and Turner celebrated
the English landscape; the Barbizon painters did the same for France.
National folklore inspired the FREISCHÜTZ of Weber, the fairy tales
of Grimm, Andrew Lang, and Hans Christian Andersen. At a time
when music was turning more and more to picturesque effects, to

color and atmosphere, the folk tunes and dances of the various racial stocks became an inexhaustible treasure-house upon which composers could draw to their hearts' content. Idiomatic melodies and characteristic rhythms united with the powerful emotional associations evoked by a patriotic program to open up a rich new field to music. Grieg became the musical voice of Norway; Tchaikovsky, Rimsky-Korsakoff, and Moussorgsky, of Russia; Weber and Wagner, of Germany; Liszt, of Hungary; Chopin, of Poland; Dvořák and Smetana, of Bohemia; Albeniz, of Spain; Elgar, of England; MacDowell,

BY PERMISSION OF THE OWNER, MRS. C. M. GOOCH, MEMPHIS, TENN.

MIDNIGHT RIDE OF PAUL REVERE   *Grant Wood*

of our own country; Debussy and Ravel, of France; Sibelius, of Finland.

A composer could use his gifts to glorify the national heritage in various ways. He could utilize folk-song and folk-dance idioms of his people, as Dvořák did in the *Slavonic Dances*, Chopin in the *Polonaises* and *Mazurkas*, Liszt in the *Hungarian Rhapsodies*. He could weave his music around the life of a national hero or king, as Wagner did in the music dramas based on the life of Siegfried, or Moussorgsky in his Boris Godunoff. He could glorify the scenic beauties, the rivers and forests of his native land, as Johann Strauss did in his *Blue Danube* and *Tales from the Vienna Woods*, Smetana in *The Moldau*, Respighi in *The Pines of Rome*, and our own Stephen Foster in such songs as *Swanee River* and *My Old Kentucky Home*. He could use an historic event that had great emotional significance to his countrymen, generally one in which his nation had been victorious, as Tchaikovsky did in the OVERTURE 1812. Or he could set his music to the work of a native poet, as Grieg did with Ibsen's *Peer Gynt*, Debussy with the poetry of Verlaine, Tchaikovsky with the dramas of Pushkin. Most nationalist composers used several of these methods and thereby communicated to their audiences the essence of the spirit of their country.

As the century wore on, the struggle for freedom on the part of the oppressed nations became ever more bitter. Music, because of its intensely emotional appeal, became a weapon of first importance. Auber's *Masaniello*, with its stirring choruses in praise of liberty, became the rallying cry of an awakening Italy against the Austrian yoke. Later, when the operas of Verdi became popular, the frenzied shouts of "Viva Verdi" that greeted his works took on the nature of a political demonstration against the Austrians: the letters of Verdi's name happened to correspond with the initials of the nationalist slogan *Vittorio Emanuele Re d'Italia* (Victor Emanuel King of Italy). So too, when Finland was struggling to liberate itself from Czarist rule, Sibelius' FINLANDIA touched off such demonstrations on the part of Finnish patriots that the Czarist officials forbade its performance. In the tragic upheavals of our own time, music has again taken on this political role.

As our essential listening for this chapter, let us hear THE MOLDAU by Smetana, the OVERTURE 1812 by Tchaikovsky, and FINLANDIA by Sibelius. A number of suggested and supplementary projects may be found at the close of the chapter.

Bedrich Smetana (1824-1884)

Biography

Bedrich Smetana (sme′tà-nà), the founder of the Czech nationalist school, was born in 1824 in Litomyschl, Bohemia. His father was a brewer and was passionately fond of music. Like Saint-Saëns and Dukas, Smetana displayed marked musical gifts at an early age: he improvised on the violin at the age of five, and made frequent public appearances as a pianist during his adolescence. Finally, after overcoming the opposition of his family, he went to Prague to study composition.

Weathering all sorts of privations—at times he practically starved —he eventually became music master in the family of Count Thun. The revolution of 1848 aroused his national consciousness as a Czech. In the next years Liszt, then at the height of his fame, became interested in him and helped him to establish a school of music. From then on his career was a slow progress to recognition and fame. He moved to Gothenburg, Sweden, where he became conductor of the new Philharmonic Society. Smetana returned to his home in Prague after the death of his wife. On his journey back from Sweden to his homeland, he stopped at Weimar to visit his benefactor, Liszt, and came strongly under the influence of the latter's symphonic poems.

Several years were spent in concert tours over the Continent before Smetana settled permanently in Prague. Here he became the leading figure in the nascent movement for a Czech national music, as composer, conductor, teacher, music critic, and writer. The production of his masterpiece, the gay folk opera THE BARTERED BRIDE, was followed by a number of successful musical-dramatic works, all strongly nationalistic, either based on the Bohemian folk idiom or on national legends. Of these, LIBUSSA, THE TWO WIDOWS, and THE KISS are best known.

In 1874, after his health had broken down under the strain of overwork, Smetana suddenly became completely deaf. It was in this final period that the composer wrote some of his greatest works—the autobiographical string quartet AUS MEINEN (From My Life) 1876, and the warmly romantic, patriotic symphonic cycle of six tone poems, MÁ VLAST (My Country), of which *Vltava* (*The Moldau*) 1874, has become popular throughout the musical world. In 1883 Smetana suffered a complete mental breakdown and died a year later in an asylum at the age of sixty.

"The Moldau" (1874)

Of the six symphonic poems that make up the cycle MÁ VLAST the description of the River Moldau is the second. The first, *Vyšehrad*, concerns the castle of popular Czech legend, its former glory conjured up by the bard Lumir. The third, *Šárka*, portrays a legendary warrior queen of Czechoslovakia who, to satisfy her hatred against men, entertains the knight Ctirad and his followers at a banquet and, after having plied them with drink, murders them. The fourth is the famous *From the Fields and Groves of Bohemia*, an idyllic pastoral poem of serene beauty. The fifth, *Tábor*, is a fantasy on an old chorale that was sung by the followers of John Huss. The sixth, *Blaník*, describes the mountain known to Czech folklore. When foreign oppressors come, the heroes, who have been hiding in the mountain, drive out the invader and restore Bohemia to her freedom.

The Moldau is one of the most successful pieces of descriptive music in the symphonic repertoire. Smetana appended the following note to the score:

Two springs gush forth in the shade of the Bohemian forest, the one warm and spouting, the other cold and tranquil. Their ripples, gaily flowing over rocky beds, unite and glisten in the morning sun. The forest brook, rushing on, becomes the River Vlatava (Moldau), which hurrying through Bohemia's valleys, grows into a mighty stream. It flows through dense woods, where the joyous noise of the hunt and the tones of the hunter's horns resound nearer and nearer. It flows through verdant meadows and lowlands where a wedding feast is celebrated with song and dancing. At night the wood nymphs and water sprites revel in its glistening waves, which reflect many fortresses and castles—witnesses of the past splendor of chivalry and the vanished martial fame of bygone days. At the Rapids of St. John the stream speeds on, winding its way over cataracts and cutting a channel with its foaming waters through the rocky chasm into the broad river bed in which it flows on in majestic calm toward Prague, welcomed by time-honored Vysehrad (the famous Bohemian castle, citadel of the ancient kings). Then it disappears in the far distance from the poet's gaze.

Smetana heard this music, which was destined to become his most popular symphonic composition, only in his imagination, for it was written in 1874, after total deafness had descended upon him.

ANALYSIS. The music opens *allegro commodo non agitato* (fast, at an easy pace, not agitated) in E minor, with a flowing sextuple meter, a rippling figure in the flutes portraying the two springs. Presently, against the rippling figure now taken by the strings the broad lyrical melody of the river emerges, played by first violins, oboes, and bassoons, a theme of great tenderness and simplicity in a minor key. Notice here, as well as in the folk-dance theme later, the regular four-measure phrase structure:

After a spacious development, the melody returns. But by raising the G to a G-sharp—that is, by using the raised third step of the scale—Smetana shifts the tune from minor to major in an extraordinarily effective transformation:

Hunting calls sound on the horns and woodwinds, at first remote, but soon approaching in a steady crescendo while the music grows more boisterous. With the next section, "Peasant Wedding," we modulate to G major. A rustic folk dance appears, abounding in gay little groups of sixteenth notes, played by strings and woodwinds:

The tune swells to a fortissimo and dies away. In the next section, "The Moon Rises—Dance of the Nymphs," we hear soft harmonies on the flutes, clarinets, and harp. The magical atmosphere of the forest permeates this section with the horns, trombones, and tuba intoning stately harmonies, as from afar, in the rhythm of a solemn march. At the section marked "The Rapids of St. John" we return to *Tempo I*, the music quickening in the original rippling figure with an upward gliding on the strings. The principal theme is heard much as before, first in the minor, then with a broad development, finally in the major. The music takes on majesty and power as "The Moldau broadens out" with the solemn motive of Vysêhrad—the historic castle—intoned triumphantly, like a hymn of praise, by brass and woodwinds against a rich orchestral background. The climax passes; the music dies down to a gentle rippling, and flows farther and farther away.

Here is heartfelt lyricism, imaginative orchestration, fantasy, and rare pictorial power blended in a work of universal appeal that well deserves its popularity.

"Overture Solennelle 1812," Op. 49 (1880), by Peter Ilyitch Tchaikovsky

In a letter from Italy to Mme. von Meck, Tchaikovsky writes:

Why is it that the simple Russian landscape, a walk in summer through Russian fields and forest or on the steppes at evening, can affect me so that I have lain on the ground numb, overcome by a wave of love for nature, by the indescribably sweet and intoxicating atmosphere that drifted over me from the forest, the steppe, the little river, the faraway village, the modest little church—in short, all that makes the poor Russian landscape?[1]

Although there were strong foreign elements in his work—he worshipped Mozart and admired Italian opera, French ballet, and German song—he considered his music Russian to the core. In response to a question of Mme. von Meck he writes (the reference to "our symphony" is to the *Fourth* which he dedicated to her):

As to the Russian element in my compositions, it is true that I often begin to write with the intention of using one or another popular song. Sometimes (as in the *Finale* of our symphony) this happens of itself, quite unexpectedly. As to the Russian element in general in my music—the relation to the popular song in melody and harmony—I grew up in a peaceful spot, saturated from earliest childhood with the miraculous beauty of Russian spirit. In short, I am a Russian through and through.[2]

This intense nationalism increased as he grew famous and began to be recognized as the foremost representative of Russian music. It was further reinforced by the personal attention and friendship that, in the last two decades of his life, members of the Imperial family bestowed upon him. In the light of all this it is not difficult to understand why the 1812 OVERTURE became one of Tchaikovsky's most popular and most overplayed works. For the average Russian, the year 1812 had an almost mystical significance: Napoleon's invasion had been thrown back, not by armies or strategic victories, but by the Russian winter. It was literally as if the country itself had arisen to hurl back the enemy.

The work was written at the request of Nicholas Rubinstein for the Moscow Exhibition of Arts and Industries, at which it was first performed, with booming cannons and other stirring effects, on August 20, 1882. Tchaikovsky was given the choice of three themes, of which he picked: "Solemn Overture on the Dedication of the Church of the Saviour in Moscow." Conceived along the broad outdoor lines proper to an exhibition, the *Overture* uses all kinds of effects designed to capture the popular fancy.

This composition offers the music listener a lucid example of how

---

[1] Catherine Drinker Bowen and B. von Meck, *Beloved Friend.* (New York: Random House, 1937.)

[2] *Ibid.*

the composer's mind works and how he handles his themes. In this case, the insight we get is particularly clear because one of the principal themes in the development of the *Overture* is the opening phrase of the *Marseillaise*, which symbolizes the approach and later the retreat of the French army. Because of its familiarity, the listener can easily follow it as the composer tosses the theme about from one choir to the next, combines it with other thematic material, presents it with all kinds of changes in timbre, dynamics, tempo, and register. By following these transformations carefully we gain an insight into one of the most important elements of symphonic style—the handling and developing of the basic musical ideas, the themes out of which a large musical form is constructed.

ANALYSIS. Tchaikovsky's *Overture* opens with a solemn chorale in E-flat major that seems to be invoking divine aid in the face of approaching calamity. Marked *largo*, the chorale is in simple four-part harmony; violas and 'cellos, playing mezzo-forte, *mf*, bring out the rich coloring of the solemn chords:

After a climax of great dignity and breadth, an oboe sings a plaintive tune. The strings sweep upward ominously; the mood becomes one of impending disaster. After a gradual crescendo and accelerando, which works up to *fff*, we hear the rattle of military drums; woodwinds and horns announce the second theme of the introduction, the famous Cavalry theme, in a martial andante, mezzo-forte:

With this, the introduction may be said to end and the movement proper to begin. The Strife theme, a grim motive of strife and anger, is played by the strings, allegro and forte, with abrupt runs and fierce accents and those upward and downward sweeps on the strings that we have already pointed out as an unmistakably characteristic of Tchaikovsky's orchestral style. There is a resemblance here to the Feud theme in the ROMEO AND JULIET OVERTURE.

Notice the change of key. The tumult mounts; we hear the opening strains of the *Marseillaise* played by trumpets and taken up by cornets, as if announcing the approach of the enemy, while vigorous upward scale passages on the strings and woodwinds provide a turbulent accompaniment. After working up to a stirring *fff* climax, the movement subsides; the second theme of the exposition emerges, a broad lyrical melody rising from the violins and violas in a broad sustained curve, a song of hope and love for the homeland, in F-sharp major:

A Cossack dance follows. Based upon one of those Russian folk tunes Tchaikovsky so loved, it is played piano by flute and English horn with tambourine accompaniment in a plaintive minor key:

The development brings us echoes of the Strife theme ingeniously combined with snatches of the *Marseillaise* bandied about among the brass and woodwind instruments. The music gradually gains momentum and surges forward with irresistible force to the point where the Strife theme reenters *fff*. The first part is recapitulated in a somewhat abridged form, the Hope theme followed by the Cossack dance, more or less as we heard them before. An imposing transitional passage, based on a downward movement in the strings, leads to the grandiose coda, which is fashioned from the material of the introduction, giving us the prelude-postlude formation as a frame for the Overture. The chorale, largo as in the introduction, is now transformed into a mighty paean of thanksgiving accompanied by pealing bells and booming percussion, while woodwinds and strings execute the characteristic upward and downward sweeps. The Cavalry theme follows, *ffff*, allegro vivace, and is repeated as a countermelody, while the lower brass and string instruments blare out the national anthem, *God Save the Czar*. Meanwhile, the *Marseillaise* has completely faded from the scene, overpowered, retreating to oblivion as booming cannon and pealing bells bring the work to a triumphant close.

Jean Sibelius—a Finnish Tone Poet

Biography

Jean Sibelius, universally recognized as one of the greatest of present-day composers, was born in Finland on December 8, 1865, the son of a well-known physician. Like Tchaikovsky, he studied law. But with him, too, the urge to compose soon proved too strong to resist. He gave up all thoughts of a legal career and entered the Conservatoire at Helsingfors, continuing his musical studies in Berlin and Vienna. Returning to Finland at the age of twenty-eight, he soon won such recognition as a national composer that in 1897 the state offered him a life grant, on which he was able to retire and devote himself entirely to composing. Since then, except for short trips abroad, he has lived in his native land, turning out the works that have spread his fame throughout the world. Just as the career of Haydn has gone down in the history of music as a singularly happy illustration of princely patronage at its best, so that of Sibelius will be remembered as a shining example of what an enlightened government can do to protect and encourage its creative artists.

Throughout his career nationalism has played a fundamental part in Sibelius' music. Springing as he did from a national minority under the yoke of Czarist oppression, his music could not but reflect the intense patriotism, the pride, the sufferings, and the aspirations of his people. So saturated is his music with the spirit of his race that it is commonly assumed that he makes extensive use of folk-song material. That such is not the case Sibelius himself has pointed out. In a letter to Rosa Newmarch he claimed the themes so often described as folk tunes are entirely his own, declaring that the thematic material employed in FINLANDIA and EN SAGA were his own invention. The fact that he had to make this explanation shows how completely he has succeeded in capturing the musical idiom of the folk.

Sibelius' music reflects not only the spirit of his people but also their natural setting—the hard soil, the wintry skies and gray horizons, the swirling snows and lonely Arctic nights of the Northland, as well as the more cheerful days of the brief season of sunshine and warmth.

Actually, the affinity of Sibelius with soil and forest is in the great "back-to-nature" tradition of the early Romanticists. (See Chapter XXIX for more about Sibelius.)

"Finlandia" (1899)

FINLANDIA, the work by which Sibelius is best known to the general public, was composed in 1899. This was two years after the composition of Dukas' SORCERER'S APPRENTICE. But there was nothing of the *fin de siècle* sophistication about it. The year was one of smoldering resentment against the oppressive measures that the Russian government had just introduced, aimed at throttling the Finnish press. The nationalist party decided to carry on a campaign for the press fund, culminating in a gala performance at Helsingfors of a series of "Tableaux from the Past" with music by Sibelius. The music for the final tableau—"Finland Awakes"—after revision became the tone poem that the world now knows as FINLANDIA. Karl Ekmann, Sibelius' biographer, states that this work was of greater value to the nationalist cause than were hundreds of pamphlets and newspaper articles. The work soon came to be considered so inflammatory by the Czarist authorities that its performance was forbidden in Finland; in other parts of the empire it was not allowed to be played under any name that indicated its patriotic character. Sibelius tells that when he conducted it in Riga in the summer of 1904 he had to program it under the politically harmless title of *Impromptu*.

After Finland gained her independence by the Treaty of Versailles, the tone poem became a kind of national symbol for the jubilant little republic. To the famous melody of the chorale have been set innumerable hymns and poems throughout the world, and in Finland it has become a national anthem.

ANALYSIS. The composition opens andante, in duple meter, with grim, snarling chords of defiance given out in the low register of the brasses, forte. The woodwinds and strings answer with a short, prayerful passage. A vigorous clarion call proclaimed by trumpets and trombones, like a summons to action, opens the allegro moderato (moderately fast) section. The orchestra leaps into activity, allegro. Over a persistent accompanying figure, reiterated by cellos and double basses, the woodwinds and violins sing a joyously defiant melody in quadruple meter, *ff*. Notice the regular formation: two four-measure periods with a semicadence in the middle and a cadence at the end:

The music works up to an exultant fortissimo climax, then suddenly subsides. There emerges the celebrated chorale, pianissimo, intoned first by the woodwinds, then in unison by 'cellos and violins: a serene, broadly flowing melody, expressing calm inner faith in the justice of the cause and in its ultimate victory:

Notice that the melody consists of three regular eight-measure periods.

The themes of conflict and defiance return and are developed with great vigor, after which, in a kind of brief coda, the wind instruments proclaim the opening of the chorale, fortissimo, bringing the work to a triumphant close.

The form of FINLANDIA is rather free. The sections follow each other—andante, allegro moderato, allegro—in accordance with the idea that the music is seeking to convey—that is, in accordance with the program rather than with any strict musical form.

Like everything else Sibelius has written, FINLANDIA reveals what Gerald Abraham has aptly called his "granite" manner of orchestration, "the fine harsh bleakness of his harmonies, . . . his marvelous exploitation of the darker colors and lower registers of the orchestra." [3] When a friend of Sibelius spoke to the composer of his first impression of Finland, "low, reddish granite rocks emerging from the pale blue sea," Sibelius replied: "Yes, and when we see those granite rocks we know why we are able to treat the orchestra as we do." In the same vein Paul Rosenfeld has spoken of the "wet grays

---

[3] Gerald Abraham, *One Hundred Years of Music.* (New York: Alfred A. Knopf, Inc., 1938.) Quoted by permission.

and blacks" of Sibelius' instrumentation: "The works are full of the gnawing of bassoons and the bleakness of the English horn, full of shattering trombones and screaming violins, full of the sinister rolling of drums, the menacing reverberation of cymbals, the icy glittering of harps." [4]

If we compare FINLANDIA with the Tchaikovsky work, we are struck first of all by Sibelius' economy of means. Here are none of the transitions, repetitions, interludes, and postludes that abound in the 1812 OVERTURE. The composer has his say; when he has had it, he closes. Sibelius' terseness seems to belong to a method diametrically opposite to that of the Russian master of tone. Where Tchaikovsky spins out, expands, and reiterates, Sibelius pares away mercilessly until nothing is left but the bare essentials, achieving thereby a compact texture of great intensity and power. It is this concision that in Sibelius' best scores gives the same impression as one has when reading a paragraph by a master of prose style—that not a single word could be omitted without marring the total effect.

In general, Sibelius' piece avoids the bombast and obviousness of Tchaikovsky's. It is less theatrical and more deeply felt. Sibelius at the beginning of his career was strongly influenced by that Russian master of tone. But he learned from the older man not only what to do, but also—what is often much more important—what to leave undone.

Although written in the same decade as SORCERER'S APPRENTICE, FINLANDIA belongs much more to the earlier Romantic tradition. This may be accounted for partly by the fact that the nationalist mood out of which Sibelius' first works stemmed definitely derived from an earlier decade, from the heyday of Smetana, Tchaikovsky, Dvořák, Grieg, and the other great nationalists rather than from the post-Romantic and more modern trends of the end of the century. Partly, too, the answer lies in Sibelius' creative personality. Although the greater part of his career fell in the twentieth century, he has never been considered one of the "moderns," and he has been influenced by the contemporary scene far less than the other important composers of our time. In a very real sense his music is a continuation of nineteenth-century Romanticism. This very timelessness, according to his admirers, gives his work a quality that lifts it far above the fads and fancies of the moment.

[4] Paul Rosenfeld, *Musical Portraits: Interpretations of Twenty Modern Composers.* (New York: Harcourt Brace and Co., Inc., 1920.) Quoted by permission.

ADDITIONAL SUGGESTIONS FOR LISTENING

THE SWAN OF TUONELA and PAHJOLA'S DAUGHTER by Sibelius; IBERIA by Albeniz; NORWEGIAN DANCES by Grieg; *Overture* to THE BARTERED BRIDE by Smetana; HARY JANOS SUITE by Kodály; RUSSIAN EASTER OVERTURE by Rimsky-Korsakoff; THE ENCHANTED LAKE by Liadov; HENRY THE EIGHTH DANCES by Edward German; GRAND CANON SUITE by Ferde Grofe; ROMANIAN RHAPSODY No. 1, by Enesco; THE SANTE FE TRAIL by Harl McDonald—this will serve as a good beginning for your own list of nationalistic music; and we wish to stress as much as we possibly can the enjoyment to be derived from making such "discoveries" for yourselves. Throughout this book we shall only suggest a beginning, never a comprehensive list, or anything near that; for such a practice would be contrary to our real purpose, which is to stimulate the listener to develop himself. The listener should have at his elbow a first-rate, up-to-date phonograph record catalogue—and leisure time to "shop" by actually hearing before he buys. The personality of the music lover is shown just as much by the record library he builds as by the friends he keeps.

Chapter XV

EXOTICISM IN MUSIC: RIMSKY-KORSAKOFF

THE glamour of the East has intrigued the European imagination ever since the Crusades and the travels of Marco Polo. The Romantic movement, with its love of the strange and the picturesque, naturally stimulated this interest in the exotic.[1] In literature of the nineteenth century we have Fitzgerald's adaptation of the *Rubáiyát* of Omar Khayyám, Burton's translation of the *Arabian Nights*, and a whole series of works laid in the East, from Scott's *Talisman* to the tales of Kipling, Rider Haggard, Pierre Loti, and Joseph Conrad. In painting, besides the oriental scenes of such great colorists as Delacroix, Géricault, Turner, Decamps and Fromentin, Bakst and Roerich, we have throughout the century a crop of highly romanticized scenes of Tunis and Morocco, with all the proper accoutrements of turbans, minarets, and camels. Music—as we have seen from Tchaikovsky's *Arab Dance*—lent itself pre-eminently to this kind of picturesqueness, especially in a period when composers were becoming increasingly preoccupied with atmosphere, orchestration, and piquant tone colors. Thus we have Saint-Saëns turning for inspiration to the Orient in his ALGERIAN SUITE and SAMSON AND DELILAH; Felicien David doing the same in his tone poem THE DESERT. Massanet's THAÏS, Verdi's AÏDA, and Puccini's MADAME BUTTERFLY, César Cui's *Orientale*, Borodin's *In the Steppes of Central Asia*, Rimsky-Korsakoff's *Song of India*, and *Hymn to the Sun* from SADKO are but a few well-known items in a list that could include many of the Romantic composers. It was inevitable that the Russian composers should play a leading part in spreading the influence of the East, springing as they did from an empire that was Asiatic as well as European. Of all the works inspired by exoticism, Rimsky-Korsakoff's Symphonic Suite SCHEHEREZADE, after *A Thousand and One Nights*, has become one of the most firmly established works of its kind.

---

[1] The reader should carefully discriminate between *exoticism* and the use of the *exotic* in art. There is a wide difference of meaning in the two expressions.

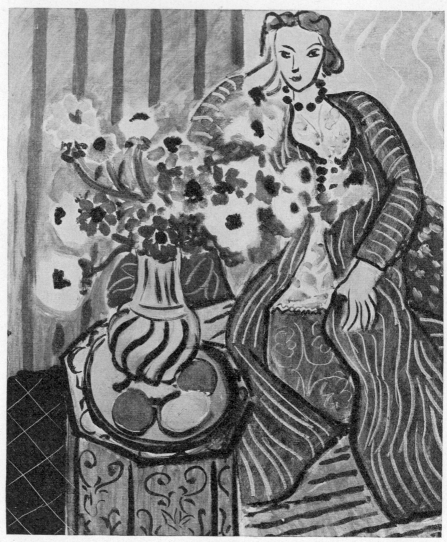

THE GIRL IN THE PURPLE ROBE
Matisse

This painting by the French artist Henri Matisse (born in 1869) is an excellent example of exoticism in European art. Here, in the decorative values of composition, internal designs, and arabesques, together with the bold use of color and the forceful resultant rhythms, concords, and dissonances, are inescapable evidences of influences from the Near and Far East. To those who are attuned, there is a strange and fascinating modern "music" in the painting of Matisse, as there is "painting" in the music of Rimsky-Korsakoff and others.

Nicholas Rimsky-Korsakoff (1844-1908)

Biography

Rimsky-Korsakoff was one of the most brilliant members of the Russian nationalist school. Like Tchaikovsky and Sibelius, he did not start out with a musical career in view. Rather, his well-to-do family intended that he should become a naval officer, and thus he studied at the Naval College in St. Petersburg for six years until he was eighteen. He also studied the 'cello and piano in dilletante fashion and learned enough to entertain his friends with the popular arias from Italian opera. At seventeen, however, he made the acquaintance of Balakirev, the leader of the new Russian nationalist school, who played so important a part in the conception of Tchaikovsky's ROMEO AND JULIET. The friendship that developed with Balakirev marked a turning point in Rimsky-Korsakoff's life. He decided to devote himself to music seriously and began to study under Balakirev. In the meantime, his course at the Naval Academy came to an end, and he was assigned to a practice cruise around the world. Despite his duties on board ship, he worked on a symphony throughout the three years of the cruise, sending the work, movement by movement, to Balakirev for correction. Balakirev conducted the symphony in St. Petersburg in 1865 when Rimsky-Korsakoff returned from the cruise; the work met with a hearty reception. The audience was astonished to see a young naval officer step forward to acknowledge the applause.

The squadron to which Rimsky-Korsakoff was assigned came to this country in 1863. The composer writes, "During the whole of our stay in the United States the Americans were engaged in their Civil War. . . . We followed the course of events with deep interest, though we kept exclusively within the Northern territory." [2]

Back in St. Petersburg, Rimsky-Korsakoff made rapid strides in his art. In 1871 he was appointed professor of composition and instrumentation at the St. Petersburg Conservatory. Two years later he retired from the navy in order to devote himself wholly to composition. At the wish of the Grand Duke Constantine he became inspector of naval bands, a post in which he exerted a strong influence on musical standards throughout Russia. He succeeded Balakirev as director of the Free School of Music in St. Petersburg and conducted the concerts of the Russian Symphony Society, at which many important works of the new Russian school received their first per-

[2] Nicholas Rimsky-Korsakoff, *My Musical Life*. (New York: Alfred A. Knopf, Inc., 1923.)

formance. He soon became the most important composer of the "Five," as they came to be known in the musical world: the group of composers in St. Petersburg who devoted all their energies toward creating a Russian national school. Besides Rimsky-Korsakoff, the group included Mily Balakirev, the leader (1837-1910), and the latter's three disciples—César Cui (1835-1918), known in this country mainly through his popular violin piece *Orientale;* Alexander Borodin (1833-1887), whose *Polovtzian Dances* from the opera PRINCE IGOR are a favorite with concert and ballet audiences; and Modeste Moussorgsky (1839-1881). Tchaikovsky considered the "Five" as amateurs, himself as a professional composer.

The "Five," whose activities centered about St. Petersburg, believed in and practiced "art for Russia's sake." Revolting against what they considered the strangling influence of Western European musical culture, they preached that genius, inspiration, and a return to the riches of the national heritage were infinitely more valuable to the composer than the technical and harmonic disciplines of the traditional European conservatory training.

The most conscientious and self-critical of the group, Rimsky-Korsakoff recognized early that there might be some truth in Tchaikovsky's charges, and that his self-education in music had possibly not prepared him thoroughly enough for his task as a composer. Despite the fact that he was already professor of composition at the Conservatory, with several important symphonic works and an opera to his credit, he put himself through a severe course in theoretical exercises—a rare example of self-discipline on the part of an artist who had already "arrived" in his field. As a result of this continual striving, he developed his genius to its full powers, became a painstaking craftsman, and was the only one of the "Five" to leave a deep imprint on the technical development of European music, especially in orchestration.

With never-failing generosity Rimsky-Korsakoff placed his brilliant technical gifts, particularly his mastery of the art of instrumentation, at the disposal of his fellow composers. He orchestrated THE STONE GUEST, which Alexander Dargomijsky (1813-1869) had tried to finish on his deathbed, as well as parts of Borodin's PRINCE IGOR and Moussorgsky's operas BORIS GODUNOFF and KHOVANTSCHINA. Throughout a long and successful career he labored unceasingly to raise the standards of musical taste in Russia, while through his classes at the Conservatoire—among his pupils were Stravinsky and Respighi

—he exerted a direct personal influence on the rising generation of composers.

Both as musician and man Rimsky-Korsakoff was singularly free from the melancholy, the moody introspection and morbidity that literary legend has attached to the artistic temperament in general and the Slavic artist in particular. It might perhaps be wise to attempt here to puncture the popularly accepted fiction of the great genius in his garret, unkempt and unbalanced, consuming himself in fiery torturings of the soul. Of the distinguished composers whose careers we have examined thus far—Saint-Saëns, Dukas, Smetana, Moussorgsky, Tchaikovsky, Sibelius, and Rimsky-Korsakoff—all but one received due public acclaim and official recognition during their lifetimes.

"*Scheherezade Suite*" (*1888*)

The sea, which plays so important a part in the SCHEHEREZADE SUITE, fascinated Rimsky-Korsakoff from his childhood. During his naval cruise, he came again under its spell; was impressed with the glowing colors of the tropical ocean and the tropical skies. In SCHE-HEREZADE, probably his most famous work, this love for the sea united with his love of exotic atmosphere, his dazzling use of orchestral color, and the bent of his imagination toward folklore and fairy tale to produce a work that captured completely the imagination and splendor of the Arabian Nights. From a purely technical standpoint, the work has come to be considered a veritable textbook for the aspiring young composer. The score reveals with salient eloquence the possibilities of the modern symphony orchestra for poetry, lyricism, humor, color, and pictorial opulence. Its influence on the younger composers at the turn of the century was incalculable.

The score, published in 1889, was titled *Scheherezade—After a Thousand and One Nights— Symphonic Suite for Orchestra, Op. 35.* The use of the term *symphonic suite* was the composer's way of indicating that he had built his work on a larger scale and with greater emphasis on the orchestral element than was the case with the ordinary suite. (*Op.* is the abbreviation of *opus*, the Latin for "work." Followed by a number, it indicates the order either of composition or publication of the particular piece among the composer's works. When a composer has written many works of the same type, as Beethoven's sonatas or Chopin's waltzes, the opus number is helpful in identifying a particular work.)

The score carried the following prefatory note:

The Sultan Schahriar, convinced of the faithlessness of women, had resolved to put to death each of his wives, after the wedding night. But the Sultana Scheherezade saved her life by diverting him with tales which she told him a thousand and one nights. Conquered by curiosity, the Sultan postponed from one day to the next the execution of his wife, and in the end renounced completely his bloody vow.

Many wonders were narrated to Schahriar by the Sultana Scheherezade. For her tales the Sultana borrowed from the poets—their verses, from the songs of the folk—the words; and she fitted them together in many tales and adventures.

ANALYSIS. The composition is scored for piccolo, two flutes, two oboes (one interchangeable with English horn), two clarinets, two bassoons, four horns, two trumpets, three trombones, bass tuba, kettle drums, snare-drum, bass drum, tambourine, cymbals, triangle, tom-tom, harp, and strings.

The Sea and the Ship of Sinbad.[3] We hear first the theme of the grim Sultan announced fortissimo by most of the orchestra and pitched in a low register:

After some mysterious chords and a pause, a solo violin soars high above the arpeggios of the harp, lento and espressivo (slow and expressive)—the tender Oriental theme of the Sultana.

The introduction over, we are ready for the wonderful sea voyage. The entire movement is built out of two melodic figures, of which the first is repeated over and over but with ever-changing colors—now the reediness of the oboe fused with the warmer tints of the viola; now the distant fogginess of horns pitted against the shimmering clarinets and violins; and now the entire orchestra rising in a surge of storm and thunder while the gentle roll of the accompaniment persists throughout, weaving its hypnotic spell over the listener and painting in tones a magnificent picture of the sea. Above all, Rimsky-Korsakoff succeeded in capturing the wonder and unreality of the

---

[3] The titles for the different movements were suggested by the composer himself.

fairy tale, the feeling of "a painted ship upon a painted ocean." There never was such a ship, there never was such a sea—save in the dreams of poets, whether of words, or pigments, or tones.

The introduction is marked *largo e maestoso* (broad and majestic), the movement proper is *allegro non troppo* (not too fast), and is in six-four time, a fine example of the use of sextuple meter to achieve a sense of spaciousness and a gently rolling effect. The Ship theme is in reality the Sultan theme shifted into six-four time and provided with a rolling accompaniment, as though the Sultan listening to the tale were in fancy projecting himself onto Sinbad's ship:

It is a regular four-measure phrase, legato, noteworthy for the trill in the third measure. The two staccato notes in the last measure are repeated pizzicato, like an afterthought, by the rest of the orchestra, making a fifth measure—a charmingly irregular formation.

This theme, worked up in a *crescendo poco a poco* (gradually louder), alternates with the Calm-of-the-Sea theme, one of Rimsky-Korsakoff's happiest inspirations—a series of chords played by clarinets and bassoon, later by flutes and clarinet:

Notice that the phrase consists of a two-measure motive repeated an octave higher. Notice also the contrast between these two themes —the Ship theme in low register with irregular rhythm formations, the Calm theme ascending to the upper register in a perfectly regular rhythm. Such contrasts are most valuable in securing variety and balance. Equally noteworthy is the contrast between the two themes of the introduction: the Sultan theme in low register announced by full orchestra, grim and brusque, in a regular four-measure phrase of which the last two notes are repeated; the Sultana theme in high register played by solo violin in a highly ornamented arabesque, a cadenza-like passage that in its freedom of form and rhythm suggests an improvisation.

The movement as a whole is free in form. Unity is achieved through the constant reiteration of the Ship theme, a reiteration that assists materially in projecting the mood of the Oriental storyteller. Variety is achieved mainly through the wonderful interplay of the different instrumental colors. Now an oboe solo plays a counter-melody to the Ship theme echoed by a clarinet, now the solo violin interposes with the Narrator (Scheherezade) theme, acting as a unifying thread to the movement. Now the Calm-of-the-Sea theme is given over to the violins, while clarinet and flute descend in broadly curving countermelody. Theme A (Ship) is finally built up on a surging crescendo to a fortissimo climax, after which the whole movement is repeated with interesting changes in instrumentation and dies away tranquillo (tranquilly), dolce (sweetly) and pianissimo.

As for the other elements—the lyrical melodic line, the sensuous harmonies, the subtle modulations from one key to the next, the steady beat of the sextuple meter, and the brilliant interplay of instrumental timbres, all fuse in one composite and unified effect. The dynamic scheme is fairly simple: forte (Sultan) and piano (Sultana) in the introduction; thereafter a piano built up to a fortissimo, repeated, and dying away in a gentle diminuendo. Notice particularly the satisfying effect of the prolonged final cadence.

The Tale of the Prince Kalender. The second movement recounts the tale of the Prince Kalender. The Kalenders were a Persian sect of wandering beggar-dervishes. There are three who figure in the story of "The Porter and the Three Ladies of Bagdad," all by a coincidence disguised as princes. Rimsky-Korsakoff was careful not to specify which one he had in mind; nor, truth to tell, does it matter much. A whimsical folk tune on the bassoon hits off perfectly the happy-go-lucky quality of the wandering beggar. The melody is repeated, each time a little faster, as the Kalender gets off on his adventure. He plods along amiably until—has he come to one of those enchanted castles in which doors open mysteriously, luring the unwary wanderer from one room to the next? Perhaps he succumbs to temptation and slips an emerald into his pocket, or—worse still—catches a glimpse of something he should not have seen. Abruptly the mood changes: a trumpet call sounds closer; the violins shudder ominously; a grim march emerges. We do not know what sentence is decreed for the luckless beggar, but that it is one of those terrible punishments that abound in the *Arabian Nights* there can be no doubt. But now we hear again the happy-go-lucky theme of the opening as he picks himself up and continues on his way.

The movement is introduced by the unifying Scheherezade theme on the solo violin, *lento* and *espressivo* (slowly and expressively), developed into a more elaborate cadenza than at the opening as though, having survived the first night, the Sultana had greater confidence in her storytelling powers. Actually, Rimsky-Korsakoff is here following one of the fundamental laws of musical esthetics: when a theme is frequently repeated, it should be varied or elaborated now and then to sustain interest.

After the introduction, the movement proper is *andantino* (somewhat slowly; faster than *andante*) and *cappricioso* (capriciously). The bassoon announces the whimsical theme of the Kalender Prince, which opens with a grace note. (This term indicates a note of little or no value used before a note of regular value; thus an ornament or "grace" note.) The Kalender Prince theme contains "grace" notes in the second and third measures as well, providing a wonderful balance within the phrase—and simulating one of the characteristics of Oriental music.

Bassoon

The melody is marked *dolce ed espressivo* (sweet and expressively), is in ⅜ meter, and in a plaintive minor mode.

The phrase is irregular, consisting of five measures. Notice the cadence effect obtained through the long note in the last measure. Throughout the movement Rimsky-Korsakoff eschews the regular four-measure structure. This irregularity, like the grace notes, contributes to the whimsical quality of the tale.

The theme is repeated several times in succession, each time in a higher register and *piu animato* (a little more animated) by the oboe, strings, and woodwinds. This continuous accelerando and climb in pitch is a wonderful buildup to the eventful middle section. The ominous trumpet call announced by trombones and tuba is echoed by muted trumpets. Notice the effective way in which the various brass instruments imitate each other. Tremolos on first and second violins complete the atmosphere of suspense. (A *tremolo*, the reader may recall, is a repetition of a note on a string instrument produced by moving the bow back and forth rapidly, giving a shuddering, scintillating, or trembling sound.)

The tempo changes to *allegro molto* (very fast). Just before the entire orchestra leaps into action we hear the unifying theme of the Narrator spun out into an elaborate cadenza on the clarinet, as if the wily Sultana were tantalizing her audience before getting to the nub of the story. The grim march is played by full orchestra in a clear-cut quadruple meter. A somewhat sorrowful cadenza on the bassoon, derived from material of the Kalender theme, leads us back to the re-appearance of the first theme where the luckless dervish proceeds on his journey.

The structure is a clear-cut basic ternary, or ABA, with the first and third sections balancing each other. The movement is unified within by the repetitions of the Kalender theme and united to the first movement by the reappearances of the Sultana theme. The clarion call and march of the middle section offer an effective contrast to the Kalender theme; particularly noteworthy is the use of special effects —tremolo, harmonics, and pizzicato—in the middle part.

The melodic line of the first section is notable for its plaintive, folk-tale flavor. In the middle section, by contrast, the melodies are brusque and vigorous. The harmonies support this contrast: in the first part, restful; in the middle section, pungent harmonic effects, abrupt contrasts, a sense of activity and suspense. The rhythmic pattern, too, contributes its part: in the opening, a flowing triple meter, gracefully nonchalant; in the middle, brusque irregular rhythms, frequent changes in tempo and meter, action and excitement. Timbre is used in the same way: in the beginning, mild strings and woodwind colors blending imperceptibly; in the middle, the sharp colors of the brasses pitted against each other, shrill harmonics, and full tonal masses in the march. We see, therefore, that all four elements—melody, harmony, rhythm, and timbre—combine to bolster up the structural contrast of the A-B-A form.

The Young Prince and the Young Princess. Again the composer has left no clue as to which prince and princess he had in mind; but that they were young and beautiful and very much in love there can be no doubt. We encounter here nothing of the narrative style that abounded in the Kalender movement. This is a mood of romantic sentiment with all the proper accoutrements. First, the young prince serenades his beloved in a lyrical melody. Then, the princess dances for her love to the muffled beat of the tambourine; and then we hear again the serenade of the prince.

First and second violins announce the melody of the Prince's serenade in a flowing sextuple meter, piano:

Here Rimsky-Korsakoff returns to the regular four-bar structure. Notice the longer notes that create the pause at the cadence. The tempo is *andantino quasi allegretto* (a subtle tempo somewhere between andantino and allegretto). When the theme is repeated, flutes and clarinets swoop up and down in broadly curving arabesques.

The graceful dance of the princess, which begins *ppp grazioso* (gracefully) with a clarinet solo, is a regular two-phrase period (symmetry of structure is essential in a dance tune) accompanied throughout by the muffled beat of the tambourine:

After the symmetrical periods of the dance we return to the love song, *dolce ed cantabile* (sweet and in singing style). As it gets under way, the unifying Narrator theme (Scheherezade) breaks in *lento* and *espressivo* in the familiar violin solo and harp accompaniment, but this time still more elaborate than before. This continual adding of ornament to each repetition of the theme is in line with the esthetic principle we pointed out a few pages back and serves to keep the theme always fresh and interesting. Besides, it is a good trick of simulating native Oriental music.

The cadenza is cleverly transformed into an accompaniment for the serenade of the prince. The flutes and clarinets now combine in languorous runs as the movement draws to a close. There is a last outburst of romantic fervor; then the music floats up in a delicate final cadence. This is the lyrical movement of the suite. The basic structure is a simple ABA; the $\frac{6}{8}$ meter makes for a broad flowing movement. The melody is smooth and gentle; the harmonies are consonant. Incidentally, notice the balance of movements: the first pictorial; the second an exciting narrative; the third lyrical; and the fourth the brilliant, vivacious, event-packed narrative of the Sultana.

Festival at Bagdad—the Ship Is Sunk. The final movement is divided into two parts. First is the *Festival at Bagdad*, a whirl of color and movement that seems to capture the pulse-beat of the ancient city at the height of its splendor under the great Haroun-al-Raschid. The exciting mood and scene of the festive day are set. Swept along by a rhythmic force that never falters, the familiar themes—the Sultan, the

Kalender, the young Princess—turn up for a moment and disappear. The riotous carnival gathers momentum; the dance works up to a climax. Suddenly we are transported back to the vessel of Sinbad. The doomed ship draws closer to the magnetic mountain on top of which stands the figure of the bronze warrior. The sea heaves and threatens; storm winds blow up on the rushing chromatic scales; the ship is swept headlong on great, surging billows of sound. Now within the magnetic pull of the mountain the nails and iron bolts fly out, the wooden planks fall apart with a great thud as the warrior lifts his trumpet and pronounces the motive of doom. There is a last growl as the wreckage sinks; and a great calm descends upon the sea.

We hear the violin cadenza of Scheherezade for the last time— her task is done. The theme of the Sultan which opened the work re- turns at the close, strangely soft and tender: the misanthropic Schah- riar has been won over at last by the wit of the fascinating Sultana.

The movement opens *allegro molto* and *fortissimo*, with a snatch of wild dance music based on the Sultan theme followed by the unify- ing Narrator theme in its most elaborate version. The dance proper is announced by flutes and taken up by the violins, *vivo* (lively). In order to get a maximum of accent, the composer needs the shortest possible measure. The music is therefore in a vigorous duple rhythm —a regular four-measure formation of four phrases, or two periods. See how unmistakably the composer turns to regular four-measure structure as soon as he has a dance pattern in mind. How Oriental this seems!

Flutes I&II

(Note the multiple time signature $\frac{2}{8}$ $(\frac{6}{16} - \frac{3}{8})$ by which means the composer has tried to indicate varying meters and rhythm that appear in the course of the melody. See if you can distinguish which is which as they appear.)

A *vivace* or *allegro* movement is most appropriate at the end of a work in several movements in order to pitch the finale in a mood of gaiety or triumph. This pattern prevails in many suites and symphonies.

Throughout the nineteenth century, composers were concerned with attaining unity not only within the separate movements of their longer works such as symphonies and suites, but also between the movements. They began more and more to introduce in one movement themes and ideas already heard in a previous one, thus knitting their movements together more closely in a cycle. This type of compositional technique is known as *cyclical* and has become very popular with composers.[4] Thus far Rimsky-Korsakoff has unified his movements by the Narrator, or Scheherezade, theme running like a thread through all of them. In the final movement he further strengthens the bond by bringing back the themes of the Sultan, the Kalender Prince, and the young Princess. We have here an excellent example of the achievement of continuity in program music through the use of the cyclical structure and musical themes attached to definite characters.

The music works up through a crescendo and accelerando to the higher and more brilliant register in a slowly accumulating climax, *fff*. Tonal masses are hurled against each other in clashing dissonance, woodwinds against brass, then against strings; but the timbre, like the melody and harmony, is here subordinated to the wild, relentless rhythm of the dance. As the climax is reached, there is an abrupt pause and the movement shifts to *allegro non troppo, maestoso* (not too fast, majestic). We now return to the $\frac{6}{4}$ meter of the first movement with the Ship theme thundered forth by trombones and tuba against a seething orchestral background. Fierce chromatic scales are whipped up to a *fff* as the ship goes down. A final "growl"; then,

---

[4] We pointed out in our discussion of form that the repetition of a theme solves the composer's problem of achieving unity in his work. As compositions grow more and more extended, there are likely to be quite a number of restatements of the original theme. To ward off the ever-present danger of monotony, composers have developed a fairly elaborate technique of varying their themes, thus achieving a kind of variety even within the unifying element.

A theme may be varied, as in Tchaikovsky's NUTCRACKER SUITE, by changes in the orchestration. The rhythm may be changed: an example is the free, cadenzalike Scheherezade theme that is shifted into a sextuple meter when it reappears in the course of the first movement. The chords in the accompaniment may be different, as was the case when the Kalender Prince theme reappeared after the middle section. The melody itself may be elaborated or ornamented, as we saw in each reappearance of the Scheherezade theme. To sum up: the composer may keep the same melody with different timbre, rhythm, or harmony; or he may vary the melody itself; or he may use several of these changes in every possible combination. How many different ways did you hear in the work just studied?

pp, dolce, we hear for the last time the Calm of the Sea, the Sultana themes soaring aloft over the orchestra in Tempo I, and the Sultan theme rising in a slow curve to the benign final cadence.

ADDITIONAL SUGGESTIONS FOR LISTENING

For Additional Suggestions for Listening see opening paragraph. It will be quite easy and very enjoyable for you to extend this list to your own pleasure. Be sure you list the CAUCASIAN SKETCHES by Ippolitov-Ivanov. Remember to include some "moderns."

Chapter XVI

THE SYMPHONIC POEM: FRANZ LISZT

No ONE sums up so well the prevailing moods of mid-nineteenth-century Romanticism—the emotional exuberance and theatricalism that found their perfect literary expression first in Byron then in Victor Hugo—as the composer of the *Liebestraume* and many *Hungarian Rhapsodies*. He was born when the Romantic movement had just got under way, and his career stretched clear across the century almost until the nineties, by which time it had exhausted itself and made way for newer modes of expression. For over half a century his star shone with extraordinary brilliance over the horizon of musical Europe. And when it set, one of the most colorful periods in the history of the art had come to a close.

Franz Liszt (1811-1886)

Biography

Franz Liszt was born in Hungary on October 22, 1811, the son of a steward on the estate of Prince Esterhazy. His father gave him his first lessons in piano playing. At the age of nine he appeared in public with such success that some Hungarian noblemen granted him a subsidy. The great master Czerny was Liszt's piano teacher. At eleven he played in Vienna where, it should be noted, Beethoven recognized his genius publicly; at twelve, in Paris where, ironically enough, the Conservatoire refused to admit the boy who was to become the greatest pianist of the age on the ground that he was a foreigner. Throughout the first phase of his career he made Paris his home and became the "fashionable" virtuoso. Here, too, he drew close to the literary leaders of French Romanticism—Victor Hugo, Lamartine, George Sand, Alfred de Musset—who exercised considerable influence on his artistic development. In 1834 he met the novelist Countess d'Agoult, known in the literary world as Daniel Stern. One of their daughters, Cosima, became the wife of Richard Wagner and, after Wagner's death, the organizing genius behind the Wagnerian festivals at Bayreuth.

Liszt concertized all over Europe for years and firmly established his reputation as a great, perhaps the greatest, pianist of all time. The emotional power and dazzling virtuosity of his playing have become a legend. Endowed with an electric personality, striking appearance, and a marvelous sensitivity to his audience, he captured the imagination of Europe much as Byron had done a generation earlier. Yet in 1847, at the height of his triumph, he gave up his public career as a pianist in order to develop himself as a composer and conductor. He was made the court conductor of the Grand Duke of Weimar; composed steadily; and became the champion of the "New Music," devoting himself to furthering the works of then unknown composers, especially Wagner, with an unselfishness and singleness of purpose which have few parallels in music. From the Weimar period, too, dates his friendship with the Princess Caroline Wittgenstein. Their home, the "Altenberg," became a center of artistic activity where the enormous musical and social influence of Liszt and the Princess were constantly exerted on behalf of all that was new and progressive in art. Some of the key events of the new movement—the production of Wagner's LOHENGRIN, TANNHÄUSER and THE FLYING DUTCHMAN, of Berlioz' BENVENUTO CELLINI, of Schumann's GENOVEVA and music to Byron's MANFRED—took place under Liszt's direction at Weimar, the city where half a century before Goethe and Schiller had been instrumental in ushering in the reign of literary Romanticism.

In the last years of his life, Liszt divided his time between Weimar, Budapest, and Rome. In Budapest, his countrymen acclaimed the composer of the fiery *Hungarian Rhapsodies* in transports of patriotic fervor. At Weimar, aspiring young pianists came to him from all over the world to be instructed in the mysteries of his art, the majority of them unfortunately carrying away a style of piano-playing that retained all the acrobatics and bombast of the master but little of his poetry or fire. In Rome, the brilliant man of the world, the former radical, who in his youth had welcomed the Revolution of 1830 and indulged in atheistic tracts, fell more and more under the sway of the religious mysticism in his nature and ended by becoming an Abbé in the church. He joined the Order of St. Francis, wore priestly garb, and composed religious works—the MASS FOR GRAN CATHEDRAL, the LEGEND OF ST. ELIZABETH, and the CHRISTUS—which contain some of his finest music. He died on July 31, 1886, appropriately enough at the Wagner festival in Bayreuth where the "Music of the Future" of his old comrade-in-arms for which he had labored so well was finally entering upon its hour of victory.

Liszt belongs to the most colorful era of the Romantic movement. His literary counterparts are Byron and Hugo; among painters, Delacroix, Géricault and Turner stand closest to him in their theatricalism, colorfulness, and grand manner. If some of his music seems oversentimental to us, the tendency of his age must be remembered. Precisely because he so perfectly expressed the prevailing tastes and ideals of his own period he was bound to suffer an eclipse as soon as the pendulum had swung the other way. As is usual in such cases, the reaction against Liszt's ostentatious expression of emotionalism went a little too far. He was unquestionably one of the most gifted of the Romanticists, a pioneer in exploiting new forms, a daring experimenter in compositional technique, harmonic invention, and creation of new orchestral effects. His ideas were borrowed not only by Wagner but to some degree by a large number of the composers in the second half of the century; and evidences of this borrowing are heard everywhere, even today!

For a time, musical criticism was excessively hostile to his music and everything he represented; but recent writers are evaluating his contribution more justly. Paul Bekker, one of the most discerning of modern critics, says of him:

Liszt was one of the great practical organizers of public musical activity. He thought of the artist as a sort of prophet—and he saw himself as one—who passes through the stage of virtuoso and champion of everything new and good, to become the high priest, the mediator between God and man. This was the course Liszt's own life took.[1]

Although program music received a great impetus fairly early in the Romantic Period—Beethoven wrote his *Pastoral* SIXTH SYMPHONY and his dramatic overtures in the first quarter of the nineteenth century—it was not until some decades later that there emerged the musical form that summed up most completely and remained most closely associated with the storytelling tendencies of Romantic music —the *Symphonic Poem*. It was Liszt who first used this somewhat romantic term to describe a musical composition, and he it was who played the decisive part in its development, with the result that he has come to be known in histories of music as the "father of the symphonic poem."

[1] Paul Bekker, *The Story of Music*. (New York: W. W. Norton and Company, Inc., 1927.)

The characteristic most frequently associated with the Lisztian tone poem is the principle of *theme transformation*, which Liszt used to unify and integrate his work. Liszt transformed and varied his themes in rhythm, harmony, timbre, tempo, and general style to mirror the development or changes in the poetic thought. He applied the principle with great ingenuity and effectiveness and through its use secured a solidity of structure and unity of mood that the symphonic poem did not always achieve in the hands of his disciples. We shall have occasion to point out some interesting theme transformations in LES PRÉLUDES.

The literary idols of the Romantic composers and painters, as we have seen, were Shakespeare, Goethe, Schiller, Dante, Petrarch. Their more immediate inspiration stemmed from Hugo, Byron, Walter Scott, Heine, and the imaginative E. T. A. Hoffmann (whose influence we noticed in the NUTCRACKER SUITE). The return to the spirit of the Middle Ages found expression in the Catholic revival of Lamartine and Chateaubriand (paralleled in England by Cardinal Newman and the Oxford movement). The pessimism of Schopenhauer and the all-embracing humanism that Goethe passed on to his disciples were no less important, while in the background stood the towering figure of Jean Jacques Rousseau with his doctrine of "the natural man" and the "return to nature."

We can see some of these influences at work in examining the titles of Liszt's symphonic poems: FUNERAL HYMN FOR A HERO, intended as the first movement of a revolutionary symphony, an intention never carried out as the young composer's radicalism subsided; TASSO: *Lament and Triumph,* depicting the tragic career of the great poet, his hopeless love for Beatrice d'Este, and the triumph of his work after his death (both Byron and Goethe had treated the subject); LES PRÉLUDES, after the mystical Lamartine's POETIC MEDITATIONS; HUNGARIA, on a patriotic theme; WHAT ONE HEARS ON THE MOUNTAIN, dedicated to nature and solitude; MAZEPPA, dealing with the hero whose adventures had inspired Hugo, Byron, and Pushkin; PROMETHEUS, on the theme that had kindled the imagination of Shelley; FESTIVAL PIECE, to commemorate the fiftieth anniversary of the first production of Schiller's *Huldigung der Künste;* ORPHEUS, conceived during the rehearsals of Gluck's ORFÉO at Weimar; THE BATTLE OF THE HUNS, a return to the setting of the Dark Ages, inspired by Kaulbach's celebrated painting; THE IDEAL, after Schiller's poem; HAMLET, an attempt to unravel in music the riddle of Shakespeare's hero; FROM THE CRADLE TO THE GRAVE, consisting of three parts: *The Cradle, The Struggle for Life,* and *At the Grave, Cradle of a Future Life.* In addition, there are the two program symphonies, the first based on Dante's *Divine Comedy,* containing an "Inferno," "Purgatory," and "Magnificat"; and the second his masterpiece, the *Faust* SYMPHONY, after Goethe, giving three magnificent tone pictures of Faust, Marguerite, and Mephistopheles. We have in these titles a veritable catalog of the literary influences in music during the Romantic Period.[2]

"Les Préludes" (1854)

For Liszt, the program was merely a point of departure, a symbol to be translated into musical terms. The music suggested the symbol with all the pomp and grandeur of which tone was capable, but it seldom imitated or gave a too literal interpretation of the symbol. Nothing better illustrates this attitude than the fact that the program of LES PRÉLUDES was attached to the tone poem after the music was written. Almost a decade before he had written the music for a choral work, THE FOUR ELEMENTS (Earth, Winds, Waves, Stars), which he laid aside, discouraged by the stupidity of the words. He then made an orchestral version, but, still dissatisfied, discarded this also. In 1854, needing a new work for a benefit concert at Weimar, he recast the abandoned sketch in its present form and looked about for an appropriate poetic motto. Struck by one of Lamartine's poems, he lifted the title, wrote a program of his own that bears some resemblance to what Lamartine actually said, and attached this to his work with the subtitle "After One of Lamartine's Poetic Meditations." Thus, music that had begun by representing earth, winds, waves, and stars ended by symbolizing love, human aspirations, nature, and immortality. Liszt then, even though he was sufficiently a Romanticist to want literary associations for his music, at the same time was musician enough to realize that these associations must of necessity be vague and that the music must present general emotional moods such as exaltation, triumph, grief, or defeat rather than the concrete details of a story.

The program that Liszt wrote for LES PRÉLUDES reads as follows:

What is life but a series of preludes to that unknown song whose initial solemn note is tolled by Death? The enchanted dawn of every life is love; but where is the destiny on whose first delicious joys some storm does not break?—a storm whose deadly blast disperses youth's illusions,

---

[2] Works of Liszt that we have mentioned, aside from LES PRÉLUDES, might well serve as supplementary listening for the chapter on Liszt.

whose fatal bolt consumes its altar. And what soul thus cruelly bruised, when the tempest rolls away, seeks not to rest its memories in the pleasant calm of rural life? Yet man allows himself not long to taste the kindly quiet which first attracted him to Nature's lap; but when the trumpet gives the signal he hastens to danger's post, whatever be the fight which draws him to its lists; that in the struggle he may once more regain full knowledge of himself and all his strength.

We have here a number of elements characteristic of literary Romanticism: the religious mysticism and "intimations of immortality"; the idealization of love; the conception of life as a struggle against destiny, cruel and disillusioning; the longing for solitude and healing in nature's lap; and the glorious return to the battle. Liszt follows his program rather loosely, treating it as a motto rather than a restriction.

ANALYSIS. Although LES PRÉLUDES is written in a single continuous movement, close inspection will reveal that it is a work of a number of episodes (some eight or nine) grouped into four contrasting sections which may be said to correspond roughly to the separate movements of a complete symphony—a sort of telescoping condensation. Then, too, most of the work is constructed out of the metamorphosis of a simple "germinal motive" which is heard in the third measure of the Introduction and which bears close observation throughout the entire symphonic poem:[3]

What we have chosen to call Part I opens with an introduction presenting the grave Questioning motive as part of the first theme, played by the strings. Note the ominous opening pizzicato (plucked) tones and, in the third measure, the "germinal motive" marked with an "a"—, played with the bow (arco):

---

[3] This musical idea seems to have some inherent universal significance, for one can find one similar to it in a number of widely separated periods, among which are: Bach's C-sharp minor Fugue (No. 4) of the *Well-tempered Clavichord*, the *Muss es sein* string quartet, Op. 135, of Beethoven, the *D-minor Symphony* of César Franck, the *Freischütz Overture* of Weber, the "Fate" motif in Wagner's "*Die Walküre*," and so forth. See footnote in Chapter XXIII, page 338.

This phrase is repeated several times, with slight changes, until the movement proper begins (*Andante maestoso*—with majestic movement), with the theme sounded loudly in the trombones, 'cellos, and basses. As we have indicated, it is formed out of the "germinal motive" marked with an ".a."

The strings frame this theme in an arpeggiated (broken-chordwise), undulated figure not unlike a wave.

Presently another theme is woven out of the germinal motive and played by the second violins, violas, and 'cellos, with a rippling figure in the first violins the while, and the basses pizzicato:

This idea is developed for some twenty measures, when the lyrical second theme proper appears in the French horns and muted violas, each divided into three parts. Though the theme is not without its trite sentimentality, it is, nevertheless, a very clever development of the germinal motive as indicated:

Liszt builds this up to a forceful and passionate climax through the use of the full orchestra, only to calm it down suddenly into a sort of brief dialogue between the strings and woodwinds (note the ethereal close with the sustained chord held by the woodwinds, delicately punctuated by harmonics on the harp—like tiny bells).

Immediately Part II, not without its parallel to a scherzo movement, appears when the tempo suddenly hastens (*allegro ma non troppo*—fast, but not too much so). Here is a storm scene, *par excellence*, with all the chromatic trappings and sound-effect "tricks" that all too often accompany such scenes in the cinema. Of course it was a remarkable bit of writing when Liszt composed it—too frequent imitation has, however, deprived the idea of its freshness.

There will be little difficulty in visualizing a tremendous wind and storm. In due time, quiet prevails and the idea set forth in Mus. Ill. 2, page 231, reappears in the woodwinds.

Part III, which follows the storm scene, might well be considered to parallel a usual romantic and lyrical Slow Movement of the symphony. Marked *Allegretto pastorale* (fairly lively and in a rustic spirit), this main theme of the section is played, *in extensio*, by the first clarinet, but not until it has been anticipated in part by the solo French horn, and then the solo oboe.

Clarinet I (as sounds)

It is a lovely theme that still brings with it the sprightliness and freshness of spring; and it still causes one to marvel at Liszt's compositional sensitiveness, for it is to be noted that the theme is not beholden to the germinal motive. The theme is tossed about between the strings and woodwinds in a frolicsome manner. Eventually a forceful climax evolves in which the theme of Mus. Ill. 3, page 231, is prominently set forth; the key changes markedly, the pulse quickens, and the brasses play bits of anticipatory fanfares—something very important is about to happen!

Part IV, parallel to the finale in a symphony, is ushered in by scale passages, lively passes between the first and second violins, while the French horns and trumpets play the martial theme "A" and the trombones interrupt with the idea "B"—which was first heard in Mus. Ill. 1, page 231. The tempo is *allegro marziale animato* (in a lively and animated martial tempo).

Horns and Trumpets   add Trombones

A complex tonal picture ensues, with the bass drums, snare drums, and cymbals adding to the volume of sound; the tempo broadens to a more majestic pace, with the trombones and strings returning to the ideas that came immediately after the introduction—serving to bring about a feeling of formal unity and coherence. Thus the symphonic poem, LES PRÉLUDES, closes in a lustily proclaimed victorious spirit, and one wonders, nevertheless, just what victory does this final section celebrate? What do you think?

SUGGESTED SUPPLEMENTARY LISTENING

Additional works of Liszt have been mentioned throughout the earlier part of the chapter.

Chapter XVII

RICHARD WAGNER AND THE LEIT MOTIF
TECHNIQUE

N O PICTURE of the orchestral idiom of the nineteenth century would be complete without a consideration of the career and achievement of Liszt's friend, Richard Wagner (1813-1883). Technically, Wagner was an opera composer, and his main reforms, as he thought of them, were carried out in the realm of dramatic music. Actually, he was one of the century's great masters of orchestral writing, whose innovations in harmony and instrumentation, as well as intensity of emotional pitch, exerted incalculable influence on the whole domain of Romantic music. Indeed, it is hardly an exaggeration to say that Wagner's music shaped the entire course of orchestral writing in the second half of the century, both through the composers who considered themselves his disciples, like Richard Strauss, Anton Bruckner, and Gustav Mahler, and those who, like Debussy, sought to shake off his influence by striking out into new paths. In any case, Wagnerism represents the very culmination of Romanticism, a brilliant, impassioned style of overwhelming—sometimes almost brutal—power, of dazzling orchestral color and virtuosity, so distinctive that some historians of nineteenth-century art use it as a landmark. In our own time, too, although his music dramas still hold the center of the operatic stage, his greatest influence is in the concert hall where symphonic excerpts from the operas, to all intents and purposes great tone poems, are among the staples of the orchestral repertoire.

Biography

The career of this volcanic iconoclast makes one of the most colorful sagas in the story of music. His life, like Liszt's, stretches well across the nineteenth century. He was born in Leipzig in 1813, two years after his great friend, and died in 1883, three years before him. As a youth, Wagner was attracted principally to literature, particularly the Greek classics. At fourteen, having discovered Shakespeare, he wrote a grand tragedy in the course of the early acts of which forty-two characters died; a number of them had to return as ghosts to keep the fifth act going. Hearing Beethoven's symphonies—the effect upon him was overwhelming—he forthwith decided that what his tragedy needed was precisely such music as this. In order to compose it he borrowed a textbook on harmony and ploughed through it; but somehow the "system" described in the text could not be made to work. A few lessons from an organist named Müller disappointed him: he thought his teacher a dry pedant, and Müller considered his pupil pigheaded and eccentric. The boy's interest now turned back to literature. He fell under the spell of E. T. A. Hoffmann, the author who exercised such an extraordinary influence on Schumann, Weber, and other Romantic composers; and in Hoffmann's tales he came across some of the material that he later used in his operas. When he was seventeen, he managed to get an overture performed at a concert. It was, he admits in his autobiography, the high peak of his absurdities. The excesses of the drummer, who was directed to play a beat *fortissimo* every four bars, amazed the audience, which grew impatient and finally dismissed the work as a joke.

At the University of Leipzig, Wagner studied composition with Theodor Weinlig for about six months, this being practically all the formal musical training he ever had. Thereafter he buried himself in the scores of his idol, Beethoven. Leaving the University at twenty, he spent the next six years knocking about the third-rate opera houses that dotted provincial Germany, acquiring through practical experience as chorus master, stage director, and conductor that intimate knowledge of the stage that is one of the prime requisites for the successful opera composer. At Königsberg he married an actress of his company, Minna Planer—he was then twenty-three—and got an engagement as conductor at Riga. Growing dissatisfied with the rut into which he had drifted, he turned his eyes, as all ambitious young artists then did, toward Paris. He completed the first two acts of his grand opera RIENZI; *Last of the Tribunes*, based on the novel by Bulwer-Lytton, and set out with his wife to seek his fortune in the French capital. During the voyage through the North Sea the legend of THE FLYING DUTCHMAN which he had come across in a story by Heine took possession of his mind. Thus the seed was planted for his first truly important work.

His life in Paris was a bitter disappointment, a grinding struggle with poverty, a futile knocking at doors that remained closed. Despite the letter of introduction given him by Meyerbeer, at that time the virtual ruler of grand opera, the young man was unable to gain a foot-hold anywhere. To support himself and his wife he was reduced to hack work, "arranging rubbish for various instruments—the cornet among them"; he wrote vaudeville airs, and at one time tried to get a job as a chorus man. "The conductor who tested my capabilities discovered that I could not sing at all, and pronounced me a hopeless case all around." Despite all obstacles, he finished RIENZI, which he dispatched to the Dresden Opera House, and set to work on the libretto of THE FLYING DUTCHMAN. (He had a distinctive literary gift and wrote the poems of all his operas.) In dire straits, he tried to write for a living and turned out some articles on music that were published in the Parisian journals. Just when the outlook was gloomiest, the news came that RIENZI had been accepted for performance at Dresden. He shook the dust of Paris from his feet and set out for his native land. With tears in his eyes, he tells us, he beheld the Rhine "and swore eternal fidelity to the German fatherland."

RIENZI scored a sensational success. Almost overnight the twenty-eight-year-old composer found himself lifted from obscurity to the position of *Kapellmeister* (conductor and general music director) to the King of Saxony. He now had everything a composer could wish for—security, a theater under his direction, an enthusiastic audience. He needed only to continue to turn out works in the conventional grand-opera manner. But his integrity as an artist would not permit him to do this. He had a vision of music drama more lofty than anything that had been done up till then and he was determined to force this vision upon the world. The audiences that had applauded the flamboyant RIENZI were totally unprepared for the stark simplicity and intensity of THE FLYING DUTCHMAN. They were repelled by the tragic ending of TANNHÄUSER and were puzzled by Wagner's new type of melody. When it came to LOHENGRIN, the second work that Wagner completed during his seven years at Dresden, the bureaucrats in charge of the royal opera did not care to continue what they considered a dangerous experiment and refused to produce the work.

Wagner realized that he could not give the public what it wanted and it would not accept what he could give it. It was borne in upon him that he would never be able to rescue operatic music from the triviality and vulgarity into which it had fallen. His projected reform for the theaters of Saxony fell on the deaf ears of the conservative ministers who expected him to supply the court with conventional pleasantries. His restless intellect led him further in his search for the original evil. He saw that in order to reform the theater, which was but a reflection of the social scene, he would have to reform the social scene itself and its basic determinant, the state. It was futile for an artist to seek to change his little corner of the universe, since what he really had to change was society as a whole. This line of reasoning led Wagner straight into the revolutionary camp and he had to flee.

With the years of political exile which he spent in Switzerland began the mature period of his creative career. He decided that the only way to create an audience for the "art work of the future" was to take up his pen to propagandize for and to explain his theories. For five years he wrote no music, turning out his chief literary works— *Art and Revolution* (1849), *The Art Work of the Future* (1850), and *Opera and Drama* (1851), besides a host of shorter essays on related subjects. Having thus cleared his mind for action, he "attempted" to put his principles into practice in the fully developed music dramas—he coined this term to distinguish his works from the conventional opera—of his maturity. How widely his practices veered from his theories is, by now, quite common knowledge.

The remaining three decades of his life he devoted, with a singleness of aim that has few parallels in the story of art, to imposing his will and his vision upon the world. How he forged ahead in a Europe that at the onset understood neither his music nor his ideas, and how he finally got the world to listen, to understand, and to worship, is one of the most incredible success stories of the nineteenth century. We get an insight into the lack of understanding he had to face at this period from the following description by Gasperini of Wagner's interview with the director of the Théâtre Lyrique in Paris where he had gone in the hope of getting TANNHÄUSER performed:

One evening, arriving at Carvalho's house, I heard an extraordinary noise! Wagner was at the piano, struggling with the finale of the second act of TANNHÄUSER. He sang, he shouted, he performed all kinds of contortions; he played with his hands, his wrists, his elbows. M. Carvalho remained impassive, waiting with a patience worthy of antiquity for the bedlam to subside. The score finished, Carvalho stammered a few polite words, turned and fled.

Fortunately, Wagner did not have to conduct the struggle completely alone. Liszt was a staunch friend who did more perhaps than any other to launch the "music of the future." Other disciples included Hans von Bülow, the great pianist and conductor, and the fiery young Nietzsche, for whom the master's music was—for a time —the revelation of a new world. Liszt produced LOHENGRIN at

Weimar; other productions of THE FLYING DUTCHMAN and TANN-
HÄUSER followed throughout Germany. Wagner was unable to hear
these, for he was still forbidden to enter his homeland. Gradually the
movement for Wagner's pardon gained strength. Through the in-
tercession of Princess Metternich, the ban of exile was finally with-
drawn and Wagner returned to Germany after an absence of eleven
years. He plunged at once into the composition of his one comic
masterpiece, THE MASTER SINGERS OF NÜREMBERG. Despite all this,
the darkest period of his life now approached. Having completed the
first two dramas of the RING OF THE NIBELUNG, he faced the realization that Europe contained neither a theater nor singers capable of
presenting them. His efforts to get TRISTAN AND ISOLDE produced fell
through. He was estranged from his wife; his romantic friendship
with Mathilde Wesendonck, who had played an important part in
the inspiration of TRISTAN, ended in an unhappy separation. At last
his power of resistance was broken. He thought of suicide, and finally
decided to give up his public career.

And then the "miracle" happened. The throne of Bavaria fell to
the eighteen-year-old Ludwig II, who had been an enthusiastic devotee
of Wagner ever since he had heard LOHENGRIN. One of the first acts
of the young King was to invite Wagner to come to Bavaria to finish
his work. Thus opened the final and triumphant chapter in Wagner's
life. He closes his autobiography at this point: "I was never again to
feel the weight of everyday hardships of existence under the protection of my exalted friend."

He settled at the capital, Munich, where in 1865 TRISTAN was
produced under his supervision, von Bülow conducting. He now
completed DIE MEISTERSINGER (*The Master Singers of Nüremberg*),
twenty-two years after his first sketch of the poem. After an interruption of nine years, he returned to the RING and finished the poem
and music of the fourth and final drama, GÖTTERDÄMMERUNG (The
Twilight of the Gods). Now he was joined by Liszt's daughter
Cosima, one of the most extraordinary women of her time, who
brought Wagner the understanding he needed, together with an un-
flagging will and energy equal to his own in building the Wagnerian
Festival Theatre at Bayreuth. The lifelong friendship between Liszt
and Wagner received its first wrench at this domestic drama, for
Cosima was the wife of Wagner's disciple von Bülow, and her decision occasioned a scandal that Wagner's enemies were only too eager
to exploit. In 1870, after all legal obstacles had been swept away,
they were married. There followed the crowning act of Wagner's

life—the building of the theater at Bayreuth, made possible by the
contributions of Wagner societies throughout the world. In 1876
the first Bayreuth Festival was given, with the four dramas of the
RING OF THE NIBELUNG (DAS RHEINGOLD, DIE WALKÜRE, SIEGFRIED,
and GÖTTERDÄMMERUNG) performed in their entirety for the first
time twenty-eight years after Wagner had begun to work on the
librettos. Bayreuth now became the Mecca of all the adherents of the
"music of the future"; the festivals, given every four years, later an-
nually, became the focal point from which Wagner's music and ideas
emanated all over the world. Every technical detail, from the seating
plan of the theater to the singing and coaching of the performers, was
superintended by Wagner himself and represented the final realization of his notions of musical-dramatic art. Here his last work,
PARSIFAL, was first produced (1882). A year later he died in Venice
at seventy and was laid to rest in Bayreuth. Ernest Newman sums
his life up well in his *Wagner as Man and Artist:*

He lived, indeed, to see himself victor everywhere, in possession of
everything for which he had struggled his whole feverish life through.
He completed and saw upon the stage every one of the great works
he had planned. He found the one woman in the world who was fitted
to share his throne with him when alive and to govern his kingdom after
his death with something of his own overbearing, inconsiderate strength.
He achieved the miracle of building in a tiny Bavarian town a theatre to
which, for more than a generation after his death, musicians would still
flock from all the ends of the earth.[1]

In his attempt to make the orchestra express all the emotional experience of his characters—love, passion, hate, despair, revenge—as
well as the pictorial and scenic aspects of the myths upon which he
built his dramas—storm, flame, the magic of the forest, the wonder of
the rainbow, the shimmering of the Rhine—Wagner made his richest
contribution to the symphonic idiom of the Romantic movement.
Through the use of new orchestral combinations, particularly in the
brass and woodwinds, through new harmonic progressions and the
use of a restlessly chromatic and contrapuntal idiom that modulated
ceaselessly from one key to the next, he immeasurably extended the
capacities of the art for emotional expression and tone painting. His
daring chordal combinations and their uses paved the way for a new
concept of harmony. His writing became the basis of most subse-

---

[1] Ernest Newman, *Wagner as Man and Artist.* (New York: Alfred A. Knopf,
Inc., 1924.)

quent developments in the final decades of the nineteenth century; and his influence carried over into the twentieth, even to this day.

Another contribution that Wagner made to music was the tremendous development and perfection of the use of leading motives, more exactly known as *leit motifs*. He is not here credited with the invention of this technique, for it was known long before; but he did perfect its use almost to the point of exhaustion of its possibilities. Since this technique is such a characteristic and large part of Wagner's style of composition, it is well to inquire into it, and we shall use the TANNHÄUSER OVERTURE as a typical example; but, first, we should acquire a better concept of the *leit motif* itself. Such a motif is a characteristic theme or musical figure that the composer attaches to a person (such as to Venus or Sirens), to a thing (such as a Sword or Holy Grail), to a condition (such as Love or Hate), or even to an abstract idea (such as Glorification of Venus or Love's Ban). Thus, whenever these ideas are pertinent to the moment in the storytelling, the appropriate motif, or motifs, will be performed. Obviously, if the listener is in possession of the composer's intentions and connotations pertaining to the motifs, a running communication and narration are quite feasible—and the extent to which Wagner made this communication intelligible without loss of musicality is one of the wonders of this many-sided genius.[2] But more of this when we analyze TANNHÄUSER.

Overture to "Tannhäuser"

The Overture to TANNHÄUSER when heard in the opera house provides an appropriate introduction to the drama. When heard—as is much more often the case—apart from the opera, it is an exciting symphonic poem built around the inner conflict within the hero of the drama. As with much program music, knowledge of the drama is an aid to the fullest appreciation of the score.

The knight Tannhäuser is torn between his love for Elisabeth,

---

[2] While it must be admitted that a *knowledge* of the "leit motifs," together with the *recognition* of them as they appear in the performance, enhances the enjoyment (and in the opera itself they are quite indispensable), it is to Wagner's everlasting credit that the music, when performed as concert music, is fully capable of standing on its own feet, so to speak; and often the difference of enjoyment between the intimate *knowing* and the *not-knowing* of the motifs is in kind rather than degree. However, "The Perfect Wagnerite" (read G. B. Shaw's book by that name) will know all the "leit motifs" as well as "The Perfect Baseball Fan" knows the rules of the game and the men who play it. It is interesting to differentiate between the "leit motif" of Wagner and the "germinal motive" as we found it in use in Liszt's *Les Préludes*.

who represents all that is best in his nature, and the pagan goddess Venus. Surfeited with the goddess' sensuous rites and revels, he tears himself away from her and returns to the world of mortals. The second act centers about the "Tournament of Song" in Wartburg, the Thuringian castle of Elisabeth's uncle, in which each of the knightly minstrels sings in praise of love. When his turn comes, Tannhäuser, under the spell of the goddess, mocks the spiritual conception of love and sings the *Hymn to Venus*, a passionate dithyramb on the pleasures of voluptuous love. Finally realizing the depravity of his soul, he undertakes a pilgrimage to Rome to do penance. But the Pope, shocked at the enormity of his sins, tells him there is as much chance for his soul to win salvation as for his withered pilgrim's staff to sprout leaves. Tannhäuser, returning home in deepest despair, is on the verge of giving himself over to Venus and eternal perdition; but the faith of Elisabeth, who dies with a prayer for him on her lips, recalls him to his better self and saves him. As he falls dead on her bier, the pilgrims returning from Rome bring news of a miracle: Tannhäuser's staff has sprouted leaves, and the sinner has won salvation through the steadfast love and sacrifice of Elisabeth.

ANALYSIS. The Overture to the opera delineates, in condensed form, the central conflict of the action that is to follow, and we shall name the leit motifs as they appear in the Overture so that their narrative function can be more clearly apprehended. First we hear the stately hymn, the *Pilgrims' Chorus*, called the "Salvation by Grace" motive (in the old Breitkopf and Härtel edition that is serving as a source book). This hymn is played softly at the beginning as though heard from afar, and it increases in volume as it approaches, in a slow and majestic pace (*andante maestoso*). It is played, at the onset, by two clarinets, two horns, and two bassoons (fagottos).

(Clarinets Bassoons & Horns) in concert key

Gradually more instruments are added until the full orchestra bursts forth with a new motif called "The Pulse of Life," or "Unfettered Passions." This is a descending sixteenth note figure that appears in the first and second violins, while the trombones and tuba blare out the melody, "Salvation by Grace," just heard. (The descending figure in the violins should be noted carefully as it assumes a most important part in the composition of the Overture.)

This motif goes on for some time, working itself up to a fortissimo climax which eventually dies down to a small volume of tone, when the "Pilgrims' Chorus" theme is heard as though it were far in the distance. (Observe how Wagner has thus provided a well-balanced section.) Notice that for the hymnlike effect Wagner has adhered to the regular, square-cut, four-measure phrase so common in actual hymns.

Suddenly, and in complete contrast, a theme appears like a whisper in the violas, amidst the tremolo figure in the violins; all is hushed, and still, and quietly subdued, suggesting the enchanted background against which the nymphs and bacchantes of Venus' train disport themselves. In fact, this theme is known as the "Venusberg" motif, or one of the nine (*sic*) "Bacchanale" motifs.

No sooner has this wisp of a suggestion passed by when another Bacchanale motif is heard, very softly in the strings and woodwinds, only to give way to the seductive Sirens motif heard in the flutes, oboes, and clarinets, with the strings playing a harplike arpeggio.

Soon the "Venusberg" theme is heard again, this time played at first by the clarinet and then tossed to the bassoons and violas, to be joined at last by the oboes. The dance becomes louder and more impassioned, and presently a new motif is heard in the first and second violins, with a rumbling and most exciting chromatic figure in the 'cellos. The new theme, in the violins, is merely another Bacchanale motif as follows:

This last motif is worked up to a loud, fortissimo, climax, where still another motif bursts forth. This time it is in the strings and woodwinds, and it is called the "Glorification of Venus" motif:

It is obviously a theme of mock majesty, of pomp and circumstance, and it is worked up to a mighty volume of tone by the full orchestra; whereupon, with a sudden drop of dynamics to a mere *piano*, the Venusberg theme appears in the violas with the Siren motif in the woodwinds. The music becomes softer and softer, and almost ethereal, as the strings put on their mutes (*sordini*) and softly trill as though the scene were in an enchanted forest. A note of melancholy, of nostalgia, now is injected into the carefree orgy of the Bacchanale by a somber melody played by the solo clarinet.

This melody is called the "Love's Ban" motif. It is promptly dispelled by the intrusion of the Venusberg motif; and still another Bacchanale motif is heard, until the full orchestra awakens into new life as though from a dream. All is alive with renewed vigor and agitation, as the Glorification of Venus motif blares forth with all its pomp and power. Without lessening, the Siren motif returns, this time played by the full orchestra, and one realizes that, finally, here is the real climax of the Overture.[3] The Venusberg and Unfettered Passions motifs assume prime importance in the scheme of the composition. Gradually the volume of tone subsides, the strings continue with the Unfettered Passions motif, while beneath is heard the *Pilgrims' Hymn*. An appropriate and brilliant coda is appended for the

[3] In the so-called "Paris Edition," which Wagner reluctantly made in 1861 to meet the demands of the Paris Opera authorities, he greatly changed the second act and added the "Bacchanale" in Act I. It is at this last point in the program that the curtain rises, revealing the Venusberg scene with the ballet in progress; of course the music continues without interruption into the opera and the ballet.

close in the concert version, providing a subject for much debate among musicians of today as of previous years. Perhaps you would like to discuss the appropriateness of the close provided for the concert version. Have you noticed the counterpoint in this work?

ADDITIONAL SUGGESTIONS FOR LISTENING

We have previously mentioned, among other works in the chapter on religious music, the *Preludes* to LOHENGRIN and PARSIFAL. For other examples of Wagner's symphonic style, listen to the *Prelude* to DIE MEISTERSINGER and to the famous excerpts from the four dramas that constitute the RING OF THE NIBELUNG. From DAS RHINEGOLD (the first of the cycle), hear the *Prelude* describing the River Rhine, and the final scene, the *Entrance of the Gods into Valhalla.*

From DIE WALKÜRE (The Valkyrie) listen to the stirring *Ride of the Valkyries* and the *Farewell of Wotan*, culminating in the "Magic Fire" scene. The "Ride" is built upon a clarion figure repeated over and over with a kind of brutal insistence, while headlong chromatic scales and a luminous orchestral background suggest the neighing of the steeds as the Valkyrie hurtle through the storm. In the "Magic Fire" scene that closes the opera, Wotan takes leave of his favorite daughter Brünnhilde. Because she has disobeyed him, Brünnhilde must lose her power as goddess and know all the sorrows of a mortal woman. But Wotan consents to ring her about with a wall of fire so that only the hero may pass through and claim her as his bride. The warrior maiden lies down on the magic rock, clad in her armor, and falls asleep as Wotan summons the god of fire, Loki, to wrap the rock in flame. Lifting his spear, Wotan proclaims that only he who knows no fear may pass through the fire. As he does so he sings the theme of Siegfried who will claim the sleeping goddess in the next opera. The curtain falls upon one of the most poetic scenes on the lyric stage.

The magic of the forest is captured in the *Forest Murmurs* from SIEGFRIED, when, as the hero lies dreaming in the woods after having killed the dragon, the forest whispers to him of his godlike ancestry and a bird tells him of the sleeping beauty who awaits him on the burning height.

From GÖTTERDÄMMERUNG listen to *Siegfried's "Rhine Journey"* which proclaims the joyously defiant clarion call of young Siegfried; and from the final act of the opera the "Death Music" for the betrayed hero, one of the mightiest laments in all music.

To round out the suggestions for additional Wagner works, listen to the *Good-Friday Spell* from his last work, PARSIVAL; and to SIEGFRIED's "FUNERAL MARCH," which has been called the "greatest threnody in all music" (Gilman), and rightly so for, with the aid of leit motifs borrowed from all the dramas of which Siegfried was a part, the life story of Wagner's hero is told in symbolic detail; and be sure to include that delightful chamber-orchestra work written as a Serenade for Cosima, SIEGFRIED IDYL. From here it will not be difficult for the music lover to make up his own list of "musts."

Chapter XVIII

RICHARD STRAUSS AND REALISM

IT WAS inevitable, once a musical form had been evolved that was expressly designed to project the message of poetry or painting by means of music, that composers should begin to experiment to achieve an even more graphic style in the depiction of programmatic values. During the decades after Liszt, the symphonic poem moved steadily closer to realism. This shift was undoubtedly accelerated by the tendency toward realism that made itself so strongly felt in the sister arts, especially in literature and painting, throughout the second half of the century. One need but mention the naturalism of Zola who dominated the literary scene in France, of Hardy in England, of Howells and Crane in this country, and the romantic realism of such painters as Courbet, Manet, and Millet. All these artists were deeply concerned with drawing their art closer to life, with transplanting the elements of reality with the closest possible fidelity into the art work.

As to composers, those who came after Liszt fell into two camps as far as their handling of the tone poem was concerned. On the one hand were composers like Tchaikovsky and Dukas, who continued in their essentially Romantic attitude toward the program, making the music suggest the symbol rather than attempting to give a literal tonal imitation of it. On the other hand were realists like Saint-Saëns who, in his *Dance of Death*, gave a graphic representation of the rattle of the skeletons' bones, the howling of the winter wind over the cemetery, the striking of the witching hour, and similar details. This tendency was brought to its high state of development by Richard Strauss, the great naturalist in tone, who adapted Liszt's romantic conception to the more sophisticated temper of our own time and brought the symphonic poem to a stage of realism that Liszt had never foreseen.

Biography

Born in 1864, a year before Sibelius, Strauss blazed a cometlike path across the musical sky of the 1890's. By this time Liszt and

PORTRAIT OF GEORG GISZE   *Holbein*

Elsewhere Romanticism, Classicism, and Impressionism have been discussed and illustrated. Here we have an excellent example of Realism, wherein the hand of the artist tries faithfully to set forth what the eye beholds. Before the advent of photography the sole means of duplicating or simulating objectivity was through man's skill in art. Since then, man has been freed from many of the responsibilities in the direction of portraying reality. With such a knowledge, one cannot but admire the truth and uncanny skill of Holbein's perception and draftsmanship.

Wagner, the high priests of Romanticism, were dead. Their successors—Saint-Saëns, Tchaikovsky, Rimsky-Korsakoff, Dvořák, Grieg—were middle-aged men entering on the final phase of their careers. They had brought the movement to its final stage; the time was ripe for a new departure. It was in this *fin de siècle* atmosphere that the young Richard Strauss wrote his witty, brilliantly original tone poems, startling and scandalizing his contemporaries, in effect ushering in the "Modern Period."

Strauss was born in Munich amidst a combination of circumstances well-nigh ideal for a future composer. His father was the leading horn player of the Munich Opera orchestra, a thorough musician who saw to it that Richard's musical training was in the strictest classical tradition. His mother came from a wealthy brewing family, so that the budding composer was spared the searing effects of poverty and insecurity. He showed his talent early: at the age of six he composed a polka and a Christmas song. By the time he entered the University of Munich at eighteen he already had had a number of compositions published and performed. Unlike Tchaikovsky and Sibelius, Strauss did not wait until his graduation to decide on a musical career. He left the university at the end of his first year and thenceforth devoted himself to composition.

His early works—a symphony, sonatas, concertos, and quartets in the conventional style—gave no hint of the future *enfant terrible* of program music. When he was nineteen he met Alexander Ritter, nephew of Wagner and one of the most fervent apostles of the "music of the future," as the new style of Wagner and Liszt was called. The young man was forthwith converted to the programmatic approach—and found his medium. To Ritter he attributed his understanding of Liszt and Wagner and the molding of his style into the poetic and expressive qualities characteristic of the "music of the future."

Strauss soon became the leader of the "Expressionist" composers, as they were then known. Their motto was: music for expression; their goal: to make music express life. Their uncompromising realism went far beyond the tentative, often naïve efforts of Saint-Saëns and his generation. They believed that there was no facet of human experience, whether abstract philosophical speculation, psychological analysis, biting satire, or raw comedy, that music could not be made to express. If the result was sometimes harshly dissonant, that too was an expression of reality: since life was at times discordant and ugly, why couldn't art be?

From his twenty-third year when he wrote DON JUAN, considered by many his masterpiece, Strauss turned out a series of tone poems and operas that made him easily the most important composer of the early 1900's, that seemed for a time to herald the dawn of a new era in music, and that captured the mood of Europe before the First World War—the fevered restlessness, the hectic gaiety, the romantic nostalgia, the wit, the disillusion, the weariness, the need of strong stimulants—as few artists and certainly no other composer succeeded in doing. Using a gigantic orchestra, which he handled in masterly fashion—his scores are of a complexity far beyond anything Wagner or Liszt had dreamed of—the young iconoclast set out to express things in music that no one had ever before attempted. Whether it was the jabbering of the market women in TILL EULENSPIEGEL, the bleating sheep and whirring windmills in DON QUIXOTE, the battle music in A HERO'S LIFE, or the inner turmoil in Don Juan's soul, there was no situation, no subtlety of characterization or quirk of plot that Strauss did not feel supremely able to depict in tones. On the one hand, he aimed to develop the descriptive powers of his art to such an extent that it would be possible "to describe a teaspoon in music" (although there might be some question whether this was worth doing). On the other hand, he was able to say of his THUS SPAKE ZARATHUSTRA, with a courage that would have abashed a more hardened philosopher, that he intended it as a musical expression of the development of the human race from its origin to Nietzsche's Superman.

We may well understand the bewilderment of the musicians of the old school. After hearing THUS SPAKE ZARATHUSTRA, Sir George Grove, the venerable author of the great musical dictionary, wrote: "What can have happened to drag down music from the high level of beauty, interest, sense, force, grace, coherence, and any other good quality which it rises to in Beethoven . . . down to the low level of ugliness and want of interest that we had in Strauss' absurd farrago? *Noise* and *effect* seem to be so much the aim now." [1] Nothing so well illustrates the forward march of history as the fact that Grove held up as the high representative of "beauty, interest, sense" and all the other good qualities Beethoven, who less than a century before had shocked and startled his contemporaries with a new conception of beauty in music.

As for Strauss himself, he not only was not crushed by the opposition, he seemed positively to thrive on it. His early works breathed an

[1] Sir George Grove, *Dictionary of Music and Musicians*. (New York: The Macmillan Company, 1927.)

amazing vitality and zest, scorching humor, buoyancy, and exuberance —the lusty defiance of a young giant with supreme confidence in his power. To the tone poems we have already mentioned may be added MACBETH and DEATH AND TRANSFIGURATION, the latter somewhat more in the poetic tradition of Liszt, and his three principal operas—SALOMÉ (1905), an extraordinarily effective setting of Oscar Wilde's one act play; ELEKTRA (1909), a powerful one-act music drama centering about the heroine of Greek tragedy; and DER ROSENKAVALIER, or CAVALIER OF THE ROSE (1911), a comedy in the eighteenth-century manner combining Mozartian grace, the Viennese waltz, and the piquant harmonies of the modern idiom.

In all these works Strauss managed in an astonishing way to fuse his Romantic heritage with the idiom of a more modern age. He will go down in the history of music as one of the first great composers of the post-Romantic era. For, although he stemmed from Romanticism—his use of strikingly dramatic plots, his reliance upon theatrical effects of orchestration, and his luscious melodies are all in the great Romantic tradition—there is an element of intellectuality in his work, of sophistication and objectivity that stamps him as a post-Romantic, a child of the twentieth century. Strauss has been called the prose artist of music, the one who substituted the tone of the modern realistic novel with its psychological probings, its devotion to detail, its objectivity for the poetic drama of the earlier epoch. In short, Strauss achieved in music what the "naturalistic" writers of the end of the century—Zola, de Maupassant, Chekhov—achieved in literature. Through his wonderful sense of musical characterization, his bold imagination, the sweep and power of his style, he was able to describe, to analyze, to satirize, to conjure up the details of a scene with a vividness never before achieved. DON JUAN, TILL EULENSPIEGEL, DON QUIXOTE—these are no mere symbols for vague, generalized poetic moods as the protagonists of the earlier tone poems had been. These are fully realized, distinctive individuals hit off with deep insight and psychological acumen, projected with merciless clarity, with an incisiveness and completeness little short of the phenomenal.

The Merry Pranks of Till Eulenspiegel (1895)

Of all Strauss' works, the brilliant portrayal of the medieval rogue, Till Eulenspiegel, has attained the widest popularity. Strauss was thirty-one when he wrote it. He had already written MACBETH, DON JUAN, DEATH AND TRANSFIGURATION, and the opera GUNTRAM. Whether because he was smarting from the reluctance of his fellow musicians to respond to his art or because his genius for comedy was coming to maturity, Strauss now turned his gifts to sarcasm and impudent waywardness. In more than one spot the mocking laughter of the vagabond-rogue seems but to echo his own. As we listen to the startling leaps of flutes and oboes, the bold curve of the melodic line, the novel harmonies and orchestral effects, it is difficult to believe that this music was written but four years after the NUTCRACKER SUITE and two years before FINLANDIA.

The young composer chose a fit symbol, for Till is one of the eternal rebels, the scoffers, who fail to fit into the accepted social patterns. He is related to François Villon and Gil Blas, to Puck and Robin Hood, to Rabelais' lusty Pantagruel and Anatole France's equally lusty Tournebroche. In German folklore he occupies a position analogous to that of our own Huckleberry Finn and the Katzenjammer Kids.

Historically, Till Eulenspiegel—the name, literally translated Till Owl-Glass, is derived from an old German proverb to the effect that "Man sees his own faults as little as an owl recognizes his ugliness in looking into a mirror"—came into German literature through a collection of folk tales and anecdotes about his doings written by Thomas Mürner (1475-1530) toward the end of the fifteenth century. It was a period of vast social change. The feudal system was breaking up under the rise of the guilds and burgesses; the semi-independent barons were being subdued by the centralized monarchy of the modern European state; the new humanism was raising its head against medieval scholasticism; the scene was being laid for the deepest upheaval of all—the revolt against the Church of Rome, the Reformation. In English literature we have a stirring expression of the period in *Piers the Plowman*, in Malory's *Death of Arthur*, and in the works of Chaucer. Mürner, in open revolt against the clergy, told the life of Till as a satire against the smug monks, the domineering lords, and the grasping bourgeois. He pictured Till as continually outsmarting the victims of his wit, dying peacefully in bed after a long and eventful career, and at the very last playing a joke on his heirs by refusing to lie still in his grave. By the end of the nineteenth century, as Strauss knew, society was much more effectively organized to deal with such spirits. His "Till" accordingly pays on the gallows for his daring.

Unlike LES PRÉLUDES and FINLANDIA, in which the music gives a vague suggestion of a vague program, the music of TILL EULENSPIEGEL depicts the adventures of the rogue in the most literal, realistic terms. Consequently, a knowledge of the program is much more important for a proper appreciation of this music than is the case with Liszt's or Sibelius's tone poems. Here the listener cannot substitute for the program of the composer whatever image happens to strike his fancy, for the music at any given moment is depicting a concrete detail of the story. If less leeway is given to the imagination of the hearer, there is compensation in following the cleverness and rich fancy with which the composer has transcribed the images of the everyday world into the world of tone. The program was derived by Strauss' closest friends from the markings of the principal themes in Strauss' own copy of the score; the music falls into several distinct episodes.

ANALYSIS. *"Once upon a time there lived a wag."* Violins announce a tender "dipping" theme, piano, setting a mood of long ago and projecting the essential lovableness of the rogue:

"Named Till Eulenspiegel." The staccato Mischief theme symbolizing the wayward side of Till's nature is announced by the horn, piano, in $\frac{6}{8}$ time—a wonderful little etching in tone of the charming scapegrace who has never learned how to stay out of trouble. Notice the subtle shift of accent in the melody whereby the little figure marked "A" begins each time on another beat in the measure.

Like all truly great orchestrators, Strauss hears his themes not as abstract melodic patterns but always in the tone color of a particular instrument. This theme is fundamentally a horn theme; it is literally molded to the personality and technical peculiarities of the instrument that announced it. It reveals the secrets of Strauss' brilliance in orchestration—he always makes the instruments do what is specially fitted for them. These two themes and their ingenious transformations will reappear throughout the work. In his use of theme transformation Strauss, a faithful disciple of Liszt, carried the device to even greater lengths than the master.

"Off for new pranks." Repeated in quick succession by various

instruments in a rapid crescendo, the Mischief theme is built up into a brilliant climax in which it is proclaimed by the entire orchestra, fortissimo. The scene is set for Till's first escapade. The tender Till theme with its characteristic "dip" is now transformed into roguishness on the clarinet, speeded up into a most flippant rhythm:

"Till in the market place." We hear the click of hoofbeats as Till approaches the market place. The two themes leap about maliciously. He catches sight of the women who sit gossiping in front of their stalls. Till's fertile brain hatches a plan. He sidles closer on his horse; looks about him innocently; suddenly jumps his horse right into the middle of the crowd. There is a terrific din and confusion: fishwives scream, pots and pans clatter, geese cackle—all of which gives Strauss an opportunity to indulge in one of those orgies of orchestral "noise" of which, as a realist, he was so fond.

"Till and the priests." The scene shifts. We hear a simple legato melody in the style of the German chorale on clarinets and bassoons:

Coming as he did at the end of the century, Strauss completely emancipated himself from the regular four-measure-phrase structure. Yet, notice that here when he wishes to give the effect of a hymn he reverts to the regular phrase pattern.

"Disguised as a pastor, he drips with unction and morals." Till seems to be taking part in one of those theological disputations that formed one of the favorite pastimes of the Middle Ages. But a clarinet sliding precariously down the "dip" of the Till theme reminds us that despite his clerical garb "out of his big toe there peeps the rogue." The priests suddenly realize that Till is mocking them. Little shuddering triplets seem to warn that the scoffer will come to no good end. The first Till theme returns, insouciantly: he isn't afraid—as yet.

"Till in love." A long glissando on the violin tells us that Till is now deep down "in the dumps," a victim of the tender passion. (A *glissando* is a wailing, gliding sound made by passing the fingers in a smooth, unbroken manner over the keys or strings—a common hu-

morous effect used in the cinema.) The present glissando goes from the topmost E flat to the G below middle C—the lowest string on the violin.[2] In this romantic episode, Strauss has had his opportunity of poking fun at the emotional extravagances of the Romantic composers. The Till themes languish, grow sick with longing, now light up with ardor. A lovely romanza (built, as a romanza should be, on the regular four-measure-phrase pattern) emerges as the impassioned swain serenades his beloved. But the lady says *no*, which only whets the suitor's ardor. The Till theme, on brass and strings, becomes agitated. He storms and fumes and threatens to depart; but the fair one remains adamant.

At this point Strauss transforms the whimsical "dip" theme into one of anger by augmenting the time values of the notes—that is, playing them as dotted quarters instead of eighth notes. This kind of transformation is called *rhythmic augmentation*. Compare this version with Mus. Ill. 1, page 251:[3]

The opposite of augmenting a theme would be to diminish the note values, speed it up, as it were. This process is known as *diminution*. We had an example of this when the Till theme reappeared in sixteenth notes on the flutes before the market episode.

Having been rejected in love, his theme is flung out angrily by the entire orchestra as poor Till storms away. A moment later, we hear again the mischievous, carefree undulation on the clarinets, and we are aware that Till is off on his next adventure.

"Till and the Philistines." A persistent, plodding rhythm in the darkest register of the winds announces the advent of the professors and pedants, the pompous mediocrities and "stuffed shirts"—in short, the pillars of society against whom the artist—especially when he is still young and unsuccessful—is in perpetual revolt. A brilliant orchestral colloquy follows, with the sparkling Till theme hurled in defiance against the plodding, nagging chords of the Philistines. The opposing tonal masses seem to represent personalities and viewpoints that can never come together.

"Till's self-questioning: should he reform?" A delightful street

---

[2] For those who can read the score, the glissando is twelve measures before Figure 15.

[3] One measure after Figure 19.

song, with something very naïve and childlike about it (quite like a polka), ushers in the next episode:

(Note that this is at Figure 26 in the printed score—Aibl Edition.) Notice that here, too, in order to give the effect of verisimilitude, Strauss uses the folk-songlike regularity in the four-measure phrase structure. As Till watches the contented folk about him, there steals into his heart that sense of loneliness that comes sooner or later to all who refuse to submit to the accepted order of things. A wave of tenderness passes over the orchestra as Till catches a glimpse of what life might really be if he would only mend his ways. The wood-winds utter a searching question (not unlike the questioning theme in LES PRÉLUDES, with an appropriate rising inflection): should he not try to reform? Just as he is about to succumb, we hear the ascending horn theme of "Mischief" followed by the whimsical "dip" motive, both slowly gathering strength, becoming louder and louder as the realization sweeps over Till that he can never change, that he must remain true to the fundamental character of his nature. Till he is and Till he must remain, come what may!—the orchestra bursts forth in triumph; the Mischief theme, originally played in staccato eighth notes, is now heard in a rhythmic augmentation played by the four French horns and two trombones (at Figure 31 in the printed score and here transposed into the concert key for convenience):

The music breaks forth presently with a joyous, furious dance. The two themes shown in Mus. Ill. 1, page 252, and Mus. Ill. 2, page 254, are developed in intricate orchestral tone patterns and tossed about cleverly from one instrument to another. "Now," thinks Till, "I can really be myself"—or words to that effect.

"The judgment of Till: his sad end." But those who dare to defy society must pay the price. At the height of the festive mood, the brasses proclaim the opening measures of the chorale—the warning of the priests is about to come true. A long drum-roll announces the

convening of the court of justice: the culprit has been arrested and brought to trial. Menacing and ponderous chords, ff, in the low, dark registers of the brasses, low woodwinds and strings over a roll in the drums, announce the ministers of the law. Unabashed, the irrepressible Till greets them with his defiant theme on the clarinet as though he were mocking them: he is confident that he will wiggle out of this fix as he has out of so many others. The drums roll again; but Till is still cocky. As the court proceeds he loses his composure; the judge obviously means business. The clarinets indicate that Till has become panicky; we hear again the shuddering little triplets from the episode with the priests. Lower strings and brasses pronounce sentence: Till is to be hanged by the neck until dead. There is a savage snarl in tubas and contrabassoons as the trap door is swung. Clarinets and flutes whine piteously. "There he swings; he gasps for air . . . the mortal part of Till is no more." (The hanging of Till is an outstanding example of stark and brutal realism.)

Epilogue. A long pause. And then we hear again the opening measures of the tone poem. "Once upon a time there was a wag named Till—and now you have heard his story." It is a gallant farewell to Till, a passage drenched in nostalgia and dreams. Perhaps he wasn't so bad after all. . . . There is a final outburst of roguery just at the end. Till is dead—but his spirit lives on!

Strauss called his work "a rondo in the old roguish manner." He had a somewhat mischievous intent in labeling his completely programmatic and realistic tone poem with a term reserved for one of the most "abstract" forms of so-called pure music. Increasingly the charge was leveled at the program composers that their music possessed no inherent musical structure, that it derived all its organization from the literary program. Strauss took up the challenge by showing his critics that his piece had a musical form, and a quite intricate one at that, at the same time that it told a highly complicated story. Strauss proved his point in more than brilliant fashion. Yet it must be remembered that any tone poem that tells the adventures of a central character can often be adapted to rondo form, if for no other reason than that the theme of the central character will reappear quite naturally after each of the episodes. If this be a rondo, it is certainly one such as the eighteenth-century masters of that form never conceived.

So firmly has the work established itself in the affections of present-day audiences that it is difficult to understand the reactions it aroused only a generation ago.

ADDITIONAL SUGGESTIONS FOR LISTENING

Among the works of Richard Strauss mentioned in the text of this chapter, we suggest that the reader listen to any or all of these Symphonic Poems: DON JUAN, DON QUIXOTE, DEATH AND TRANSFIGURATION, HELDEN-LEBEN (A Hero's Life) and THUS SPAKE ZARATHUSTRA. It will not be difficult to add to this list, if the reader is eager to hear more of this composer's works.

It will be a splendid challenge to the listener, at this point, to review and compare the character and use of the "germinal motive" of Liszt, the "leit motif" of Wagner, and the realistic "descriptive theme" of Richard Strauss.

Chapter XIX

THE SONATA AND THE SYMPHONY:
A ROMANTIC SYMPHONIST—DVOŘÁK

W E HAVE, up to this point, occupied ourselves largely with various kinds of programmatic music, or music that had extra-musical values—the symphonic poem, opera, and music drama, oratorio, suite, ballet, the different kinds of songs, and so forth. We now come to the domain of so-called *absolute* music in which the composer does not necessarily rely on extra-musical associations, either literary or pictorial; in other words, where the "story" of the music is the music itself, and the action consists of the working out of musical themes to their fullest possibilities, as the composer sees them.[1]

Since in *absolute* music, as we here use the word, there is no external literary plot to hold the music together, the form naturally plays a most important part in supplying cohesion and clarity. We may therefore expect to find that the flowering of absolute music is bound up with the emergence of extensive musical forms. Of these, unquestionably the most important is the *sonata* (from *sonare*, to sound, indicating a piece to be sounded as distinct from *cantata*, a piece to be sung). The sonata is an extended musical composition in several contrasting movements, generally three or four, of which the first usually is designed in the sonata-allegro form. It is well to emphasize the word "usually." For just as every novel presents another version of the basic formula of development, climax, and denouement, so here there are so many variations of the form of the sonata as a whole, so many exceptions to rule, that only the most generalized picture of the entire structure can be drawn. Actually, in our study of the sonata we shall aim principally at understanding the basic esthetic principles that underlie it rather than the technical details of which these are but a manifestation.

---

[1] See article "Absolute Music" in Grove's *Dictionary of Music and Musicians* for more detailed explanation of the term.

The Sonata

The sonata, as signifying a work of several movements, is a form used for all the instruments. There are solo sonatas for piano, for violin, 'cello, organ, and the like, or for any two instruments. If three instruments are involved, we speak of a trio sonata; if four, of a quartet. Quintets, sextets, septets, octets—all refer to the same form, the difference in title merely indicating the number of instruments used. Naturally, the more instruments the greater the opportunity for interplay and contrast among them and the more extended and elaborate the basic form becomes. If the form as a whole is used for solo instrument and orchestra, we have a concerto: thus, we speak of Beethoven's *Piano Concerto*, or Mendelssohn's *Violin Concerto*. And if the form is written for full orchestra, we have one of the noblest and most ambitious types of composition in music: the symphony.[2]

The rise of the sonata was intimately bound up with two of the most important developments in the history of Western European music: the shift in emphasis from vocal to instrumental forms, and the establishment of our major-minor system of keys. We have had occasion to touch on both. It took a long time to realize that instruments could play an independent part in music instead of being merely an adjunct of vocal or dance music. The interludes inserted in the madrigals and operas, the overtures that preceded the performance of vocal works, gradually gave rise to a distinctive instrumental style independent of the older vocal style.

Throughout the seventeenth century instrumental music was emancipating itself from bondage to the voice. The technique of playing rose steadily. The organ, the violin, the harpsichord, and the clavichord came into prominence. Composers faced a new esthetic problem. As long as they set their music to a text, whether religious, dramatic, or poetic, the meaning of the words furnished a skeleton upon which they could drape their musical inspiration. But in attempting to write for instruments alone they had to organize their musical thinking without any assistance from verbal association or dramatic plot: they had, in other words, to learn to think along purely

---

[2] When we speak of a *sonata*, we refer to an entire work of several movements; but when we use the term *sonata form*, we refer to a specific first-movement, or *sonata-allegro*, structure consisting of three sections: exposition, development, and reprise. For a fuller description and history of the sonata than we can give here, see articles "Sonata" and "Symphony" in Grove's *Dictionary*, Thompson's *International Cyclopedia of Music*, Hadow's *Sonata Form*, or any standard reference in music.

musical lines. At first they clung for support to the popular dance rhythms of the day and developed the *suite*, a group of fairly short movements based on popular dances in various rhythms and tempos but all in the same key. As they grew more confident of their ability to think along purely musical lines, they branched off into the more extensive form of the *sonata*.

At the same time that instrumental modes of thought were shaking the supremacy of the vocal style, the new major and minor system of keys was supplanting the modes or scales that had been the foundation of medieval church music. The two tendencies amalgamated in the sonata. Not only did this form represent a more highly organized attempt than had ever been made before to think in terms of pure music by presenting and developing themes that had a distinct personality of their own, but in an even deeper sense the sonata became a drama of contrasting tonalities in which the action shifted from the home-key center, the tonic, to surrounding tonalities, mainly the dominant, and then triumphantly fought its way back to the original key. The plan of the sonata came to be based upon the new awareness of keys and their relationships, upon what were then daring experiments in modulation and transposition. Throughout the eighteenth century composers experimented with this new drama of keys and themes. Their experiments bore fruit, in the second half of the century, in a magnificent flowering of the Classic sonata form, which reached its peak in the art of the two masters, Haydn and Mozart. Inside of two centuries music had evolved a new language and a new technique, the sheer perfection of which still dazzles us.

The first movement of a typical nineteenth-century sonata is generally allegro. This is, as a rule, the most important of the movements as regards structure, wealth of thematic material, and ingenuity of development. The second movement, for contrast, is andante or adagio in tempo, and cantabile; this is the most lyrical and melodic movement of the set. The third movement, often a minuet, or scherzo vivace in character, is the dance movement, strongly rhythmical and sprightly. The fourth movement, like the first, is elaborate and structurally of impressive dimensions. In the Classical symphony it is generally a rondo—an allegro molto or a vivace built on a dance pattern. In the nineteenth century, the fourth movement more often became a triumphal climax in which the struggle and aspiration of earlier movements were brought to their resolution. Sometimes composers reviewed in the final movement the themes of the previous movements, thus unifying their work most effectively. (Of course it is to be understood that the foregoing is intended only as suggestive generalities, for there are actually no hard and fixed rules.)

We have, then, in the typical sonata, a sequence of four movements, of which the first and fourth are fast and intricate; the second slow and lyrical; the third lively, strongly rhythmic, and dancelike. Sometimes composers switch the second and third movements about; in his *Pathétique Symphony*, Tchaikovsky transposes the slow movement as the Finale.[3] In the celebrated *Moonlight Sonata*, Beethoven began with an adagio and followed it with a minuet and a presto.

We may at this point differentiate between the sonata and the suite of the eighteenth century, which also had several movements. The suite movements were each based on the persistence of a uniform dance rhythm. They were all in the same key. They therefore exhibited none of the dramatic contrast of key and theme, of theme development and organization, which was the very basis of the sonata. In short, the movements of the suite did not aim at that impression of organic unity, of architectural organization, of diversity of mood and material, which distinguished the sonata.

The Symphony

We have, so far, referred to the sonata as being played by a solo instrument, or by several such instruments grouped into a small chamber ensemble; but we now come to the use of the form in a composition to be played by the large number of instruments comprising the modern symphony orchestra—and we appropriately refer to the form thus used also as a *symphony*. Therefore, in a general way, we may think of a symphony as a sonata performed by an orchestra. Of course we realize that countless qualifications and exceptions might be made to such a generality, and we shall soon experience some of the conformities as well as exceptions as we go along in our study. For the present, the general definition is adequate and provocative.

Of course it is to be expected that this larger playing organization, the orchestra, should enrich the structure of the sonata, and the form, in turn, bind together the many different instruments and players that might otherwise seem to be antagonistic to each other or even to fall apart—the form unifies the performing medium. The inherent musical possibilities of the different instruments making up the orchestra, separately and in innumerable combinations, gave a new life and

---

[3] The author has always considered this a mechanical rather than a compositional transposition and the third movement to be, in reality, the *Finale proper*, from a compositional standpoint. Witness audience reactions.

value to the sonata form. Composers were not slow in realizing these
possibilities, and their imaginations were awakened as if by magic;
they gave free rein to their inventiveness and experimented with new
ideas and effects. Out of this has emerged the modern symphony—
both the form and the performing medium. Composers dreamed of
new vistas and made them come true; and they are still dreaming and
experimenting with this seemingly inexhaustible combination of idea
and reality—the sonata form and the symphony orchestra.

We thus have an extraordinary growth in the power and sweep of
the nineteenth-century symphony that spread like wildfire over the
entire musical world. The symphony became the most important
form in music—the equivalent in the tonal art of the fully developed
novel of Tolstoy, Thackeray, or Balzac. Just as in the great novel,
we have in the symphony the sense of an intensely concentrated
emotional experience; the satisfaction of realizing the perfection of
the minute parts in their relationship to the nobility and sweeping
power of the grand structure; and, withal, the feeling of having
actually lived with the varicolored and vitalized themes for a space
of time, and of having watched them grow, develop and pass on, as
we do with the leading characters in a great novel.

And all these desiderata can be accomplished with or without

COURTESY OF THE BOSTON SYMPHONY ORCHESTRA

BOSTON SYMPHONY ORCHESTRA   *Sergei Koussevitzky, conductor* extra-musical implications. Truly a great and noble instrument had come into the hands of the composer, and the rich symphonic literature that is our heritage stands as eloquent evidence to the justification of the efforts and circumstances that brought both the large symphonic form and the large symphonic orchestra to their present high state of perfection.[4] The years have shown, and continue to show, the adaptability of both form and medium to the highly diversified individual needs of our great composers, not the least among these being the symphonic poet of the common folk—Antonin Dvořák (dvôr'zhäk).

Antonin Dvořák (1841-1904) and His Symphony "From the New World"

We begin our listening study with the perennially popular *From the New World* SYMPHONY IN E MINOR, Op. 95, of Antonin Dvořák. This has a special interest for Americans since it was written while the composer was living in this country, and it presents some of his impressions of the New World. By far the most generally accepted of his works in this form, the vigorous rhythms and lovely melodies of this symphony have won for it a high place in the affections of the public, and it is today, half a century after it was written, one of the most widely and frequently played compositions in symphonic literature.

Biography

The composer of the universally beloved *Humoresque* and *Songs My Mother Taught Me* was born in 1841, a year after Tchaikovsky, near Prague. His father, a village butcher and innkeeper, could do little for the boy, whose musical gifts were evident from childhood. Local musicians who believed in Antonin's talents helped him through the period when poverty threatened to put an end to his musical aspirations. But when he reached the age of sixteen, he was able to get to Prague where he pursued his musical education in earnest.

For more than ten years, during which he supported himself by playing viola in the orchestra of the Czech National Theatre in Prague and by giving private lessons, only a few of his intimate friends knew

---

[4] It would be traditional to stop here for an inquiry into the technical details of the sonata-symphony form and to use them as a basis of intellection; but, as has been our philosophy and practice, we shall do so—if at all then necessary—only after we have enjoyed to the full the uniqueness of the listening experience.

anything about his attempts at composition. Gradually, though, his works made headway and began to attract the attention of the musical world. His first great success came in 1873, when he was thirty-two, with his HYMNUS, a work for voices and orchestra infused with intense devotion to his fatherland, which was under Hapsburg dominion. From then on he espoused the cause of Czech nationalism, turned to the folk songs, dances, and legends of his beloved Bohemia and, under the influence of his older contemporary, Smetana, became one of the leading figures of the Czech nationalist school. The songs and dances of the Gypsy fiddlers who had passed through his father's tavern, the songs and dances of the village folk among whom he had grown up, formed the chief source of his inspiration.

Enabled by his success to devote himself exclusively to composition, he produced a series of works that spread his fame and the cause of Czech music throughout the world. Among the works directly inspired by his nationalism may be mentioned the MORAVIAN DUETS, the popular SLAVONIC DANCES, the three SLAVONIC RHAPSODIES for orchestra, the dramatic overture HUSITSKA, dedicated to the national ideal of religious freedom as symbolized by the martyr Jan Huss and the Hussite movement, the oratorio LUDMILLA, and the folk operas, RUSALKA, KING AND COLLIER, THE CUNNING PEASANT, THE PIG-HEADED PEASANT, all set to the works of Czech nationalist poets and suffused with the folklore and folkways of Bohemia.

Like Tchaikovsky and Sibelius, Dvořák was not only a nationalist. Besides the program works directly inspired by his love of country, he wrote much in the "absolute" forms, carrying on the great tradition of Beethoven and Schubert, Schumann and Mendelssohn. His symphonies, trios, quartets, and quintet, while adapting the hallowed Classical forms to his needs as a Romantic and a nationalist, nevertheless show an impressive command of musical structure and an ability to think in the classical spirit, or temper. In this domain he was influenced and encouraged by Brahms, who became his staunch friend.

Toward the end of the century, Dvořák was recognized as one of the ranking composers of his time. In 1891, at the tercentenary celebration of Cambridge University, he was among the musicians—Tchaikovsky was another—who were given the honorary degree of Doctor of Music. He was made professor of composition at the Prague Conservatoire, elected to the Czech Academy of Art and Science, and decorated by the Austrian government. In 1892—a year after Tchaikovsky's visit to America—he was invited to come to New York and direct the National Conservatory of Music. He was enthusiastically welcomed here and remained for three years, achieving great success as teacher, conductor of his own works, and composer. He traveled through the country, responding to its vastness, its great cities, its sense of power and promise. His summers he spent in the simple, intimate atmosphere of the Czech colony at Spillville, Iowa, where he could almost fancy himself back in his native land.

Despite his great success in this country, his homesickness grew apace. In 1895 he returned to Europe. His joy at the prospect of homecoming found expression in a series of short piano pieces, the *Humoresques*, of which the seventh has become a most popular gem. After his return he took up his post at the Prague Conservatoire, becoming director of the school in 1901. In the final period of his career he devoted himself exclusively to symphonic poems and operas based on legendary material. His best work along these lines, the poetic opera RUSALKA, belongs to these years. His death in 1904 at the age of sixty-three was mourned by the entire Czech nation as well as by music lovers all over the world.

He was a master of warm, spontaneous melody, of poetic and lyrical moods. His peasant stock and his love for the folk came out in his vigorous rhythms and his strongly accented musical speech. He was one of the masters of orchestration, achieving magical effects with the subtlest of means, especially in his works for smaller instrumental combinations. A poet of nature, he was steeped in the music of the rivers and prairies of his fatherland. There is a warmth and freshness of feeling about his music, a verve and manliness, a tenderness and a humanity that have endeared him to the multitude.

"Symphony in E Minor" (From the New World), Op. 95

The most famous of Dvořák's orchestral works was completed in 1893 in the Bohemian colony at Spillville, Iowa, where the homesick composer had gone to be as close as possible to the language and customs of his native land. It aroused a violent controversy when it was first performed: did it really capture the spirit of the New World, or was it, despite the Negro and Indian flavor of some of its themes, a work fundamentally Czech in character and outlook? The issue no longer seems as crucial as it once did. There can be no question that Dvořák, a great nationalist composer acting as teacher and guide to the younger generation of American musicians, gave much thought to the establishment of an American school and the development of a musical idiom that would express the spirit and strivings of the new continent. Music in America at that time was largely in the hands of

men who had been trained abroad in the traditions of German Romanticism and who simply transplanted those traditions to another soil.
Edward MacDowell, the first American composer to make an impression on the world scene, was still a young man. Stephen Foster's
songs, in the true folk style, had been thus far the only real attempt to
discover a distinctively American vein. Dvořák naturally felt that
his students ought to do the same thing that he and Smetana had done
in Bohemia, that Tchaikovsky and Rimsky-Korsakoff had done in
Russia: they should turn to the indigenous rhythms and melodies of
the folk. In attempting to portray in music his impressions of the
New World and the emotions that it aroused in him Dvořák is said
to have turned, in parts of the Symphony, to the inspiration of the
Negro and Indian musical idiom, though the composer himself denied
the contention. At the same time he was a European writing in the
musical language that was natural for him. It would therefore be
erroneous to regard the Symphony as American music. Rather it
presents the impressions of a gifted and sensitive visitor, just as does the
Italian Caprice of Tchaikovsky, or the *Spanish Caprice* of Rimsky-
Korsakoff.

In any case, the *New World* SYMPHONY reveals Dvořák's gifts—
spontaneous melody, vigorous rhythms, colorful orchestration, firm
grasp of form, and a natural flow of ideas—at their best. Note how
Dvořák obtains a feeling of unity and coherence between the several
movements of the Symphony by restating themes that had appeared
in previous movements—a species of "cyclical" treatment. See if you
can discover the reappearances of such themes. The structure and
form of the Symphony, as a whole and in parts, is very orthodox and
"classical."

ANALYSIS. FIRST MOVEMENT: *Adagio—allegro molto. E
minor.* $\frac{2}{4}$ *time.* The slow introduction gives a sense of mystery and
spaciousness, beginning pianissimo and bearing traces of Indian song.
The opening phrase of the 'cellos is answered by flutes and oboes.
The music seems to draw nearer and nearer in a great swell and
plunges us into the brusqueness and vigor of the movement proper,
allegro molto.

The principal theme is announced by the horns in E minor, *mf*
(*mezzo forte*), a bold arpeggio ascending and descending along the
tones of the chord in the syncopated rhythm that already at that time
impressed Dvořák as characteristic of the American musical idiom.
(*Syncopation* means that the accent falls not on the strong beat of
the measure, where we normally expect it, but on the weak beat, the

"offbeat," producing an effect of waywardness and irregularity that adds a pleasant "snap" to the rhythmic effect. Thus, in the theme below we have in the second and fourth measures an unaccented eighth note falling on the principal beat of the measure, the "one," while the accented quarter note is shifted to the offbeat. This effect, characteristic of the shuffling dance steps of the Negroes of the South, became one of the most distinctive features of American dance music.)

The vigorous syncopation is retained as the theme is unfolded, first *ff* by the strings in unison, then *fff* by the entire orchestra. A short bridge, which modulates to G minor, leads to the first part of the second theme, announced by flutes and oboes, pianissimo, that has all the poignance of a Bohemian folk tune.

The naïve character of this melody is accentuated by the regular phrase structure. Shifted into the major mode, it is ingeniously transformed into a typical frontier song and has been used as accompaniment for countless Western scenes in the movies. Notice the engaging syncopation of the rhythm and the F natural in the last measure.

The second part (or real second theme) follows and, for reasons of comparison, the original *Swing Low* melody is shown below it.

Notice the regularity of phrase structure, the effect of the syncopation in the second and sixth measures, and the major mode. With the fortissimo repetition of this theme we come to the double bar, whereupon the entire section is repeated.

In the next section the themes are developed, or worked out. Fragments of the *Swing Low* melody are tossed about among the various choirs. The ascending-descending arpeggio figure of the first theme is hurled forth intermittently by the bass instruments. The themes take on new life from these startling juxtapositions; the music modulates frequently, shifting us from one tonality to another. After a fortissimo climax, a gradual retransition leads us back to the home tonality of E minor, where we hear the first theme as we heard it originally.

From then on we hear the three themes substantially as they appeared in the first section. For reasons that we shall soon consider, they are not in the same key as they were in the first section of the movement; they have been shifted bodily, or transposed, to other keys. But the melodies themselves are unchanged.

The third theme is followed by a coda marked by impetuously descending chromatic scale passages. The first theme, boomed forth triumphantly at the end by strings and trombones, leads into the stirring final cadence.

We therefore see that the *first-movement form* consists of three sections. In the first the themes are presented, or exposed; hence this section is known as the *exposition*. In the second, the development, the themes are developed or worked out. In the third, the *recapitulation*, or *reprise*, the themes are repeated or reviewed as at first. An introduction may often open the movement and a coda (a tailpiece) usually brings it to a close.

At this point the reader will quite naturally see a resemblance between the *sonata-allegro*, or *first-movement*, *form* and *ternary*, or *A-B-A, form*.[5] While the first-movement form contains three sections, of which the first and third are similar, the structural principle is not quite the same as in A-B-A form. In the latter we have unity in the two "A" sections and contrast in the "B." In first-movement form, the exposition (the "A") contains a contrast within itself, since two or more themes and keys are presented. The development (the "B"), although it contains contrast and variety, nevertheless uses the same basic thematic material as the first section presented in a new guise. The third section, the recapitulation, restores the themes in their original form to the home key. We have here the same basic effect of unity, contrast, and variety as in the simple A-B-A form, but this is achieved in a far more intricate design. These two forms satisfy a similar fundamental human desire for balance and symmetry. If the first-movement form had for its object merely the presentation of a succession of pleasant melodies, it would not differ substantially

---

[5] The terms *first-movement form* and *sonata-allegro form* are here used interchangeably.

from the suite, or any of the lighter forms, such as Salon music. But because it presents these melodies of a more serious vein in an intricate, highly co-ordinated key organization, the first-movement form takes its place as one of the most ingenious and significant structural forms in music. Here key and modulation become the very determinants of form, and they do this, as we shall see, efficiently and subtly.

SECOND MOVEMENT: *Largo, D-flat major.* ¼ *Three-part, or song, form.* Mysterious chords, *ppp*, on bassoons and brass instruments usher in as a solo on the English horn one of the most famous melodies in symphonic literature.

The reedy, yearning quality of the instrument brings out to the full its poignant wistfulness. Here the son of a Bohemian village merchant has caught a world-wide feeling and has expressed it eloquently. It has been said that Dvořák was thinking of "Hiawatha's Wooing," but there is little substantiation. Set to the words of "Going Home," the melody has become widely popular with singing groups.

After the unfolding of the melody, which is based on a three-phrase pattern, we are shifted from the serene major mode into a dark, somber minor, pianissimo, in a passage of brooding tenderness. It argues well for the universal quality of music that while for some this part has the flavor of a Bohemian lullaby, for others it might have the awesome beauty of a night on the prairie or a connotation closer to the individual listener's fancy.

Now the oboes and flutes begin to trill in what might conceivably be a nature scene.

Violins follow suit; the tempo quickens; the whole orchestra becomes tremulous with excitement. When it subsides we return to *Tempo 1;* the *Going Home* melody is sung by the English horn; the movement flows on for a little while and then dissolves in a pianissimo chord for double basses.

THIRD MOVEMENT: Scherzo. Molto vivace. ¾ *time. E minor. Minuet and trio (A-B-A) form.*[6] In the "Scherzo" Dvořák forgets all about the New World and lets himself be swept away in a wave of nostalgia for the folk dances of his native land. A strumming accompaniment on violins and 'cellos introduces the first theme, its gaiety subtly overcast, as so often happens in Slav dances, by the minor mode. (The student may have noticed from the heading that we are now back in the E-minor tonality of the first movement.) An abrupt, twitching rhythm imparts a curious zest to the theme, which is piped staccato in high register by flutes and oboes:

As in many folk dances, the structure here is based on the regular four-measure phrase. The melodic imitation in this passage is interesting to follow.

After a repetition of this section we are brought into a suave major mode, *poco sostenuto* (a little sustained), where a gracefully swaying, almost languid dance is intoned by flutes and oboes against a string accompaniment. The asymmetrical formation—a three-measure phrase answered by one of five phrases—lends an elusive charm to the movement (Goetschius calls this the first Trio):

The melody is brought back in the bass, sung in mellow tones by bassoons and 'cellos, while the chords of the accompaniment soar high above. Then, *a tempo* (in the prevailing time), we return to

---

[6] According to the eminent American theorist, Percy Goetschius, this is a song-form with *Two* Trios; according to an equally eminent English theorist and program annotator, Donald Tovey, the Scherzo is a simple song-form with *One* Trio, Mus. Ill. 2, page 269, being considered merely an interlude. Others describe the form as a Minuet and Trio with *Two* themes each.

the brittle staccato of the opening theme. Presently, in what Goetschius calls the *second* Trio and what many others call the *one* Trio proper, the strings play a bell-like reiteration over which the woodwinds play a motive not unlike a trumpet call.

The *Da Capo Scherzo* (repeat the scherzo from the beginning) rounds off the contrast with the "Trio." In the coda the reminiscence of the first movement suddenly returns, but this time it materializes into a full-fledged appearance, *fff*, of the ascending-and-descending arpeggio theme. As it fades, the rhythm of the opening of the Scherzo flits past, *ppp*, and a fortissimo final chord brings the movement to an abrupt close.

FOURTH MOVEMENT: *Allegro con fuoco (fast, with fire).* E *minor.* ⁴⁄₄ *time. First-movement, or sonata-allegro form.* Out of a tempestuous introduction emerges a marching song given out fortissimo by horns and trombones. Even the minor mode cannot dim the sense of power and promise, the high determination and courage that breathe through this music.[7]

(Note that the D natural at the mark N.B. shows the underlying scale structure to be the Aeolian Mode, an old Church "scale.") The theme is repeated with heightened color by violins and woodwinds in high register. The music broadens into a torrent of triplets that courses onward, sweeping everything before it. There is a terrific energy and exultance about this transitional passage that leads to the second theme.

The mood changes to one of reverie. The second theme, given to

---

[7] Dr. Sigmund Spaeth, in his book *A Guide to Great Orchestral Music* (New York: Random House, 1943), suggests that the opening theme of the final movement might have been influenced by an American folk song, "Peter Gray," and, further, that the final gay theme resembles "Yankee Doodle."

the solo clarinet, unfolds in broad curves of melody to a climax on the strings (note the frequent interruptions by the 'cellos):

We are plunged into a popular fortissimo melody, each of whose phrases ends with three detached descending notes. This third (or closing) theme is sung by flutes and violins:

Expansive and joyous, it is a song for vast multitudes. The three descending notes at the end are repeated in the bass by 'cellos and basses and then blossom out as the opening of the familiar tune "Three Blind Mice" bandied about by the orchestra with humor and imagination. Now deep down amidst the bass strings, now high up on the woodwinds, this distinctive descending motive persists in imitative style against an intricate countermelody and finally disappears, imitated by a number of instruments at various registers in a continuous downward curve.

The development section is a rich mosaic of the three themes, the connective material, plus reminiscences of previously heard themes. The March theme on the horns, sounding mysteriously as from a distance, is pitted against fragments of the "Three Blind Mice" theme. Familiar melodies heard in new rhythmic patterns are interspersed among the energetic triplets that lent such verve to the exposition. Echoes of the "Going Home" theme from the *Largo* wreathe about the March theme like a pale memory. The syncopated arpeggio of the opening theme of the Symphony suddenly spurts upward in a surge of excitement, ever more pressing, until the March theme appears fortissimo against downward chromatic scales. The music veers toward the home key of E minor.

In the recapitulation, Dvořák touches upon the thematic material of the exposition. The March theme appears in E minor, strangely subdued. The dreaming second theme rises to a sonorous curve as before, but its orchestral coloring is altered. The popular song (third theme) has a plaintiveness about it. The recapitulation is in the nature of a brief review, preparing the way for the electrifying coda. The ascending-and-descending arpeggio of the opening movement gives way to a fortissimo entrance of the March theme. From a headlong climax we are thrust into the opening chords of the *Largo*, while the strings produce an upward thrust of great billows of sound. An abrupt diminuendo and a fragment of the "Going Home" theme sweep past in startling juxtaposition to the twitching opening rhythm of the *Scherzo*. It is as though all the themes we watched grow and expand in the earlier movements were hurrying past for a brief summation before the close. A last solemn announcement of the March theme, and we are swept into the final broad cadence on an E major—instead of minor—chord, an ending called, *Tierce de Picardie*.

Schematic Outline of a Symphony as a Whole

The first-movement, or sonata-allegro, form

The first movement is often the most important of the entire work. It carries, in the sonata-allegro form, the fundamental principles of musical structure—unity and variety—to their utmost realization. Just as in the novel the action consists of the psychological and emotional interaction between several clearly defined personalities and the working out of their destiny in relation to one another, so here we are presented with two well-defined themes or groups of themes in contrasting character and tonalities, the action consisting in exploring their possibilities as independent entities and in working out their relationship—their "struggle"—with each other.

Since the first movement of the sonata was generally allegro, the first-movement form came to be known as *sonata-allegro form*. The term is not entirely satisfactory, since it is easy to confuse *sonata-allegro*, which refers specifically to the first movement, with *sonata*, which covers the three or four movements of the entire work. For this reason, many theorists in this country prefer to use *first-movement form*, which is not a good term either, since the form is sometimes used also for other movements, notably the fourth; but it is the best nomenclature we have.

We have seen that the first-movement form consists of an exposition, a development, and a recapitulation, which work out the contrast or "conflict" between two groups of themes in contrasting keys. Let us now see how this theme and key organization is worked out.

The exposition. The function of the exposition is to present the two themes or groups of themes out of which the movement is to be constructed. The first theme or group of themes is placed in the home, or tonic, key; the second theme or group of themes is in a foreign key. (In the typical Classical symphony, the second theme was generally in the key of the dominant—the key, that is, whose tonic was a fifth above—when the first theme was in the major. If the first theme was in the minor, the second theme was in the relative major; that is, the major key whose signature is the same as that of the minor. Thus, if the first theme was in C major, the second was in G major. If the first was in A minor, the second was in C major.)

A few words of advice to the listener: Listen intently to the themes in the exposition, over and over again until they are memorized and can be readily recalled at will, either for enjoyment in themselves or for the added pleasure of making comparisons with what the composer might be doing with the theme, or themes, at the moment—so necessary in the development section. Again—memorize the themes and carefully watch their adventures throughout the movement, or symphony as a whole. If you will do this very simple thing, your enjoyment will be more certain.

In the first-movement form, the contrast in character between first and second theme may be reinforced by a contrast in dynamics (such as first theme *f*, second *p*); in register (first theme high, second low); in tempo (first theme fast, second slow); in rhythm (first theme vigorous and strongly accented, second languid); in phrase structure (first theme regular, second irregular); in tone quality (first theme legato, second staccato); in timbre (first theme given to strings, second to woodwinds or brass); above all in mode, by far the most effective contrast of all (first theme major, second minor). It is apparent that a striking combination of these contrasting elements will produce a complete emotional and psychological opposition between the two themes. Thus, in Beethoven's FIFTH SYMPHONY the first theme is brusque, passionate, choppy, in a somber minor—"masculine" and commanding (in C minor):

The second is serenely lyrical, tender, legato, in major—"femininely" yielding (in E-flat major, the relative major key):

Similarly, in Tchaikovsky's FIFTH SYMPHONY, the first theme is staccato, rhythmically abrupt, in minor mode, intoned by the wood-winds (in E minor):

The second is legato, molto cantabile ed espressivo, flowing, in major, sung by the strings (in B minor—an unusual relative key):

In musical texts the first theme is generally referred to as the principal theme; the second, as the subordinate. This terminology is somewhat misleading, since it implies that the first is more important than the other, whereas what is meant is simply that the first is in the tonic, or home, key, and the second in the foreign key. Many theorists are therefore abandoning these terms and speaking of the first, second, and third themes.

Between the first and second themes or groups of themes comes a transition, or bridge, whose function it is to lead us from the home key to the foreign key. This bridge plays a most important part in the design, since its function is to carry us through the modulation from the tonality of the first theme to that of the second theme. Besides the first theme, bridge, and second theme, the exposition may contain an introduction, generally slow, before the composer plunges into the allegro of the movement proper, and a coda or codetta to round out the exposition of the themes. The introduction, which precedes the first theme, will be in the home key. The coda or codetta, which follows the second theme, will be in the foreign key, the same as the second theme. The composer sometimes employs a third, or closing, theme in the exposition, often in the home key.

The development. In the exposition, the composer makes use of his ability to create memorable themes; in the development, he exhibits his ingenuity in working them out: he displays his mastery over the technical resources of his art. He may take a snatch of his principal theme and combine it with a few bars of the subordinate theme, exhibiting both in an altogether new light. Or strains of his slow introduction may be used with various combinations of either of his themes. The development explores the latent possibilities of thematic material; reveals it in an altogether new light. The development is